NEXT FRIEND:

The Journal of a Foster Parent

NEXT FRIEND:

The Journal of a Foster Parent

anne southworth

Next Friend Press
Cleveland Heights, Ohio

Next Friend Press

12699 Cedar Road

Cleveland Heights, OH 44106-3332

Phone: 216.225.1829

Fax: 216.932.0964

Designed by Barb Rosenbaum

Text set in Arial Narrow and Garamond

Printed in the United States of America

Library of Congress Control Number: 2006906676

ISBN: 978-0-9747937-1-9

So many people have been part of this story. Foster parent friends like Pennie and Vince Riha and Roberta Canant. Therapist friends like JoAnn Beckman, Sondra Gardner, Andrea Goodman, Mary Kameya, and Lesley Lake. Neighbor friends like Barbara Kahn, Pam and Ken Pim, Maureen Weigand and Pat Wren. Others like Joe Donohue, Shirley Griffin, Glynnis King, Mary Paolano and Carol Sattelmeyer. They all played major roles in keeping me sane and helping me figure out behavior that puzzled me. I have no adequate way to thank them other than by putting them in this book, where the reader can see their help directly, on every page. In most cases I have changed their names in the book, as I have every member of my family.

I also thank the discerning eye of editor Jan C. Snow and the talents of graphic designer Barb Rosenbaum.

There's a term in civil procedure that I've always liked: next friend. It's an old term still used in pleading a legal case. Traditionally the next friend is the one who brings suit on behalf of a minor. Usually that would be the parent, and the caption of the case would read "Jane Doe, a minor, by Her Mother and Next Friend, Plaintiff." But if the child has no parent, the caption would begin "Jane Doe, by Her Next Friend." I don't know how the term "next friend" evolved, but I like it. The next friend is the advocate for the child, and that's what a foster parent is. I feel more like Nikki's next friend than her parent.

SUMMARY FOR TRANSFER:

ADOPTION UNIT TO FOSTER CARE UNIT

Subject: Nikki D., age 16, white female.

Agency received temporary custody when Nikki was 6; Agency received permanent custody when Nikki was 10.

Parents both dead. Parents never married. Father never involved with family.

Initial agency involvement at age 6 was precipitated by hospitalization of child. Hospital staff identified drugs in bloodstream not prescribed by doctors.

Child removed from home for one year during which she was placed in two foster homes.

Age 7-10: Returned to mother.

Age 10: Mother died of drug overdose. Placement made with grandmother. Unsuccessful.

Two foster placements made.

Age 12: First adoptive placement made. Unsuccessful. Two additional foster placements made.

Age 14: Second adoptive placement made. Unsuccessful.

Age 16: Worker and child both concur that no further adoptive placement should be sought. Case is therefore transferred to Foster Care.

February 1981

We're desperate for places for teen-agers," Jean had said on that snowy January day four years ago. "Can you take someone?" We'd said yes three times to teens from Jean's church youth group. Each girl was eighteen when she came to us, each had family waiting in the wings for current difficulties to resolve, and each placement was shorter than six months. The short placements gave us time to regroup as a family.

But now there's a question from an agency. Can we take Nikki as a foster daughter? Can we take her for three years until she's through high school? It's a tough question. There's an image of a foster mother that haunts me. She's middle-aged, rotund. She has a size XL heart, and she knows instinctively how to handle children. She bakes cookies in a warm kitchen, surrounded by three or four kids who watch and talk with her. She listens to them, understands them, loves them. And she works miracles. Kids nobody else can reach call her "Mom" and bring her little presents.

I am not like that. By now I have met some other foster parents, and they are not like that either. I am middle-aged, and though my heart may be a little larger than some, it's not XL. I'm a lawyer who is hardly ever found baking cookies in a kitchen full of children. Although we've had three teenagers with us so far—Molly, Kate and Beth—I don't know that I'm ready for a kid like Nikki. I wonder what the story is beyond the bare facts of her placements with other families. It's unusual for a kid to be moved that many times, especially to have had two adoptive placements fail. Even the placement with a relative didn't work, and that's uncommon.

Nikki's a difficult kid, her caseworker acknowledges, but she's at a loss to tell us just how. "She's kind of a square peg in a round hole," Kirsten says, shaking her blonde head. There is no major and obvious problem she can point to. Nikki doesn't do drugs, she doesn't drink, and she doesn't run around. She's just difficult in some way that can't be articulated.

I know that if I think about this, I'll say no. If I begin asking Kirsten questions about all of these placements—why didn't Nikki's grandmother keep her and why didn't the adoptive families keep her—I'll get answers that will lead me to say no. When I got that call from my friend Jean, a youth minister, I knew instinctively that if I thought about adding a teen-ager, I'd say no. But if I went with that first warm feeling of wanting to help a kid, I'd do it.

It's been over a year now since we've had a teen-ager with us, and I miss the vitality of that age. Ben, our five year-old, misses Beth, too, not only because she was the most recent, but because of all the girls, she's the one who's most in tune with little kids and gets a real kick out of them.

But three years is so different from six months. I don't know that I or my husband Will or Ben or Nikki herself could make a three-year promise at this point. Neighbors and friends have asked me why we take these kids, as though this were a question with a one-syllable answer. Yes, I can give an answer that's really plausible, maybe even a bit poetic, but I really don't know all of my own motivations. There's a phrase that a foster father used that keeps coming back to me. "A foster child is your child without you." Maybe it really is that simple. If we weren't here, I'd want somebody to step forward for Ben.

March 1981

We've had the first of three weekend visits with Nikki now. She looks like Molly with that long, reddish hair. When I open the door Friday evening, I am startled by that resemblance. Somehow it hadn't struck me during our brief afternoon meeting with Nikki and Kirsten. I feel a hesitation before I say, "Come on in." Is it the remembrance of Molly's distance and coolness, or is it a separate premonition? Molly was casual, but Nikki is downright sloppy. She's about thirty pounds overweight and doesn't seem to care about how she looks. Her hair is really a gorgeous color, but it hasn't encountered a comb for some time.

And Nikki is not distant at all. In fact, she wears me out. She wants attention every minute. Friday evening she comes in with a tape recorder and a backpack and immediately begins to play me all of her Barry Manilow tapes. I don't mind Barry, though I prefer country and blues. Saturday she talks about collecting on her paper route but takes hours to get organized. She sits on the living room floor with all of the cards spread around her and talks without seeming to breathe.

Finally I go to the third floor to do paperwork, figuring that if I weren't there to talk to, she'd get organized. Before disappearing, I tell her that I never make breakfasts or lunches for anyone except Ben but that supper is my job. I tell her that she can make a sandwich, cook macaroni and cheese, etc., and that I'll be glad to buy things she likes to eat so long as they aren't junk food.

No sooner had I started working than she appears. "This is neat!" she says, surveying the third floor. "We could make this into a TV room. I have a TV that we could put up here."

"No, Nikki," I hasten to say. "This is my work space."

"I've made a list of everything in the refrigerator that I could eat for lunch."

"Nikki," I say, in what I hope is a gentle manner. "Just pick something. I really need to work."

Eventually she does go out collecting. She offers to take Ben with her, but he doesn't seem interested. He and I have had some talks about Nikki. "There's a girl who has a problem at her house," I'd said.

"Let's get that girl," he'd responded immediately, but he doesn't seem to be warming to her. She's certainly not Beth. She's basically ignoring Ben, whereas Beth really paid attention to him. I'm not overly worried about that. By this time it's evident that Ben is going to be an only child, which is something that I didn't choose. I think it's important for Ben to know that he's not the only star in the sky. Lord knows, siblings don't always get along. So I'm not unduly worried that there's not much interaction between him and Nikki at this point.

Will is giving Ben time this weekend. Will seems to be comfortable with Nikki, but then, I have yet to meet the person that Will cannot get along with. He's big and tall and quiet, and to take a line from Peter Fonda in a long-ago movie, "He's doing his own thing in his own time." Kate and I had given him a birthday present once of a carved wooden snail with the words "Slow is beautiful." He has it at work where everybody concurs that it suits him

Nikki and I go to church on Sunday morning. I am not a church person, but I want to be supportive about her being involved with church. She chatters constantly on our fifteen-minute walk. She joined this church with her adoptive family although she was raised Catholic.

"Well," I say, "you can go back to the Catholic church now. There's one right around the corner from us."

No, she says and begins to talk about Matt again. Her boyfriend goes to this church. He and his dad always come in late, and they always sit right behind her. It is very clear that Matt is the attraction and not the church service. Nikki talks until the start of the service forces quiet, then nudges me later when Matt and his dad sit down behind us. Then we are alone with our thoughts, Nikki with hers of Matt, and me with my remembrances of the '40s and '50s in church with my family.

We spend part of Sunday afternoon looking over the mammoth catalog of classes for Nikki's first year at the high school, which begins in the tenth grade in our district. It's time to plan for that coming year, and I don't know where to begin. I think we had one mimeographed page at my high school for all three "tracks." This looks like a college catalog in comparison. Nikki leaves it so that Will and I can look it over.

When she leaves that night, I feel drained. A friend characterizes certain people as taking up more than their share of the oxygen. I feel that way about Nikki. Once, after dinner Saturday evening, she seemed to catch herself. "I talk too much," she said, jumping up from the table and carrying dishes out to the sink. She began running water for the dishes, but I stopped her, saying we'd do them later. Eventually I'll expect her to help, but I don't want her to feel that we're taking her just to get dishes washed and the house cleaned and Ben cared for.

A conversation earlier that week with another mother at Ben's daycare home touched on that point. "We're getting another teen-ager," I said. I've been excited about each kid. People talk about their pregnancies and new babies don't they? Adding a foster child is not that different.

"Oh," said the other mother. "Is she going to help you with the cooking and things?" This woman teaches at the college level, but her statement shows the power of the stereotype of the foster child as Cinderella.

March 1981

Things have been happening so fast that I'm trying to think back over how all this has come about. There are three people involved with finding a home for Nikki—two here in Cleveland and one in her home county. I think it was Mary, her school social worker, who called me first.

Mary is a friend of Ellen, a psychiatric social worker. I specialize in juvenile law, and together Ellen and I rent office space for our individual practices. When Mary called me, she said that Ellen had told her about the three girls we'd had, and she was wondering if we'd be interested in Nikki. "Nikki seems to be a neat kid. I think the problem is with the adoptive parents. They've decided to get a divorce."

We talk about that for awhile. I could hear Mary's concern for this kid in her husky, friendly voice. "Nikki wants to stay in this suburb. She's made some friends here, and she's got a boyfriend."

How long has she been with this family? "About a year and a half. I know that's longer than most placements would be if there's not going to be an adoption, but probably some of the issues surrounding the divorce made the time stretch out."

Is Nikki the only child in the family? "No. There are two younger biological children, a boy in sixth grade and a girl in eighth grade. But I

NEXT FRIEND: The Journal of a Foster Parent

really don't know all that much about it. I've been involved because I'm at Nikki's school. I'd like to give you two numbers. One is for a psychologist the family has been seeing. He can fill you in on some things, and then there's Nikki's agency worker, Kirsten. She'll really be in charge of placing Nikki."

I think it was a day or two later when I called Paul, the psychologist. Something has been bothering me about this situation with a family and two biological kids. Mary said that she thought the problem was really the parents. But they had two children before they added a third. They must have liked kids. If they'd been a childless couple who had tried to take on a teen-ager and failed, that would have been easier to understand. There must be some reason that a family would work out child custody with biological children and yet not work it out with an adoptive child. Could it be for purely financial reasons?

When I talk to Paul, I ask about that first. "Isn't it unusual for a family to add an adoptive child as the oldest?"

Yes. Paul seems to think that maybe adding Nikki was like having a baby in the hopes that it would keep the marriage together. He's not sure. He says that the couple tried very hard to separate their decision about the divorce from their decision about the adoption, insofar as that was possible. It seemed to be a split decision, but, warns Paul, the motivations could be unclear.

What was Nikki told? Paul thinks that she was given the divorce as the only reason. Paul talks a little about his work with the family. He seems to use behavior modification as the basic therapy. He had all the kids assigned specific tasks. The boy had to take out the trash, and the girls had to do the dishes. This strikes me as a bit sexist, but I don't get into that.

Nikki? Paul feels that she's made some real progress while with this family. She's lost some weight and has learned some things about managing money. She has a paper route. Part of Paul's behavior mod program for Nikki is that she has to take a shower every other day. This strikes me as unusual. Most sixteen-year-olds have to be pried out of the bathroom.

But, overall, Paul is saying that Nikki is pretty much an average kid who needs direction. Mom is quite eager at this point to have Nikki moved into a new home, so would I please talk with her caseworker, Kirsten? It's going to be Kirsten's task to deal with Nikki about this disrupted adoption, as it seems to be called in the trade.

When I call Kirsten, she is eager to meet with us as soon as possible.

"You can come now," I say, "but Will is off on his annual mountain-climb. He's attacking a mountain near Mexico City, and Ben and I will meet him in El Paso in a week or so."

Kirsten does come right away. She doesn't want to lose the chance to find a home in Nikki's old neighborhood. This way Nikki won't have to change schools or give up her paper route.

I ask how Nikki is taking all this. "Philosophically," says Kirsten. "She's not looking for another adoptive placement."

I voice something that's been bothering me. "Even if we know, and Nikki knows, that we're not adoptive parents, will we end up being de facto adoptive parents? If we're her last placement, where else will she have to come back to? And I really don't want to be an adoptive parent."

Kirsten sees my point, but she thinks the understanding is clear all around. "It has to be," I tell her. "Nikki has to know that when she graduates from high school, she'll be expected to move on."

Although Kirsten assures me that Nikki is clear about this, already I have a nagging worry that it's going to be awfully hard for me to push her out if she doesn't seem ready to go. And yet I truly am not interested in an adoptive relationship. I don't know why, but even when we thought we might never be able to have a biological child, I was not interested in adoption. I was interested in foster care, though I never talked with any of the agencies that place foster children. Then Ben came along. Kirsten and I talk until it is time for Kirsten to pick Nikki up at school. They come in, talking together, Nikki in the middle of some saga of ninth-grade intrigue.

Kirsten has asked Nikki to make up a list of questions for us.

She's written the questions on paper that she's folded very carefully into the shape of a fat arrow.

"Look at that, Ben," I say, "maybe Nikki can teach you how to make an arrow like that." Ben has been sitting very quietly, watching all of us.

"Sure," says Nikki, carefully unfolding the arrow and reading from the list. Her first question is "Can I keep my paper route?"

"Of course. It's just on the next street, isn't it? As long as you can handle it, there's no reason that I can think of why you shouldn't keep the route."

The second question is, "Can I have my hamsters?"

"Sure." Hamsters don't bother me, although they may bother our border collie, Taco. We discuss that a little. Her current family has a dog, says Nikki, but since the hamsters stay in their cages, it worked out okay.

Her third question is, "Can I keep my baby-sitting and dog-and-cat-sitting jobs?"

Why not? Later I say to Ellen, "Isn't it sad that someone even has to ask those questions?"

"Perhaps they're rhetorical questions," she replies. "They're really statements that say 'Look what a good kid I am. I have a paper route. I babysit. I cat-and-dog sit. I am industrious.'"

When this visit with Nikki is over, Kirsten says that although she's Nikki's caseworker, she's in the adoptive section of her agency and that someone from Home Finding will have to come up to see us. I shudder inwardly. It was so simple working with Jean, who knew us, and whom we trusted in turn. "Our suburb has some regulations of its own," I say. "We'll have to get a conditional use permit. You have your person come up, and I'll check city hall to see what they want.

Will stays home one morning so that we can both meet with Joan, the worker from the home-finding unit. Since the time that Kirsten came, Ben and I had a mini-vacation wherein we flew to El Paso to meet Will. Unfortunately, he hadn't reached his goal of getting to the top of the mountain, but he'll try again. We relaxed by visiting friends in New Mexico for four days. During that visit I'd tried to fill Will in on everything that's been happening about Nikki. I guess that his head must have still been in the high altitudes, because when we sit down in the nook with Joan, his first comment is that he's not sure what's really going on.

I almost bury my head on the table. Joan must wonder about the communication in this household. But she seems to take it in stride and explains to Will a little of Nikki's situation. I feel like kicking Will under the table. Sometimes slow is not beautiful! Have we given some thought to what having a teen will be like, asks Joan. We tell her briefly about the three that we've already had. Is there any type of teen that we don't think we can handle? "Well," I say, "I think I'd have a hard time with a kid who had a drug problem or a girl who was sexually promiscuous."

"From what I understand, Nikki is neither." Only later do I recall that Molly was an alcoholic and that Beth's sexual involvement with a specific fellow was what had estranged her from her family. But Molly was involved with AA, and we barely got to know her. Within a few months she had decided that she could live at home again. Beth was certainly no problem to us, and she'd never given me any trouble about my rule of no guys on the second floor. Kate was the one kid who had no visible problems. She was an all-around sensible, mature kid who, for whatever private reasons, simply did not get along with her mother.

Had we thought what we might do about planning outings with Nikki?

No, not really. The other kids each had their own circles and their own interests. We'd just wait to see what things seemed to interest Nikki.

Joan has had one foster teen in her own home, and she seems to have a good grasp of teen behavior. She laughs about the behavior she calls "claiming"—the tendency for a foster kid to look carefully through an entire house, noting everything in the new environment. "Just ask Nikki where something is if you think you've lost it."

Funny. If Molly or Kate or Beth ever did that, I was unaware of it. I do remember, though, that Kate said she'd taken Beth around, showed her how the washing machine worked, how we liked the dishes stacked, and how you had to be sure that the shower curtain hung a certain way if you didn't want to get water all over the floor. Kate was the one who had brought Beth to us, and she had simply taken it upon herself to "train" Beth.

Joan is pleased with her interview and our house. She leaves us official application blanks and a ton of material. Her agency has put together a foster parent handbook, and there's a goodly amount of material on money matters. This is something that we really hadn't gotten into with the other girls. Jean had decreed that each would pay us $15.00 per week, based mostly on their earnings as waitresses, etc. But now we'd be "official" foster parents, licensed by the state, and we'd get a monthly check from Nikki's county. We would get $4.99 per day, and each month there would be $24.00 for clothing. Twice yearly there would be an extra $90.00 or $100.00 for spring and fall clothing needs. How anyone can accuse foster parents of being in it for the money is beyond me. In fact, the application contains an acknowledgement by the parents that they have sufficient income to support a child regardless of any agency stipend.

When Joan is leaving, I say that I'll handle the local conditional use permit and will return her agency's application to her. We have to supply three references, something that Jean hadn't needed.

March 1981

For her second weekend with us, Nikki has brought an armload of photo albums and a couple of boxes of loose pictures instead of the tape recorder. She shows me all her friends. Some of the loose pictures are from Matt's seventh-grade dance and from her two birthday parties at the

Yanceys. But I am most interested in two of the albums. One is a baby book of the commercial variety, kept by her mom in a somewhat sketchy fashion. The other is hand-lettered on the cover: Life Story. Her caseworker has helped her make this book. There are pages of printing and pages of pictures. The book tells, in very simple words, the story that Kirsten has already told me.

I love the pictures—all the way from the usual wet-rat infant picture through the one year-old with the cute curl on top of her head to the pretty, long-haired four-year-old. There are pictures of most of the families that she's stayed with as well as some of her own family. This book is important not only to Nikki but to me as well. It is the history that I never had with her. I need to know what those earlier years were like, and this book is my memory bank.

Not, of course, that it really makes up for the lack of personal knowledge of that earlier time. Nikki is not a kid that one warms to. There's an insolence that flickers on her face like the warning light on the dashboard of a car when a system is starting to fail. Nikki's systems do not work well. She has no grace, no warmth, no sensitivity. When I feel the insolence and the anger, I want to smack her. But I know that none of Nikki's systems have ever been given preventive maintenance.

March 1981

It is inspection day, a cool but very bright and sunny morning. Our suburb is dispatching three men to look over our house: a fire warden, a health inspector and a building inspector. My attitude about all of this is that it is a tremendous pain in the ass, to say nothing of an invasion of my civil liberties. However, I figure that our house will pass easily. If it doesn't, I can act like a lawyer. On my return from taking Ben to the babysitter, the fire warden and the building inspector are waiting. As we expected, the fire warden decrees that we must have a smoke alarm in the house. He also talks with me about some hairline cracks in the fireplace brick, but all that he notes on his official sheet is the lack of a smoke alarm.

While he is doing this, the building inspector is carefully measuring the house, making sure that the square footage is sufficient to sustain what will become a family of four. How silly it is that we are reduced to measuring square footage because we can't calculate the atmosphere of love and caring that is far more important. Fine, he says, there is no problem with the square footage except that the ceiling on the third floor is too low to allow any sleeping room up there.

The third floor is my hideaway anyway. I've worked so hard to paper and paint it and have splurged on lovely forest green carpeting. My home desk is up there, and I have plans for a couch and a bed that will be a guest bed—not that I see fit to mention that latter point. I'd really begun feeling the need for third floor space with the other teens. Our downstairs is small and completely open, and the third floor is a perfect get-away.

Before all of this is over, a tiny little man appears, bearing a city business card with the title of Sanitarian. He is there to look at the bathrooms, I guess. "Oh," says he, with one quick look at Nikki's "suite" and the second-floor full bath, "I have no problems with this at all." And he disappears. Now it is just a matter of waiting until the city manager approves the application.

March 1981

I'm trying to remember when it was that I met Peggy for the first time. She's Nikki's adoptive mom. On one of those weekend visits, Nikki, Ben and I walked over to Peggy's house to pick up some item that Nikki had forgotten. I was a little apprehensive, but both Peggy and Russ were quite hospitable. Peggy is a very slender, attractive woman, and Russ is a dark-haired fellow who's putting on a bit of weight. I know that this must be an extremely difficult time, waiting until physical arrangements are set. Nikki will be leaving, and Russ will move to a job out of state.

Kirsten asks Peggy and me to meet her for lunch to talk over some elements of this transition. Peggy seems to be handling the strain well. She's chosen not only to divorce her husband, but, in a very real sense, Nikki, too. But she's polite and gracious. I don't expect her to discuss why she feels the way that she does about Nikki. After all, she wants me to take this child. And I don't really want to know, because then I won't even give Nikki a chance. So I ask questions about their household routine— bedtime, chores, etc. As we part, Peggy encourages me to call her with any concerns. I thank her for that, and I mean it. Since Russ will be taking a job out of town, I can't turn to him. I only talked with him once other than that day at their house. He had phoned for Nikki during one of the visiting weekends. "She's out somewhere," I said. "Would you like me to have her call you when she comes in?"

"No. Just tell her to come over and get her bike out of the way. She's not to leave it there!" The anger in his voice was very clear. I wondered just how much was a product of the current difficult period and how much was a product of Nikki's individual temperament, which I was already realizing doesn't lend itself to following instructions. I do recall Paul's saying that Russ was the one who'd taken Nikki in hand about managing money so that she was doing a very good job now. Russ insisted that she bank a certain amount of her paper route proceeds.

I find myself wondering if Nikki's weight loss—and she's already gained most of the weight back, according to Kirsten—was to please an adoptive mom who is very slender. As we leave the restaurant, Kirsten tells us that Nikki has expressed a desire to keep in touch with the Yancey family. Peggy says that she will try to maintain some contact. "After all, she'll still be our paper girl!"

Kirsten has been calling about the permits; Peggy has been calling about the permits. No word has been received. Yet this morning Nikki arrives before school, saying that she and Peggy had a terrible fight, and could she just move in? "Okay," I say. It is a Friday, and she'll be coming for the weekend anyway. She can just bring over additional things. Later I call a city councilwoman I know. "Help! Can you do anything to find out what happened to our permit? Nikki and Peggy had a blow-out, and I told her to just move in. So she's here, but we don't have the permit."

My friend calls back later. "It's okay. The permit is on the city manager's desk, and he's going to sign it today."

April 1981

Nikki is a trip. She's pulled two hustles already. As the first Sunday approached, she said, "You'll get out the car and help me with my paper route, won't you." It is definitely a statement, not a question.

"No," I say. "We took you for better or worse, but not for the Sunday paper." She seems to accept that, probably on the basis that there's "no harm in asking" or perhaps she senses the irritation in my voice.

A few nights after that, she is scheduled to babysit at 8:30 for a regular customer. At 8:25 she is still in the kitchen, talking on the phone. At 8:27 she flies into the dining room, where we are sitting with guests after dinner. "Will somebody please drive me over? I'm going to be late!"

"No." I say. "You were standing there in the kitchen, right under the clock." I tell our guests that I figure we've just got to get this transportation issue sorted out early. None of the other kids ever asked us for a ride. I had voluntarily given Molly a ride to work once, when she had missed her bus. Later her AA sponsor told me not to bail her out. I'm resenting Nikki's attempts to make chauffeurs out of us, and I truly hope that I am conveying that to her.

April 1981

I've been trying to arrange with Peggy for a time when Nikki and I can come over to pick up the rest of her belongings. Nikki's brought over armloads of things, since she doesn't even own a suitcase. "I hate the thought of moving Nikki again," Kirsten had said. I'd told her not to worry, that I'd take care of it. But I couldn't seem to pin Peggy down to a time. She was not responding like the person who wanted Nikki out of her house as soon as possible.

But finally we have a date, and Nikki and I go over in the station wagon. There are so many boxes, and I have to remember that some are boxes of things that Nikki really keeps in storage—her childhood toys, for instance. All that this child has in the world is in these cartons. Peggy gets out her wagon, and we make a couple of trips while Nikki supposedly puts other things from her room into boxes. Peggy seems really exasperated with Nikki's slowness and berates her for overfilling a trash bag that then bursts all over the floor.

Finally everything is moved. While Nikki arranges all the upstairs things—the storage boxes having been stashed in the basement—I begin dinner. Later she comes down to the kitchen. "Peggy was really mean to me," she says.

"Yes, she was," I agree. "Perhaps it was harder for her to see you go than she realized. After all, you all had good wishes when you went there to live, and there has to be a sadness that it didn't work out." It was a good speech, but I really didn't believe it myself—at least not all of it. I knew that Peggy was not totally sorry to see Nikki go.

But she was probably very sad at the end of a dream—of a happy marriage and three kids. I don't expect Nikki to be able to understand what Peggy is feeling; Nikki has enough of her own feelings to handle. I recall something that Kirsten had said. "Foster kids have a very difficult time putting themselves in someone else's shoes. It's almost as though they're trying so hard to keep themselves balanced that they can't really think about anybody else."

April 1981

Perhaps there's an underlying motive for Nikki's persistent requests for chauffeuring. Today she pipes up brightly with, "Kirsten

But this news about my bright and beautiful cousin has sent me into a panic.

My first experience with parenting came after my mother died. I still remember standing in that farmhouse kitchen, after the funeral, and hearing my brother Tom say, "I guess I'm your little boy now." He was nine, and I was eighteen. I'd taken care of him during my mother's last year of incoherent illness. He was fun. I had found that I liked "doing for him," as they say in that rural area. I liked taking him shopping for clothes, liked cooking. We developed a rather free-wheeling life-style. I let Tom and my sister Alice choose the menu for one evening meal each per week, and sometimes we had ice cream for breakfast because it was fun and tasted good.

It's strange. Even today I sometimes call Ben, "Tom." My first memories of dealing with a little boy are of Tom, and I guess that's just embedded. I find parenting Ben easy. I fear that parenting Nikki will be just as difficult as parenting my sister, who is four and one-half years younger than I am. In truth, I couldn't parent Alice. There is no thirteen and one-half year old anywhere who is going to take orders from an eighteen year-old. And maybe I can't parent Nikki either.

Sometimes I'm struck by the cold fear of the pattern of time. As Nikki grows to eighteen, will I die? Has she come to take care of Ben? That's part of the "cancer crazy," and it's so private that outside of two very close friends, I just don't discuss it. I have to deal with it myself, as I've always dealt with the concept of a shortened lifetime. If I'm alive at fifty, I intend to throw one hell of a party.

April 1981

I've been busy at Juvenile Court again. I've always got about six cases pending, and some of them are always bears. Once in awhile, one will hibernate for a few months, but eventually most of them get up on all fours and begin roaring. Paying attention to these cases frees my mind from constant thoughts about how best to handle Nikki.

Even though the cases wear me out, I like the work. For four years now, I've been participating in something called the Guardian ad Litem project. A GAL is a person whose task is to represent the best interests of the ward—usually a child or a minor parent or an incompetent parent. The Project also assigns counsel in many cases, where the attorney plays the usual role of advocate for the client. The difference is that the GAL makes his or her own determination of the ward's best interests—which sometimes varies from the ward's perception.

I've tried to explain to people—and to myself—what it is that I like about the juvenile cases. I don't think it's the lawyer in me, even though juvenile court is widely underestimated. Very few practitioners realize the power of that court. It can permanently separate parents and children, and it can lock children up in jails—forget the euphemism "institution."

The stakes can be very high in juvenile court, and most of the people who appear there are indigent. I think of us GAL/Counsel as the interns and residents of the legal system. I've learned my trade on these indigents, but I'm not going to move on. I take about ten cases a year. One or two might be delinquency cases, but the rest are neglect, dependency and abuse cases. In the latter I'm often assigned not to the child but to the parents when children's services wants to take the children away from the parents, either temporarily or permanently.

I've thought that it might be the social worker in me that is drawn to these situations. That's a family tradition. My mother was a social worker, and I was going to follow in those footsteps. But a money shortage— among other things—led me to get a one-year master's in library science rather than the two-year master's in social work.

A good bit of the skill needed in these cases is social work—getting people to open up, analyzing what it is they need and helping them find the right sources of help. I have become very cynical about the help that social agencies promise. As far as I can tell, help is the exception rather than the rule.

I think that it's the writer in me that is most drawn to juvenile court, which I have came to call, not without fondness, the East 22nd Street Theatre of the Performing Arts. Where else would I find these characters and these stories? Where else would I meet this range of people? Although all qualify as indigent under the court's guidelines for appointed counsel, all classes and types of people arrive at that court. And each has a story.

April 1981

Nikki has certainly snuck one by me about the hamsters. "Can I have my hamsters?" she asked at our first interview, leading me to think that she already had hamsters. But no. She indeed had a number of hamsters while she was at the Yanceys, but all died, and Russ finally said that he didn't think that he could take any more hamster deaths, and she could have no more hamsters.

However, she has all of their cages, toys, houses, tunnels, and food. And I stuck to my word. She has now bought two hamsters: a brown female with a white ring around her middle, named Oreo, and an angora male, Fluffy. She has two cages going for these two, as I have definitely said that I don't want baby hamsters.

The first few days she had the animals with her all over the house. She'd sit on the couch, letting Oreo crawl from one hand to the other. At night before bedtime she'd let them run around on her covers. They strike me as being her family, more important to her than pets are to most kids. After all, in the "hamster family," she can be the mom, can have a measure of control that she's never had with other families. I'm not too fond of Fluffy. He's ratty looking, but I do like Oreo. She's cute, and I like the way she stuffs food into her pouches.

A few weeks after the hamsters arrive, Nikki takes a bus trip to see two friends from her first adoptive placement. She's just going to be gone for two nights, but she gives me full instructions on the care of Oreo and Fluffy. The first morning that I go in to check the beasts, Oreo has already maneuvered her cage cover aside, despite the brick on top, and is nowhere to be seen. Cursing, I get down on my hands and knees and look around the room. Finally I see a pair of beady eyes under the dresser. Somehow I rout her out, and eventually she gets to a point in the room where I can catch her. I grab her by the scruff of her neck and drop her into her cage a little faster than I'd intended. I watch carefully for four or five minutes, but she seems okay. I find another brick and put both on top of the cage.

May 1981

Nikki comes home from school every day with a litany of complaints. This teacher gave too much work. That kid made a remark about her clothes. Another kid threatens to kick her tail. Our before-dinner conversation is virtually all negative. She is like a porcupine with her quills up. Only after supper does she seems to relax. Supper is usually a good time. Will's home to share the kids, and once I've quit running around and have gotten dinner on the table, I can relax.

I am concerned about the fact that she doesn't get along well with the other kids. I've talked to Peggy about that. She's been very helpful. "You know how junior high schoolers are," she'd said. "And Nikki is a perfect victim for them to pick on because she shows that it gets to her. I got really upset once because someone wrote in lipstick on the back of her white jacket. The jacket was new, and it had to be cleaned. I talked to the principal, but I didn't get anywhere."

I've heard from my neighbors that the junior high is really tough these days. Part of it seems to be racial and part of it seems to be just plain fighting, even between girls. When I went to school, that just didn't happen. Girls were certainly catty, but they never hit each other.

"I know," Peggy says in that delicate little voice. "But that's what Nikki's getting into now. If she'd learn to keep her mouth shut, it would help."

May 1981

Of all her subjects, Nikki is having the most trouble with algebra. Will sits with her nightly for at least an hour and a half, going over problems with her. I ask him if he thinks she stretches the time out for attention. I know that Ben usually gets Will's evening time and that it is hard for him to see his dad giving this time to Nikki.

No, Will says, he doesn't think that Nikki is angling for attention. He thinks that Nikki is one of those kids that just has no feeling whatsoever for math at that level. From what one of my friends on her paper route says, she doesn't even have a feel for basic arithmetic.

"I wish I knew how to handle this," says Will, who is really a good teacher. "We go over and over the same thing, and by the end of each session it looks as though she's got it. But by the next night, it's as though she's never seen these problems before."

"I guess you'll have to consult with your mom," I laugh. Will's mom teaches what she lovingly calls "bonehead math" at a community college.

May 1981

Nikki seems to have so many activities that I'm wondering if she spends enough time on her school work. She does her paper route, she visits with friends, she takes piano lessons, she goes to the church youth group, and there doesn't seem to be time left for doing schoolwork. I call Peggy to ask how she had handled that. "I made her study one half-hour for each course. She had to be in her room—no radio, no music, no phone calls."

I tell Nikki that I think that schedule is sensible, and that furthermore, she can use my desk on the third floor to study. The first afternoon that she goes up to work at the desk, I am sorting laundry in my bedroom directly underneath. There are some amazing bangs and crashes. I run up the third-floor stairs. "What in the hell are you doing?"

She is sitting at the desk looking surprised. "There was a lot of banging," I say. And as soon as I return to the second floor, the noises begin again.

"Look," I say, from the third-floor stairwell, "if I hear any more noises, you can study in your own room." For the time being, the noises cease.

May 1981

"I'm going to Juilliard and be a singer," Nikki has been saying from the start. Why? "Barry Manilow went to Juilliard." Why a singer? "I have a good voice. I'm in the junior high choir, and I've auditioned for Heights Choir and made it."

That's true, and I have heard that Choir is quite an honor. But Nikki's never gotten solo parts in junior high, even though she's tried out for them. And I'd expect a singer to sing. Singers sing. They trill as they go around the house, they hum as they put on their shoes. One night Will takes her to the library to look at the Juilliard catalog. "Secondary piano competence," he says upon their return.

"That is more than the little red books," I tell her. Nikki is taking piano lessons, and after two years, she's still in the little red books. She's been told that she can practice at her church, since we don't have a piano, but she hardly ever goes. I remember my Oberlin classmates who were in the conservatory. Getting them to play or sing was never the problem. Getting them to stop long enough to do something else sometimes was.

May 1981

Will and I go to hear Nikki sing in her junior high school choir spring program. We got a babysitter for Ben. Nikki came home from school saying that one of the black girls picked a fight with her and gave her a knot on the head and a bruise on her leg. The bruise doesn't look too bad to me, but it is a bruise. I didn't get a good look at the knot.

The program goes well. I'm surprised at the talent of some of the singers. Nikki has a special part in a trio, but compared to the soloists, her voice is just average. It's fun for me to look around the auditorium to see which people I know have junior high-schoolers.

It's a nice spring evening, and the three of us walk home. When we get on our street, Nikki whispers "Uh oh. See those kids up there? Those are the preps. They give me a rough time."

"Don't worry about it," I say, knowing that Will's six foot plus height is with us. The kids are standing on the sidewalk, and they do not move. I just get off and walk around them. One says "Good evening, sir" to Will but doesn't move.

The next morning I am reading the paper and having tea when Nikki comes through on her way to school. "What am I supposed to do if those girls beat on me again? A whole bunch of us were in a fight at the beginning of the year, and any of us could get suspended if we fight again. My mother always told me not to start a fight but that if someone picked on me, I could hit back."

I sigh. "I really don't know," I say. "Maybe I ought to call the principal."

So before I leave for work, I do call the principal. "I'm Nikki's foster mother," I say. "I'm sure you know that she's left the Yanceys. I'm calling because a girl hit her yesterday and has apparently threatened to hit her again. I'm pretty new at this, and I'm not sure what to do."

"Well, we've had trouble with Nikki before." He sounds truculent.

I decide to be nice. "I can understand that, after living with her for awhile. However, it appears that she didn't start this particular fight, and when she asked me how to handle the situation, I wasn't sure what to tell her."

He says a few things that don't really make any sense to me.

"Okay," I say, "here's my plan. I'm a lawyer, and I specialize in juvenile law. I'm down at juvenile court a lot. Why don't I just file on Ruth, and we'll let a referee hear it?"

"Aaaahhhh, I think I might be able to do something about it."

"Very good. I'll leave you my work number if there's a problem." When Nikki comes home, she says that she and Ruth had to go to the office and write narratives of what happened. I hear no more about it, and I don't worry because school will end in a few weeks.

May 1981

I'm sitting in the backyard with a friend when Nikki comes home from a session with Paul. She's barely off her bike before saying, "Anne, you may have to talk to Nancy. She says that Matt can't take me to the dance." She looks stricken.

"Why not?"

"I don't know. She says he has to take someone else. I've got to call Dana." She vanishes into the house.

I turn to my friend. "This is big tragedy. Matt is Nikki's boyfriend. Or at least that's what she calls him. I really don't know that he considers her his girlfriend. To my knowledge, they've gone to one movie since she's been here. He's two years younger, and, given Nikki's immaturity, that's fine. He lives near her adoptive home, and she really seems to care about him.

"This dance is the big year-end thing at his school—he's in private school. She went last year, and she never stops talking about it. She's got all of the pictures. His dad drove, and they went out for pizza afterward. It was a Very Big Deal. And she's been talking about this year's dance since she met us. But as you just heard, it looks like she's not going. This is stuff for Shakespeare."

My friend mused. "Do you think it's really his mother? Or do you think that's his excuse?"

"I don't know, but I'm inclined to think it's his mother. What I'm wondering about is whether it's overprotectiveness or some kind of rejection of Nikki."

"What do you mean, 'rejection'?"

"I don't know if I'm very articulate about it, but I'm wondering whether Nikki's changed status—adoptive child to foster child—means something to Nancy. She and the Yanceys are neighbors. Maybe Nikki was okay when she was being adopted, but now she's just a crumby foster kid. Nancy doesn't know us."

My friend shudders. "That's horrible."

"It is, but I don't think it's an unusual reaction. The other possibility is that Nikki's just made too much of a nuisance of herself. She phones constantly, and every morning she goes over on her bike to accompany Matt to the bus stop. Maybe Nancy is just tired of that.

Later, getting supper, I think back over what Nikki has told me about Matt's family. Three children in that family died of congenital heart defects. Somehow Matt escaped the malady. That could certainly make a parent overprotective.

At dinner Nikki still seems worried and preoccupied. "Did you talk to Paul about this today?" I ask.

"Yes. He said to be sure that it was Nancy and not Matt. He said that maybe Nancy is taking Peggy's side or something."

"That's occurred to me, too. Well, talk with Matt, and see what you think."

May 1981

We're going to have to make some decision about the telephone. When Molly was with us, she asked if she could put in a phone at her expense. It was important to her to be able to call AA friends at any hour, and we certainly had no problem with that.

Neither Kate nor Beth seemed to use the phone very much, but no sooner did Nikki discover the phone jack near her bed than she wanted to know what it was. When she found that it was to a separate line, she was barely restrainable. She'd pay for a phone with her paper route money, could she have one, could she, could she?

From my personal point of view, it's fine if she has her own phone because it will get her off our phone. She's been pretty good, but she's not like Beth who was always careful to ask if we were expecting a call or might be needing to make one. Will it be indulging Nikki to let her get a phone? I think back to my own teen-age years on a ten-party line. I also went to a school district that was a toll call from our tiny exchange. "Does your phone ever ring?" a sympathetic friend once asked.

There would be one additional benefit. I can certainly do without the irate calls from paper route customers. Nikki can give them her number and take her own flak. The route is in her adoptive neighborhood, and most of the people know Nikki and her situation. A psychologist called recently to complain that Nikki taped a collection envelope right smack in the center of a window and that the tape wouldn't come off. We commiserate. "That's what deprivation will do," says she.

We decide for the phone, and on a Saturday, an ecstatic Nikki and one of her friends go with me to the phone company store. She ends up with a blue trimline and requests two special features, speed dialing and call waiting. "Come on," I say. "Let's not get ridiculous about this!" But it's a nice day, and she's so excited that I decide we'll talk about speed dialing at home during the fifteen-day trial period. Call waiting I have some sympathy for, but speed dialing for her nimble, teenage fingers?

Nikki is barely able to wait until the phone is turned on. I don't think it is ever out of her hands now, and I wonder if the plastic will melt.

Nikki's been seeing Paul every other week or so since she came to us, although she hasn't been extra careful in keeping appointments. But now she's come home saying that Paul says her next session is her "graduation," and that he'd like us to come, too.

We all go, Will, Ben and I. Paul's office is in a perfectly awful cinder-block-ugly building. The decor is not much at all, but I do like the poster in the waiting room that says, "You're not okay; I'm not okay; and that's okay."

I'm puzzled by Nikki's attitude when we go into Paul's office. She seems hostile, slouching in her chair with her legs shoved out in a not-too-relaxed manner. Paul asks her how things are going and gets an "Okay." So he turns to me.

"There's only one major thing that I'm worried about," I say. "I'm concerned about Nikki's attitude toward Ben. It's not a friendly attitude. Whenever she speaks to him it's in a negative tone. It's 'Why did you leave your truck there, Ben. I fell over it.' There's no kindness there."

Paul nods understandingly. He's a big bear of a guy with black hair and beard. "Ben is your child. He has your acceptance in a way that Nikki envies. What you need to do is catch her right at the time that she's being negative and point it out to her."

Did it have anything to do with Nikki's dislike of the youngest Yancey child, also a boy? Probably, says Paul, looking at Nikki for a response that is not forthcoming. I'm very unclear as to why Paul feels that this girl is ready to "graduate" from therapy.

He begins talking about the culture clashes that Nikki has had throughout these moves. Now that certainly is perceptive. Judging by the pictures that Nikki's shown us, her own family was definitely blue-collar. And most foster homes are blue-collar. But her two adoptive homes were white-collar, as are we. Paul talks about the clash of different values and the confusion that these things have caused Nikki.

"I think I see what you mean," I say. "Let me give you an example and ask you a question at the same time. I don't agree at all with the way in which Nikki handles her paper route. She doesn't get the papers out on time, and if she's short of papers, she doesn't call in, she just goes off to school. I wouldn't do a route that way, and I would not let Ben do a route that way. But my feeling has been that those values are so settled in Nikki that there's no point in my trying to change her. My solution has been to just stay out of the paper route altogether."

Paul seems to agree with this. "You're right. There are things that you just have no control over with a teenager. With a younger child it might be a different story."

Will has a question about the driving issue. He's wondering about Nikki's level of responsibility. Paul stresses what a serious responsibility driving is. "You got stuck with that," says Paul to Will. "The Yanceys knew by the time that Nikki turned sixteen that she wouldn't be staying with them. But she didn't know, and they weren't ready to tell her. So they just kept on saying that she could take driver's ed in the fall. Well, you'll have to work it out, but, Nikki, it's definitely not a right that you have just because you've turned sixteen. It's clearly a privilege."

Paul then speaks a bit about the fact that he's worked with the Yancey family as far as he can. He apparently has been working with Peggy and Russ on the divorce issue and working with the kids separately on their individual issues. Although he doesn't really say so, I catch the drift that money is a question. At this point, Nikki is not covered by the Yancey's insurance, and her agency seems to be questioning further therapy. But we leave with Paul encouraging us to call him if we run into a snag in the fall. He'll be away for a part of the summer and will be moving his office when he returns. But we're more than welcome to call him with problems.

June 1981

It's now quite clear that Nikki isn't going to Matt's prom. Nancy has simply refused to let him go. She's insisting that he go with the daughter of one of her friends. Matt says that there is just no arguing with her.

Nikki is desolate. Will and I are sympathetic enough that we offer her a trip to Cedar Point on the day of the dance. CP is a huge amusement park, and Nikki is a CP freak. She asks if she can take along her friend Stacy, (Spacey, as I call her), who I think is at least half a bubble out of plumb. But I agree, and we also ask a neighbor and her kids. All of us have a bang-up day, and I'm wondering if Nikki's mind has been sufficiently diverted. I think so until, on the ride home, late at night, she looks at her watch and says, "I'll bet they're having pizza now."

Notwithstanding this setback to the relationship, Nikki keeps pushing for us to invite Matt over for dinner. "I'd really like to have him." I say, "That's not the problem. But I'd hate to set up a situation where Nancy could forbid him to come."

I've been trying to help Nikki's relationship with Nancy in at least one way. Nikki must call Matt three or four times a night, and she's always very brusque. "Matt there?"

I've suggested "Hello, Nancy, this is Nikki. Is this a good time for Matt to come to the phone?" She's actually tried it at least once in my hearing. It certainly can't hurt.

Finally I decide that I will call Nancy. To my happy surprise, we have quite a nice conversation. I tell her that I've heard she's passed the bar and that congratulations are in order. I ask her if she has any interest in the program at juvenile court that I've been working in. Then I say that I just wanted to touch base with her because I know Nikki's invited Matt to dinner and I wanted her to know that it's perfectly all right with me. "I know that sometimes with these kids you never know what they've checked out with parents and what they haven't."

Nancy laughs. She says that certainly Matt can come. We make big plans for pizza, and Nikki cleans her room completely. We've decided that so long as she leaves the door wide open, Matt can go up to see Oreo the hamster and can play checkers.

Matt is great. Nikki's told us all about his home computer and his great interest in it. Will gets him talking about it, and the two of them really have fun. Will even gets out some old Scientific American magazines, and the two of them work on some of the mathematical puzzles. Will is clearly impressed with Matt's mathematical abilities and later wonders aloud to me how Nikki will ever fit into the computer world.

All in all, it is a very successful evening. I think that Nikki is pleased.

July 1981

I finally get a chance to observe directly Nikki's difficulties with math. She has failed algebra and is taking a basic math course in summer school. This will supply the necessary credit that she needs to get from junior high to senior high. I can see from the assignment papers she brings home that one of the things they're working on is area problems. Good old square feet.

Fine. I have a very practical problem to give her. We've been talking since our first foster teen about painting and papering the tiny lav that's part of the "teen suite." For some reason, a previous owner painted it a horrible electric blue. It's really ugly, with wrecked linoleum floor, but none of the other teens ever took me up on my offer of sharing painting and papering with them. However, right away, Nikki had.

So I tell Nikki that if she figures out the square footage of the bathroom walls, we'll know how much paper to buy. She likes this idea very much and goes immediately to find the yardstick. However, she's back downstairs in a minute, clearly not understanding where to begin.

I go back up with her. "Let's start with this small wall behind the toilet. We measure its width, then we measure the height. Since the walls are conveniently divided into two of a kind, our work is cut in half. We measure one of each and multiply by two. Then later we'll subtract for the door and the little window."

I return downstairs and soon hear a terrible banging. I fly back upstairs to find that Nikki has taken her fist and knocked out the shelf that's across the wall above the toilet. Luckily the shelf simply rested on two molding strips and was not nailed in. "What are you doing?"

"I couldn't measure the height of the wall with the shelf in the way."

I have to stop to think very carefully before I dare to answer. "Sure you could. You measure up to it, measure beyond it, and add the width of the shelf. But there's a much easier way. The ceiling is the same height everywhere in the room. So just pick a clear shot and get your measurement."

She is looking at me in a way that very clearly says that she does not understand at all what I'm talking about. I take the yardstick and go over the process for her. I multiply, I add, I subtract the window and door space, and I tell her that this figure is our wallpaper figure. Later I tell this to Will. "I do not believe that she knocked out that shelf. I just do not believe it. What a one-way mind!"

"Now maybe you begin to understand what I was going through with the math." Will grins.

June 1981

I've become almost obsessed recently with talking about Nikki. We went to a dinner party last night, and I found myself just holding forth about our experiences with Nikki. I see a couple of elements there. First I do seem to be looking for a pat on the head. "Gosh, that's really great of you, taking in foster kids." Somehow I need that.

There's another need, too. I'm so unsure of myself. I'd know how to deal with another baby, but I don't know how to deal with a sixteen- year-old newcomer. There's so much about teenagers that I once knew firsthand but now don't remember. I need people's advice and ideas.

In truth, the subject seems to be interesting to people. They get really involved in the conversation, and many of them are genuinely helpful. They share experiences of their own in child-rearing. Everybody has ideas about raising kids. The ones that aren't helpful are the ones who say, "Well, she's just a normal teen-ager." In that she makes us uncomfortable, this may be true. But probably the reasons for our discomfort have little to do with the reasons for the discomfort of other parents of teen-agers. Nikki is hardly a normal teen-ager in any sense of the word.

July 1981

As a compromise to driving the car, Will gets out his ancient Honda 50, still sporting New Mexico plates. We laughed recently upon seeing an ad for that same model—at about three times the price Will paid in 1964. Will's been using it sporadically—never for long enough to think about getting new plates.

Nikki seems to like this idea. We insist that she wear Will's helmet, and pretty soon she's tooling around the block. "Okay," I say. "If we're going to do this, let's get legal about it. Will, you get the registration and license updated. Nikki, you get yourself licensed to drive the thing."

She promises to find out what she needs to do. The next day Peggy calls to say that she'd rather Nikki didn't give the kids rides. She's told Nikki this, but she wants me to know what Nikki's up to. I should have realized that she'd have to show off.

"No rides," I tell her. "You're not licensed, and that thing is not insured. This is no joke." So far as I know, that solves the problem.

August 1981

A neighbor has dropped by, and we're watching our little boys play. She's in the throes of deciding whether to have a second. Her career is important to her, and she's wondering whether she can handle two kids. "I looked at our dinette set the other morning, and I asked myself who was missing. It's like we're supposed to have two kids."

I laugh. "There's obviously a lot of that in me, and I don't know where it came from. Sometimes I think I had an unhappy childhood, but there must have been something more positive there than I thought."

"How many were in your family?" she asks.

"Three. Four. One child died. I barely remember her, but I always think of four when I'm asked the question. We really grew up as a family of three children. It took me years to realize that my younger brother and the sister that died were never alive at the same time.

"I've wondered, too, about the books that our mothers read and that I've seen or picked up—Jean Kerr and Peg Bracken, for example. They were about women and families."

My friend nods. A lot of her academic work has been in women's studies, and she knows all too well the role models we've had. "Those things are really strong. I know the dinette set represents an average, it's not a mandate. But the push for two is a very hard push in our society."

"Well," I say, "there were times when I did feel that somebody was missing, but right now I have the feeling that everybody who ought to be

27

here is here."

August 1981

Kirsten comes up for a visit this week. She wants to talk to me first, then she and Nikki will go out for lunch. "How's it going?" is her big question, of course.

Overall okay, I tell her, though there are some problem spots. Nikki's still snappish with Ben, and she's so wearing for me. She just talks incessantly.

Yes, Kirsten is aware of that. "These kids are so needy. It's as though they can never get enough attention. It's awfully hard on the parent, though."

"It sure is. There's been one place that I just won't give. When I get up in the morning, I make a cup of tea, and I read the paper. That's the start of my day, and I'm off-center without it. Even when Ben was a baby, I insisted on that time, even though it got cut down a bit. But the first morning that Nikki was here, she bounced in from her paper route, plopped down next to me at the table where I was reading, and just started in on a monologue. 'Whoa,' I told her. 'This is my time to read the paper. You can talk later.'"

Kirsten laughs. "You really do have to do that with her."

"I was just thinking of something else. Last week I was picking up some of Ben's things in the sunroom when she came in from summer school. She was talking about some school problem, but every time I offered a suggestion, she had some reason to turn it down. It finally hit me that she was just being argumentative."

"At least you recognize it for what it is! There was one placement where she just drove the father up the wall. He didn't understand what she was doing."

As Kirsten talks, I realize that that particular placement lasted only a short time. The dad was a minister of a small, strict sect, which may have contributed to his unwillingness to put up with Nikki's constant hassling. But it isn't easy for me, either. "My problem is that I'm argumentative, too. I often find myself giving her a fight for a fight's sake. The trick is to just say, 'Look, I'm really not interested in a debate, so let's end this conversation.'"

Kirsten laughs but then becomes serious, saying that she's tried to put this off, but that she's been asked to transfer Nikki's case now that Nikki is not going to be in any further adoptive placements. "I'm in the adoptions department, and we're short-staffed, so my supervisor wants me to transfer Nikki's case to foster care."

I sigh. "Lord knows, I've worked in and around enough bureaucracies to know how they work, but it just strikes me that no one knows this girl as well as you do. You've had her case for five years. She's got three more years with the agency. What would be the harm in just letting you continue with her? At this point you wouldn't have to see her very often."

"I know, but I'm really getting pressure to transfer the case. I'm going to tell Nikki at lunch, and I don't look forward to it."

"One thing you and Nikki might work on before you get the case transferred is bringing her Life Book up to date."

"That's a good idea. I know we're behind on it."

Sometime later I tell Nikki that I'm sorry that Kirsten is going to have to transfer the case. To my surprise—and maybe relief—Nikki doesn't seem unduly concerned. Maybe with all the people that have come and gone in her life, she doesn't expect any permanency.

August 1981

The first "big" clothing check has come, so I've asked Nikki to make a list of her fall clothing needs. I realize what a pathetic amount of money $24.00 per month is for clothes for a teenager, but I've chosen to make her stay pretty much within those guidelines for several reasons. The first is the need for her to learn to budget money and to be independent about doing that. She needs to learn how to plan her spending. The second is that teens these days dress pretty casually. Nikki seems to have an endless supply of T-shirts and jerseys, and that's what the kids wear. Third, as Peggy pointed out, Nikki earns a lot of money from the paper route, babysitting, etc., so it's not unfair to ask her to put some of that on clothing that she needs.

I'm all for the casual dress of these kids. After being a teenager in the fifties, I was sick and tired of the hair curlers, of the starched and ironed baby-doll blouses, of the bulky crinolines, of not wearing boots in winter snow because "nobody" did, and for that matter, of having to dress exactly like everybody else. When I went off to Oberlin and found that I could wear the same jeans and sweatshirts that I wore at home on the farm, I rejoiced. What a glory it was to be free of the time and effort that went into trying to look like the fifties' model teen. Around 1970, when I routinely caught the bus downtown on the corner where Nikki's high-school stands, I chuckled at the jeaned and t-shirted high schoolers.

Nikki's generation is far less raggedy andy than the '70s teens, but they're still far less appearance conscious than my own.

On our first shopping trip, back in April, we'd spent ahead a number of months just getting lingerie and a pair of Nikes. And now we are looking for jeans and winter boots. Kirsten asked us to save all of the tags in case we were one of the lucky files that the state auditor decided to pull. I can just see some CPA with the gall to imagine that a foster parent could clothe a teen on about $450.00 per year. I'd like to see that fellow eyeball to eyeball. Maybe he'd also like to tell me that we have plenty left over on the $4.99 per day that goes toward food, toiletries, school supplies and anything else out of pocket.

Nikki's real lack in the clothing department is a really good outfit for special occasions. Will and I have discussed putting Christmas and birthday money into clothing for Nikki, and it looks as though that's what we'll do.

August 1981

One of my friends who lives on Nikki's paper route has asked Nikki to feed her cat while she's on vacation. Pat knows that she has me for insurance. Nikki does not have a sterling record with Pat either as a paper girl or as a cat-sitter. Once before she simply skipped the cat's meal when she couldn't get the lid off the can. So Pat called me before she left, saying that she'd left Nikki a note with her vacation telephone number and the back-door key.

The first day of the endeavor seemed to go okay. However, the second morning Nikki came in saying that she hadn't been able to open the back door. "I'll just wait until tonight."

"No, that's not fair to the cat. We'll stop on our way." I was driving Nikki to a babysitting job and taking Ben to Emily's on my way to the office. Will followed us over, and even he could not unlock the back door.

After dinner that evening, Will and Nikki went back over for a concerted effort. Ultimately they had to tear a screen so that Nikki could climb in through a kitchen window, let Will in and feed the cat. They could not get the door to lock again. "Guess I should call the locksmith," I said. "We really can't leave that back door unlocked."

I had a few minutes the next afternoon, and I called the locksmith, who said that he could meet me there in twenty minutes. He asked me to bring the key, so I phoned Nikki to meet me there. When I arrived, the locksmith was pulling up, but there was no sign of Nikki. "Excuse me for a moment," I said and came flying home. I was yelling when I came in the door.

"I just found the key!" was Nikki's response.

That night at dinner I told everybody that the locksmith said the lock was broken and would simply have to be replaced. "We'll have to call Pat to see what she wants us to do, what kind of lock she wants put on. Go look for her number, Nikki."

That night's search through the flotsam and jetsam didn't turn up the number, so I told Nikki that she couldn't leave the house the next day until she found it. By early afternoon, I was running out of patience, so I called Pat's office and got the number. The locksmith returned and replaced the lock.

That evening I gave Nikki a lecture on the evils of a disorganized room. "I am going to buy you a small filing cabinet. You are going to get some file folders and label them for keeping things like phone numbers and keys." I know there's something humorous about this entire sequence, but I am too peeved to laugh.

August 1981

Nikki has a three-week job babysitting for a little girl on her paper route. The mom is a nurse, and her regular full-time daycare mother is taking her own vacation. By the end of the first week, Nikki is saying how boring it is to stay with a little kid—Lia is just a year old—all day. Yes, it certainly is, I point out, hoping to encourage the truth of this observation, at least insofar as a sixteen-year-old girl goes. I don't want Nikki to think that there would be anything neat about being a teenage mother.

To ease her boredom, Nikki falls into bringing Lia over here when I'm not at the office. Oh, is Lia a cutie! And for some reason, she takes to me. One afternoon when I come back from running an errand, Lia comes toddling over with a big smile on her face. "Get the look on her," says Nikki in disgust. "She's been whiny with me."

Since Nikki is engrossed in something on TV, I say I'll take Lia for a walk around the block. I get Ben's old umbrella stroller, which he and a little friend have been using for a doll, put Lia in it, and walk around the block. Pretty soon I am making up a little song. I certainly won't tell Nikki how much I am enjoying mothering a young baby.

But I did, and the part of me that wanted a second has still not healed. There were two miscarriages before Ben and two after, and when I felt the depression descending, I simply made the decision that one child would have to be enough. I'd known too much depression in my twenties to take a chance on its return for any reason.

How much does this unfulfilled need of mine have to do with my decision to foster parent? I don't know, I truly don't. I don't feel any particular drive to take an infant or toddler in foster care. That would mean cutting back on my work time, and that's too important to me to give up. And if Jean hadn't called me, I don't know that I'd have actively sought out taking teens. There's just something about being approached directly, by a friend, that makes a kid's needs immediate.

But I truly didn't reckon on how much work having this teenager would be. I guess I thought that she'd be more like Molly, Kate and Beth, who were all quite self-sufficient. Perhaps in some ways they were old for their ages while Nikki is very much young for hers. She's very sloppy. She plunks stuff down just any old where, and I'm getting awfully tired of constantly telling her to move her things. The nook table, for instance, was not put there for the express purpose of holding her belongings.

She has a room—the largest bedroom in the house—to put things in. And in general, I'm not going to fuss about her room. Even Beth and Kate let the room get messy. I remember all of the wasted time I spent nit-picking with my sister over her room. After our mother died, I would nag Alice about cleaning up her room as though it were a major deal. I guess I learned then that there are some things that just aren't worth the time. So I don't worry about the "teen room" until the ants begin to crawl, as they did with Molly's crackers. But I do expect Nikki to keep her backpack, shoes, books, etc., in her room and not scattered over the downstairs.

I've included Nikki's laundry with ours all along, but I'm surprised at how much longer it takes to do a wash for four people than a wash for three people. Likewise, I'm surprised at how many more dishes there are. Cooking doesn't take any longer although I've had to revise some recipes. Nikki is a big eater.

I think it's taken me three or four months to revamp the household routines so that I don't feel that I'm always behind. My best neighborhood friend, Pam, keeps saying that I should ask Nikki to do more. Maybe I should, but it takes constant nagging . How many times have mothers said, "It's easier to do it myself?"

But it would be nice to get a little gratitude once in awhile. This child has never once offered an unsolicited "thank you." It's not just the extra housework. It's running errands for her, taking her places—though I'm pretty insistent on the bike and the bus. But there's never an expression of appreciation. "Oh, teens are just that way," people say.

Nikki is an interesting phenomenon. I still have a piece of notebook paper taped to the back of our bedroom door. "Thanks for everything. Love, Beth." She left that for us the first night she was here. But then, she's a normal kid.

September 1981

Liz calls about something, and we have the best talk. We've been friends for years. She's a clinical psychologist at a residential center for emotionally disturbed children. She asks how we're getting along with Nikki, and I say that my biggest worry is her treatment of Ben. In fact, I'm more upset about it now than when we talked with Paul about it last spring. That conversation didn't seem to mean a thing to Nikki.

Well, it won't, says Liz, not right away, at least. "You've got your hands full with a disrupted adoption. She's going through a lot of anger and upset. You've gotten her at the worst possible time, but you can't sacrifice Ben to her. You might just have to let her go."

"There are days when I feel like it."

"Look, you should be getting some therapy with her."

"Can anyone at your agency work with her?"

"Maybe so. Our residential kids are younger, but we've taken older kids on a counselling basis. Let me see what I can do."

September 1981

Nikki came bouncing in yesterday afternoon with a surprised look on her face. "I don't get it! I was coming down the street past two little kids, and they ran away from me. One said I looked mean."

I know exactly what the little kid meant, but I was at a loss to explain to Nikki how she looks sometimes. She'd have to see it on videotape. Her walk is almost explosive, as though she's barely managing to stay on the ground. It's anger.

September 1981

Liz has worked her magic, and I'm scheduled to see a therapist, Mara, for an intake interview. The first interview will be with me alone, for background, but the therapy will be family therapy.

I like Mara at first meeting. She seems to have what I call the "hearing ear." New York, her accent tells me. I outline Nikki's history and our sixth months with her. I'm basically worried about two things, I tell her. First, there's Nikki's constant unkindness to Ben. Second, Nikki just plain wears me out. I'm not a bad talker, but Nikki will talk from morning until night about absolutely nothing. Somehow the sight of another human form triggers her tongue.

We agree that we'll come every Tuesday at five. I leave feeling relieved already. Once a week I can come on a pleasant drive to this center situated in a lovely rural area and bring all of my worries to this brown-haired New Yorker who wears blue jeans and sits in a rocking chair.

October 1981

We had a session with Mara yesterday. Nikki is clearly not thrilled with these sessions, but she knows that she doesn't really have a choice about going. This time the topic is schoolwork.

"I'm having some problems with this school work," I say. "Nikki doesn't seem to be spending any time at all on her homework. I saw one of her teachers on the street, and she told me that Nikki needs to set time aside to go over the work for that course."

"Why is that your problem if Nikki doesn't study?"

I am both surprised and relieved. "Do you mean that it's not my problem?"

Mara looks at Nikki. "Nikki is sixteen. She's old enough to decide whether she wants to do her work or not. That's her responsibility."

Nikki doesn't really respond, except perhaps with a cursory nod. "There's one other thing that I need a little help with," I say. "I figured that Nikki needed a place to study, so I offered to let her use my big desk on the third floor. But I don't feel comfortable about her using it, and I'm trying to figure out why. First of all, I've found Nikki up there lying on the couch reading. I figure that she can lie on her own bed to read. I've offered her the desk, not the couch."

Mara responds, "You're a professional person. To you work means a special location. You go to your desk, and that environment says 'work' to you. You'd like Nikki to develop these same habits. You're certainly giving her the opportunity."

"Yes, but there's also something about having her in that space that bothers me. The best way that I can figure it out is this. That space is my psychological space. I planned to use it for a getaway back when we had Molly and Kate. The truth is that I don't use it very often, but it's there if

I need it. When Nikki's in it, it's not free. Even though there are other parts of the house that are free when she's there." I am not feeling very articulate. "I guess this doesn't make much sense."

"Sure it does," said Mara. "A lot of what we've been talking about here is personal space. Nikki invades your personal space with requests for attention. She wants to talk to you all the time. She wants to bring her friends over. She wants to drive your car. Now she wants your desk."

This is reminding me of something. I begin slowly. "Nikki, do you remember the first weekend that you were with us? I was up at my desk, working, and you came up to the third floor. You looked around, and you said, 'Hey, this would make a great TV room.' All I said at the time was that the attic was my very own space, but my feeling was stronger than that. Maybe what I really wanted to say was that the third floor is off-limits."

I feel that I can speak openly when we're with Mara. To me Mara is a moderator, an arbitrator. I don't trust myself to deal directly with Nikki sometimes. I need Mara there to put me on a leash. We talk some more about the studying. Mara is sticking to the position that Will and I should have very little to do with Nikki's schoolwork.

Needless to say, Nikki seems to like that idea. It's fine with me, too. That's one less worry for me. Nikki is enrolled in a program called New School. Some of its less attractive names are No School and Zoo School. No School seems to suit it best in Nikki's case, because it seems to be that the policy is for students to do what they want.

From one of my friends, I've found that N.S. was a seventies innovation at High. At its peak there were around six hundred students enrolled. The idea was to create a learning community where students and faculty could work together. Students could create courses, if they wished and if they could find a faculty sponsor. I'd read a very positive article in the local paper that included a quote from a parent who really praised the attitude of cooperation among the students.

My favorite high-schooler and ace babysitter, Glynnis, has told me that N.S.'s enrollment has fallen to a record low and that it probably wouldn't survive much longer. "The kids who are going to college usually want regular transcripts. Also, you really have to be self-disciplined to do N.S. If you've got that kind of discipline, then maybe it can work for you, but not that many kids do."

Certainly not Nikki, I think. However, I've been told that it's not my worry, and, as I think about it, it isn't.

October 1981

We've met Nikki's new social worker now. Do I feel old! Lee is just out of school, and I'm having the feeling that I'm training her. Now I'm beginning to understand how crazy it is to think that the social worker assigned to a case can possibly know a child as well as the foster family. The worker sees the child occasionally, but within a week the foster family has had seven days of exposure to the child and has learned more about that kid than the worker could in two years.

I'll still make some exceptions for workers who've had long-term involvement with a kid, such as Kirsten has had with Nikki, but even there, I can see that Kirsten has often been puzzled about Nikki's behavior. She's blamed herself for picking poor adoptive homes, but it seems to me that what Kirsten hasn't understood is that Nikki is an uncommonly difficult kid. Kirsten sees Nikki for an hour here or there, and Nikki looks okay on the surface. But Nikki isn't okay, and only long-term therapy will make her okay.

Even if we were geographically closer to Nikki's agency, could her agency worker provide that therapy? Even if the worker were prepared professionally to do that, would her caseload permit her to take the time?

I'm sure these factors are behind the fact that her agency has given no resistance at all to our doing therapy at a private agency. Even if Jane's not able through experience to offer real help, I don't think she'll be a hindrance. In my juvenile cases I've seen some workers who are disasters. I'd rather have hands-off than hands-on in one of those situations, thank you.

October 1981

What a week! I was beaten up by the Court of Appeals. They questioned me past my allotted fifteen minutes of oral argument. What a deluge of questions, usually having to do with my lack of objections on the record from the court below. I have learned something very valuable here. The next case I have that goes like this one, I will wallpaper the goddamned courthouse with objections.

And there will be another. That is the tragedy. There will be another parent who shouldn't lose her child to the custody of children's services. There will be the same endless continuances and delays. There will be the same built-in sympathy for the argument made by Children's Services.

That's true at both the juvenile court level and the Court of Appeals.

That appellate panel of three elderly white male judges did not want to hear about this mother whose tenth child is now in the permanent custody of Children's Services. Despite strong positive testimony for the mother by a visiting nurse, past history was enough to take this child away.

I feel sad, but I expected it. The hard thing is going to be to tell the mother. This was my first trip to the Court of Appeals, and I will do some things differently the next time. I had prepared a very scholarly argument, but that was useless. I need to tell a story, not be scholarly.

October 1981

Last night I went to my first meeting of the county foster care association. I'd gotten a letter inviting me to a special program to talk about county-wide planning for problems of foster care. The Juvenile Court administrator was there, as was a psychologist I've met who's worked with foster families. She's great. I think that I was invited because I've gained a small amount of notoriety for an article on foster parenting and since I work in a special program at Juvenile Court that provides counsel to parents accused of neglecting or abusing their children.

I was really impressed with the dedication of those foster parents. There are some 800 foster families in this county, but as usual, only a small number of them become active. Many are afraid to rock the agency's boat. The parents who have became active find themselves forced to tackle the agency on policy issues related to foster care.

A number of people came up after the meeting to talk, and they all had horror stories of being treated like interchangeable families with interchangeable foster kids. It's been hard for me to understand how cavalierly the system treats foster parents. Children's Services talks of "slots" instead of "homes."

I began to realize these things when I met Shirley Griffin. I'd heard about a special program for foster parents at Tri-C, the local community college, and when I did the newspaper piece, I called her for information. I found her to be an outspoken advocate for foster parents. A tall, blonde woman with a gravelly voice, she has raised three kids and said that there was no way she'd ever be a foster parent herself. It was just too hard.

"Foster parents have responsibility for a kid twenty-four hours a day, but everybody knows more than they do. Caseworkers. School officials. Psychologists. A lot of parents take our course because it allows them to build up some credibility, to say to all those officials, 'Hey, I have some credentials, too!'"

Shirley and I met for breakfast one morning so that I could learn more about her program. She brought along a book that Pennie Riha had written and illustrated for foster children. When Shirley told me about it over the phone, her voice fairly crackled with enthusiasm. When I saw the book, I could see why. The text was clear and sympathetic to the child's point of view, and the illustrations in pen and ink were charming.

I met Pennie in person for the first time last night, too, although we've talked on the phone before. She's dynamic and a real child advocate. Her husband is the current president of the association. They've been foster parents for fifteen years, and I'm amazed at the problems they've tackled.

It's not hard for me to see where the politics of foster parenting lie. The great majority of foster parents are blue collar. They don't have access to the levers of power in the community. They get pushed around by the agency that licenses them. I'm a professional person, and I've had virtually no problems dealing with Nikki's agency. That may be in part because Nikki's agency is smaller—and since it's located some distance away, it's harder for the worker to keep in touch. Actually, most foster parents complain about lack of contact—especially helpful contact.

I left impressed out of my head with those people who just keep on doing an incredibly tough job. They are the only ones who really know what this job of foster parenting is all about. They understand how tough these kids can be. As I fell asleep, I recalled one woman's telling me that she'd banked all the payments the agency sent her for a teenage girl. When that girl left to get married, the mom gave her the money to get started in life. And this woman and her family didn't have any extra money. Now children's services has taken away a baby put in her care for some less than clear reason and given the baby to another foster family. How can this woman continue to foster parent?

November 1981

I've had my fall interview with Ben's kindergarten teacher. I left just walking on air. My son is good, true and beautiful, as well as smart, and may even be a leader. It seems that we made the right choice of a kindergarten, despite some philosophical doubts. We live in a suburb with a good public school system—with certain reservations—and there are a number of private schools to be considered.

I was raised in a family with a strong allegiance to public education. My maternal grandfather taught high school mathematics in the days when the profession required the wearing of a three-piece suit. He died when I was an infant, but I've seen pictures of a handsome gentleman with a Phi Beta Kappa key and chain across his vest.

My own experience in the public schools was certainly mixed. I went off to Oberlin with a mediocre, small-town high-school education, and I was on the academic ropes for two years. Will's experiences were similar, even though we grew up in different states. Yet both of us felt that the public school system in our town was worth considering for two reasons. First of all, it was reported to have some strengths. Second, I'd been involved in community groups long enough to know how important a good school system is to the health of a community.

In truth, our community is involved in a struggle to remain integrated. The black population of the city seems to have stabilized at 25%. Yet the black population in the school system approaches 50%. Everyone has a pet theory for this, but it is obvious that the system can ill afford to lose white kids to private schools.

Yet Ben is in a private kindergarten. High on our list of necessities was a full-day kindergarten. Our neighborhood elementary school operates on the old-fashioned half-day—and to frustrate the working mother even further, the half-days "flip" at the semester. The system does have one extended kindergarten, although it's not at our neighborhood school. I visited it and found it depressing.

So I followed up a number of neighborhood recommendations of a private, Jewish school with an extended kindergarten. It's Montessori in concept, something of which I still know relatively little. We intend to enroll Ben in our neighborhood school for first grade, but we've picked this school for kindergarten.

It has seemed to work well. At the beginning of the year, I told Mrs. Farr, Ben's teacher, that we had a new foster daughter in our family and that I thought Ben might be having same reactions to her. I said that she was the hardest kid we'd had yet, and that I was having some difficulty, too. But at the conference, Mrs. Farr says that she hasn't noticed any upset in Ben about anything. I left floating and could hardly wait to tell Will.

November 1981

An interesting thing happened at the last session of my writing workshop. Not having anything else ready to read, I read an entry from this journal. Usually that group is very professional, very conscious of style and form. But everybody plunged in with "Why did you say that?

Why did you do that?" This journal is about family, and family is such a universal that we all get right into content. We wouldn't dream of criticizing anyone's fiction on those grounds—though we might ask "Do you think that's realistic?"—but after all, this isn't fiction. It's real life and therefore open to question.

November 1981

Today's session with Mara was so helpful. I started the day in anger. I wasn't feeling great physically, either, because I had a gall-bladder attack the night before. I ultimately gave up and took medicine for the pain. That always leaves me feeling groggy the next morning.

I wake up to the noise of the garbage trucks outside. I told Nikki to get her trash ready while we were eating supper last night. She said that she couldn't do it until after choir practice, so I said okay. As I recall, she came home from choir practice, got on the phone and talked until bedtime.

I get up, put on my robe and go down to the kitchen. But on the way I glance into Nikki's room, where I see a positively overflowing wastebasket. I am getting some tea when she comes in from her paper route. "Did you put out the trash?"

"There's hardly anything down there."

"When you add in the junk from your room, there will be plenty."

"I don't see what the point is in putting out a partially-filled bag."

"I am tired of your lip. You will either get the wastebaskets and put out the trash, or I will take the phone out of your room for today."

She looks amazed, then angry, then both together. She slams upstairs and returns immediately with the wastebaskets.

"I guess the phone is the way to get to you."

"It didn't have to be the phone. It could have been any threat."

"Why does it have to be a threat? Why can't you just do what you're asked?" I follow her to the top of the basement stairs, but then I stop, retreat to the dining room, and try to read the morning paper.

I do not read calmly. I am shaking. The adrenaline is overcoming the grogginess. I don't like confrontations. I think for the millionth time about how much more complicated my life has gotten since Nikki came. I feel that I have bitten off more than I may well be able to chew.

I go to the office, and on my way there, a fragment of her weekend commentary came to me. "I knew just how far I could push Russ before he would sit on me." Is there a pattern here? What is it? Why does she have to push us? We're doing the best we can. We're out there on a limb; do we really need to hear the sound of the saws?

The anger washes away during the day as I work. I am struck again by how much I like what I'm doing—this mixture of juvenile and probate work. The anger begins to return when I pick up Nikki for our drive to the agency. Today is sunny, clear, and cool, just the way fall weather should be.

Nikki seems careful. She doesn't aggravate. She's happy about her school pictures, and she's proud of them. They are good. We have a pleasant ride. I do not mention the morning's unpleasantness, having decided that the person to deal with it is Mara.

Will is there, waiting for us. We sit for a few minutes, looking at Nikki's pictures. Then Mara arrives, and we follow her to her office. Nikki chatters about her pictures and about Rob, her current boyfriend. Will displays ignorance of this guy, who is coming to dinner at the end of the week.

I am eager to get started on the trash rebellion, but Will says he wants to finish the subject of Nikki's driving. He wants to make a long-range prediction that in a year Nikki will be driving. Mara probes to see if he has a definite time frame in mind. He doesn't. Nonetheless, Nikki looks pleased, very much like the cat that swallowed the canary.

I am aggravated. Here is this kid who is giving me great grief, and she's getting exactly what she wants. Further, Will looks like a nice guy, and I get to be the trash lady. When we're finished with the driving, I say that I am angry about something.

Mara asks me about it, and I tell the trash story. Mara asks Nikki what she feels happened, and Nikki says that what I said is true. Then Mara talks about what is negotiable and what isn't insofar as household chores and assignments go. Basically she is saying that a family can't negotiate everything, and that Nikki needs to do what she's assigned to do without a hassle.

I am watching Nikki. For the first time I find myself the observer, the third party in the room with the behavior that is usually directed at me. There is Nikki—eyes down, legs crossed, feet shoved out, lower lip about five feet forward, contesting everything that Mara says. Nikki is giving short, flip answers but arguing wherever she can. I am surprised. I feel better. For the first time I see that this behavior isn't reserved solely for me. It gives me an entirely different perspective.

Then Mara moves to a consideration of Nikki's feelings. She is saying,

"You have a lot of angry feelings inside." Nikki says that she does, that she's the only person she knows whose two parents are dead and that it hasn't been easy to live with nine other families, about one a year.

"That's right,"Mara says. "I bet you have a lot of anger that your parents died and left you." Nikki nods. Mara looks at her from under her cloud of hair. "It might help you to talk about those feelings sometime."

"I don't like to talk about them," Nikki says. "It's too depressing. I just tell people they croaked."

I can see the pain now. I've heard the bit about how they croaked, but I haven't seen the pain before.

"Yes," Mara continues, "It is depressing to talk about those feelings. But if you don't talk about them, you'll go from being an angry teenager to being an angry young woman." Mara says that her father died when she was eighteen and that she knows the feelings are hard.

I speak up. "You're right. My mother died when I was eighteen, and I started taking care of the kids. If we had talked about our feelings, all three of us kids would have had a much easier time. I'm forty-one years old, and I'm still dealing with feelings I didn't deal with at twenty."

There is more talk, but I feel relaxed. My anger is all smoothed out, folded up and put away. When I see Nikki as a person in pain, I can stretch my coping a little bit. I can try a little harder.

As we drive out of the grounds I say, "I think Mara is very helpful."

"She's a nice lady," Nikki answers, "but every time I've gone to counselling sessions, they've turned out to be gripe sessions."

"Hmmm. Maybe I have been using them like that. But I need that. I need Mara there to put me on a leash. If I didn't have her, I might beat up on you verbally. You were telling us how hard it's been to be a foster kid in nine different families. Well, it's not easy to be a foster parent, either. I want to make this work. I want to keep you with us. You're worth it. But I couldn't do it without Mara. When something happens like that number this morning, I think, 'I don't need this crap.' If it weren't for coming here, I might have asked your caseworker to find you another home by now."

I look across the front seat to see if I can see an expression. It is dark, and Nikki is looking straight ahead, but I think she looks serious. We talk more on the way home, comfortably, and I tell her that maybe we should discuss with Mara her feelings that counselling sessions are gripe sessions. We have a good time as we get supper. We joke.

Later I find myself thinking that with Nikki I'm either up or down. With Ben I'm usually in the middle ground. I'm comfortable with Ben and usually calm about him. I'll have a few days when I'm super-pleased with him and a few days when I'm really ticked at him. But for the most part, I'm comfortable. With Nikki, though, I'm either thinking she's the greatest or thinking she's the pits. I wonder if this is a typical foster parent reaction.

November 1981

My neighbor Pam and I spend a good part of Saturday picking up the oranges, the grapefruits and the tangelos, and I spend a good part of Sunday delivering them. This is another of those interminable choir fund-raisers. I don't know that I have anything good to say about my participation as a "choir parent." It's been a pain in the butt to me since Nikki joined. I learned slowly about the $225.00 for spring tour and all of the endless additional expenses.

This fruit thing has been hopelessly poorly organized. The truck was to have been in on Friday evening but didn't arrive until Saturday morning. Every parent had been asked to sign up for a pick-up time on Saturday, and Pam had said she'd help me load stuff in her big wagon. She would be taking her daughter to the high school for swimming on Saturday morning anyway. So we signed up for a time that would work with the pool time.

While the kids are getting the fruit off the truck and into the loading area, Pam and I troop over to McDonald's to warm our insides with coffee and thaw out our feet. When the fruit is finally unloaded, nobody pays any attention whatsoever to the fact that some of us have been waiting for hours. It is a free-for-all. Then, of course, only some of the buyers are at home, and we end up with thirty-three cartons still in the basement.

Sunday morning Nikki and I have another encounter that is virtually a replay of the trash rebellion but with different verbal content. The feeling is absolutely the same, and this time I am able to characterize it as feeling abused. Mara has been telling me that my perceptions are good. "If you feel you've been burned, you've been burned." I feel like burnt offerings.

After Nikki has disappeared into her room, I go up, knock and tell her that she has hurt my feelings badly. She seems chastened. I tell her that she and I have to get some things straight if we are to continue living in the same house. She seems to be aware of what I mean.

I leave her alone that afternoon, telling her that I will be available to deliver the fruit whenever she is ready. That was dumb. I should have said "I'll be available between two and five."

I have never seen less organization, except perhaps on the collecting for her paper route. She had all afternoon to get organized, and we leave the house at five, in the darkness, when the roads are turning to ice because of falling temperature.

Will gives us a flashlight so that we can read the slips. There are two slips per box, but for some reason Nikki has tucked them both into the boxes, which doesn't allow for efficient route planning. It is all that I can do to keep my mouth shut. But somehow I do, and we finish the afternoon on a happier note.

November 1981

At our next session with Mara, I explain how I felt after the recent altercations. I say that every neuron in my body short-circuited and that I felt I had footprints going right up my front and down my back. Mara knows exactly what I mean by the low reservoir and the gas tank on "E." She asks Nikki if Nikki understands that we are talking heavy duty. Nikki nods.

I need to be with Mara before I talk about those feelings. It's so hard to talk about them without threatening that Nikki will have to leave. I'd like to think of it more as an action and a consequence. If this is the way that Nikki is going to act, there are certain consequences that she can expect.

Mara points out to Nikki the power she has to hurt my feelings. I guess Nikki needs to feel that she has some power too. My power is frightening to me because it is so final. I want to use it responsibly and not in anger. I don't want to scream "You're through. Get the hell out of here."

That's why we need Mara. I want to give Nikki every chance I can. If it comes to the point where she's used up all the breaks and the gas is gone, I know I'll have regrets. But I'll know, too, that I got every mile I could out of that tank. Before the session ended, Mara said to Nikki, "Anne wouldn't be here if she didn't want to keep you."

Thanksgiving 1981

We're going out to my father's farm. It's an in-between point for us and for the relatives from Toledo. Plus, Dad not only has a huge table with extra leaves, but he can roast a turkey to a turn. He tells of his childhood Thanksgivings in Glendale, Ohio, where he grew up in a doctor's family. There was a woman in town so adept at telling when turkeys were done that you could retain her for the big day. She'd make her rounds, telling everyone just when they could expect to sit down to eat.

We'll have a nice day with my aunt and uncle and at least one of their sons. Their daughter Stevie was with us just two Thanksgivings before, and now she's dead of cancer. I'm so glad that I saw her then. It must have been ten years earlier that I'd seen her last. My aunt and uncle haven't met Nikki yet, but they'll make her feel welcome.

She's already met Dad. On a summer trip, she'd brought along her tape recorder and earplugs so that she could listen in the car, but she'd jammed the machine somehow. Dad was very nice about working on it, although he shook his head and clucked his tongue over her obviously heavy hand. He, too, made her feel welcome.

Dad is not demonstrative. He never was. Once, when Ben was an infant, Aunt Rosemary took him from me and plunked him down in Dad's lap. "That's the only way these men get to know their grandchildren," she said. Dad looked quite uncomfortable, so I retrieved Ben shortly.

Will's Mom and Dad are more like storybook grandparents. There are hugs and kisses and presents and cards in the mail. I hope that Ben knows that my Dad loves him. I've tried to explain that some people aren't huggers and kissers.

I wasn't either until I had Ben. That experience opened some closed gates. I got almost sappy about keeping a baby book, for instance. But I'm glad that I did. The feelings have always been there, if not their direct expression. It's still hard for me to be demonstrative with Nikki. I know the kid needs a hug or a kiss now and then, but it's one thing to begin with an infant and quite another to begin with a teenager!

December 1981

We've been devoting some thought to the music question. Nikki is paying for her piano lessons out of her paper route money, so if she doesn't practice very often, we feel she's making her own choice about getting her money's worth.

Yet it's voice she keeps talking about as a career interest. She's singing in the choir every day, but she's not getting any individual coaching. We ask her whether she is interested enough to take private lessons, and she says she is. So we ask around and find that one University Circle institution might be just right.

When I call for information, I am told that every student gets an audition for proper class placement. I'm also told that the voice doesn't really mature until late adolescence or older so that it's not a hindrance for

Nikki to be starting now. This is just the proper time. Someone will call me to schedule the audition.

But no one does, and it takes more calls on my part and more weeks to connect. But finally we have a date, and Nikki, Ben and I drive to the Circle after school on a freezing cold day. The big old building reminds me so much of the old Conservatory at Oberlin. I remember the day I took an accordion there, to rehearse with a trio from my dorm. The looks I got! It was as though possession of an accordion might be a felony

We leave Nikki with her teacher, a kind man who is braiding the hair of his little daughter. His studio is on the top floor, with a grand piano and all sorts of odd-shaped windows. Ben had spied a candy machine on the first floor, so we wander down while Nikki auditions. I love hearing all the music flowing out from under the studio doors.

When I mastered the accordion, I started taking organ lessons. My mother talked to me about taking a double major at Oberlin, but in her sickness and death, all that faded away—and probably just as well. If I'd really wanted to take lessons, I could have, although I'd started organ so late that I'd never have been on a comparable basis with Conservatory students. And Oberlin introduced me to folk and blues, which became far more compelling for me than classical music.

We get the candy and return to fetch Nikki. She'll be in a group lesson at one every Saturday afternoon. The individual lesson slots are filled from the group as the teacher decides that someone is ready.

We had a few hassles about getting Nikki to and fro each Saturday. Much as I would like to hold out for public transportation, the weekend schedules are bad, and the weather is cold. Will decides that he can grab some library time while Nikki's lesson is going on, and it becomes part of his Saturday afternoon routine to take Nikki to her lesson.

December 1981

This week's session with Mara is tough. To make it worse, we have to leave without getting the issues completely worked out because Nikki has an absolutely-must-attend choir practice. Then, in the snowy night, I try to take a shortcut and get lost. So Nikki misses the rehearsal, because one of the dicta was that absolutely nobody would be admitted late.

But we get home in better spirits. We throw in some frozen dinners, and Nikki gets out her choir gown to mark the length for hemming as I try to get the house tidied up for an evening coffee for some new neighbors.

That damned choir. It's not enough that there are all of these stupid rules. It's not enough that we have to spend $25.00 to hem the robe and to fix its zipper. Now we have this gown (in addition to the robe) that needs to be hemmed. I have two trials this week, and hemming a gown is low on my list of priority uses for my time. However, Nikki doesn't really know how to do this chore. I intend to show her, since it certainly qualifies as a basic skill.

I return my thoughts to the session with Mara. We are talking about the relationship between Nikki and Ben and the way that it worries me at a low level. Will characterizes Nikki as "overbearing." Nikki is not taking any of this well. The old lip goes out, and it looks as though her eyes might be a little damp. Then we have to leave before Mara completely finishes her explanation to Nikki as to why the balance of power isn't the same in a foster family as it is in a biological family. Nikki does not understand. She seems to feel that each kid should be completely equal.

She and I continue this discussion on the way home. It turns out that she doesn't know what the phrase "balance of power" means. I really am surprised that a seventeen-year-old in this country does not understand the meaning of that phrase. I tell her that what it means for our purposes is that the parents have the power. "Oh, sure," she says, "anybody knows that the parents make the decisions."

But it's much more than that too. I think that what it really means is that there is a different balance of power in a foster family and that a foster family is not so stable as a biological family. The power to end the family is an immediate option with the foster family, but it's the court of last resort in a biological family.

Again Nikki mentions that she thinks of our sessions with Mara as "gripe sessions." I worry about that sufficiently to give Mara a call. When I suggest that I shouldn't unload so much, she says "Don't censor your material. What happens in therapy is a microcosm of what happens at home. I'd guess that right now your feelings are mostly negative."

That sounds so harsh, yet I have to admit that it's accurate. At this point having Nikki with us is more pain than pleasure. She's not easy to live with. And yet we have good moments. I think of her red and white striped socks under her choir gown—Raggedy Ann joins choir. And I make up a letter to cover for her absence from the rehearsal because I don't think the director would buy the truth—that mom got lost in a snowstorm. There are some positive moments.

Christmas 1981

Nikki loves mail, and she's been going to the mailbox regularly during this holiday season. I think there have been only two envelopes for her—one from Kirsten and one from her first adoptive mother. Her grandmother and sister are Jehovah's Witnesses, who, according to Nikki, don't celebrate Christmas. Still, though, couldn't they send her a little note?

Will and I have already decided to try to overcome the ridiculous clothing budget by giving her clothing for Christmas and her birthday, which comes soon after Christmas. I mentioned this to my sister, who has a sharp eye for clothing, and she said she'd pick out some blouses.

I write notes to my brother and sister-in-law, saying that while I don't expect them to consider Nikki as part of our extended family, I would really appreciate their putting in some little item for her with whatever they are sending Ben. I don't feel guilty about this at all, considering that each of those families has two children for whom Will and I send presents. Monetarily it would be an even trade, and it would mean so much to Nikki.

Both sets of "grandparents" respond beautifully. Will's folks send a present, and my father gives Nikki a check. I insist that Nikki give first priority in spending to a set of headphones for her stereo. I'm tired of finding our set in her room!

Christmas 1981

Kate and Beth came over for a visit yesterday. I was on my hands and knees in Nikki's lav, trying to cut bathroom carpeting to fit when they called. Kate was home on vacation, and they wanted to stop by.

I was really sorry that Nikki was out for the afternoon. It would have been fun to have them meet. In truth, I would have liked their feedback on Nikki. Once Mara rebuked me for referring to them so often, and my response was that perhaps I had felt successful with them, whereas I don't feel successful with Nikki.

Kate and Beth brought some homemade Christmas candy for us, and we sat in the living room talking. Ben was virtually hanging on Beth, and he soon dragged her off to see his room and some of his newer toys. It was just delightful to see them together.

Kate was poised, as always. She's in college and stays out from time to time to earn money, but she's got a goal and a direction. From what Kate said, Beth is still floundering. She tried college and didn't stay, so she's been waitressing here and there. She's still sorting out some romantic problems.

Later Will and I talked. "It made me so happy to see Ben with Beth," I said. "It made me doubt my own perceptions less about Ben's current problems being from outside rather than inside. It's so easy to blame the effect of Nikki that I want to be sure. There's something sad, too, in that Nikki can't really enjoy a little kid for the fun that a little kid can genuinely be. She's so involved in competing. That's too bad."

New Year's Day 1982

Will and I go to a New Year's Eve party at a house on Nikki's paper route. When people find that we are Nikki's foster parents, we get lots of reaction. There is some expression of puzzlement over how she could have been left without a home, but most comment focused on her role as a paper girl. One dapper gentleman says that he respects her for doing her paper route. He says he was a paper boy, and he personally doesn't care if he gets his paper until eight o'clock. The complete opposite is an intense young woman who says that Nikki is incompetent, loud, noisy and unable to deliver a paper so that it doesn't blow into six sections.

January 1982

I'm angry with Nikki this morning, but I'm not sure why. We had a session with Mara yesterday that seemed to go well. I've also been very surprised at how well the Christmas vacation went. I had especially feared the five days that Will's folks would be here. I knew that there would be more work, and I knew that I wouldn't have my third-floor retreat, because they'd have that space.

But I needn't have worried . There was so much to do at the office that I was gone a lot. This was a contrast to the vacation last Easter when Will's folks were here, and Nikki was on one of her first weekends with us. They had been puzzled about her. "You're adopting her?"

"No, she's a foster child to us, like the other girls have been." Even now I remember one scene. Mac, Will's father, had fixed her bike seat, and when she offered no "thank you," I suggested one. "Oh, yeah, thanks," she said in a way that really didn't sound very grateful. As she rode off on her bike, Mac and I looked at each other and shrugged.

In the session with Mara we got into the whole issue of Nikki and chores. Mara thinks I'm too easy on Nikki. I say that I expect a hassle if I tell her to do something, which makes me think twice before giving an order. "No hassle," Mara says. "You tell her, and she does it."

Then we get into some of the "whys." I say I don't like being the heavy. Mara wants to know if that means that I want Will to do more of the assigning of chores. Yes, I guess I would like that. But it also ticks me off that I have to tell Nikki to do things that she already knows she's supposed to do. Will and Mara both take the position that you've just got to take a hard line with teens because they won't do anything by themselves.

"I just can't relate to that. When I was Nikki's age—seventeen—my mother was dying of cancer, and there were two younger kids to take care of. So I did it."

"You didn't have an adolescence," said Mara.

"Probably not." In truth, it doesn't sound as though I missed much. Kids are more able to work—and willing—than we give them credit for. But their contribution has to be needed; it can't just be make-work.

As I sit reflecting on that, I begin to feel differently—and better—about Nikki's going out on her own at nineteen. Here I've been feeling guilty, or at least sad, that she has to be on her own so early. But she can do it! I did it! Not in the same way, but maybe I had even more responsibility at that age than she'll have. She'll just have herself.

Mara seems to know what I am thinking. She asks me if I felt angry that I hadn't had somebody to mother me. I tell her about a recent conversation with Ellen that stopped me in my tracks. I had been griping about something or other that Nikki hadn't done, and Ellen said, "Nobody took care of you, did they?"

No. Should they have? That was the next question, wasn't it? I was seventeen when I began running the house. Nikki's seventeen, and I'm taking care of her. I'll be damned. But no, I said to Mara. I don't think I have any deep and abiding anger over the whole matter. I had pretty high-quality mothering for sixteen years, and by the time I was called upon to be an adult, I was able to respond. I don't say it out loud, but it crosses my mind that maybe my willingness to care for a seventeen-year-old is my acknowledgement that I hadn't really been ready to be on my own.

I end up sitting here with this journal, thinking how nice it was when Aunt Rosemary sewed up the parka for me last fall. Of course I miss being mothered. We all need that. I remember having a difficult time a year or so ago when a friend had her second baby. At first I thought it was just the old grief about my own inability to have a second. But then I realized that what I really envied was that her mother came to help her. It was her being mothered, not her mothering, that I envied.

January 1982

What a great weekend we all had! It couldn't have come at a better time for me. I've been feeling really stressed about all the legal work that I have to do. I've been feeling hassled and extremely tense. By the time I'd clocked pulse rates between 90 and 110 for about a week, I figured that I'd call Dr. Young.

He and I go back to my diagnosis of Hodgkin's Disease when I was a graduate student. I really think that my psyche took a far worse beating than my body, and Dr. Young has been very understanding of that. I left a call at his office on Friday afternoon, and Will and I went off that evening to a really nice dinner party.

I awake to the phone's ring on Saturday morning. "Why don't you come in?" asks the doctor. "We'll do some blood tests to be sure it's not thyroid, even though you're probably right about it's being stress. It's a bad morning, though."

"It's not an emergency. If you're busy, let's let it go."

"What I mean is that there's seven inches of new snow out there."

"Oh. Well, I'll see what I can do."

I tell Will that I'll be trying to start for Dr. Young's office in a little while, and would he please start the snow blower for me? He says yes and goes back to sleep while I eat a leisurely breakfast. Will comes down in his bathrobe, drags the snowblower from the basement to the back landing and turns it on.

It starts right away. "Great! Put it out on the porch."

Will turns it off to move it outdoors, and I go crazy. Once things are running, I do not believe in turning them off, a little belief picked up from childhood confrontations with power lawnmowers. This particular snowblower is extremely stubborn. But not to worry, says Will, putting the snowblower outdoors. When he pulls the cord, it comes off in his hand. Now we're both angry.

I grab the snow shovel and head out the door. I figure that my heart should really be pounding by the time I shovel the drive out—if I don't have a heart attack—but I'm too angry to be reasonable. I figure that I'll try to back out as far as I can, and I make it almost to the end of the drive, which settles me down. I get to Dr. Young's office with no problem, have a nice chat, leave some of my blood for testing, and then even run a few errands at a nearby mall.

When I get home, there is a car with Maryland plates in the drive. I come in to find Joe, an old friend from the late sixties. He'd been working on his Ph.D. in information science—he'd been a mathematician—while I was a librarian, my first career incarnation. We'd lost track of him, but he'd come to Cleveland with three friends for a weekend of seminars. Unfortunately for him, the place they planned to stay has cats, and Joe is already sneezing.

"Stay here," we both tell him. I say I'll cook up a big pot of chili.

"I don't want to lay a trip on you, but I've been doing some macrobiotic cooking, and if you think you'd like to try some of the dishes, I'd like to cook you a meal."

I am totally happy to let Joe cook whatever he wants to cook. We go off to the local vegetarian store. The snow has stopped falling, and it is bright and cold. Joe has a great time picking out food, and we return with two large shopping bags. Not only does Joe cook, he cleans up. I find myself wondering how it is that this man is divorced.

He's such a nice guy, much mellower than I remember. He's a little person, my size; we weigh absolutely the same. He's got my wound-up temperament, too. He's an Irish Catholic, one of six kids, and he is great with Nikki.

He even helps her with her paper route Sunday morning. She is flapping around Saturday night, trying to get her friends to help her deliver the paper. She is offering to pay them an even split of the profits, but nobody will agree. It is simply too damned cold. "What's involved?" Joe asks.

"Well, you have to get up at five, and you have to go over to where the papers are and put them together."

"I've never done that before. Once in a lifetime it might be a lark."

Joe is so protective of Nikki. They bring the papers back here because he says it is too cold on the porch. One of the families on the route has been kind enough to let Nikki have the papers delivered to their porch. Joe also says that Nikki should have some warmer jeans or even long underwear. He takes his car, helps her, and insists that both of them get back in the car to warm up after every third house.

However, he also takes her in hand about the papers that she is missing. He takes her up to the drugstore, has her buy three papers, and tells her to deduct those from the bill that the route man gives her. How many times have I tried to convince her that this is proper procedure? It is very nice to have Joe do this on his own.

Later I go with Joe to a lecture at the Unitarian Society. The speaker talks about meditation in a very sensible way. I learn more in twenty minutes than I'd ever learned from reading or talking. Anyone with a heartbeat of 110 can certainly stand to learn something about relaxation.

Joe stays two nights and really shouldn't have left when he did. The weather forecasts are of bad weather all the way back East; that original seven inches of snow has been followed by more snow and the most godawful cold. But Joe is eager to get back, and so are the people he'd driven with.

Joe insists on giving me a cookbook that he'd bought at the store. I really do love it—especially the soup recipes. One TGIF evening, Pam and I get a little high on wine and groove on the philosophies expressed in the book. There is something about "What has a front has a back." The corollary is "The bigger the front, the bigger the back."

But what I like most are the instructions for cooking soup. The idea is to layer all the vegetables in the pan and then to pour the liquid slowly down the side of the pan. This is to keep everything calm. The layers are not to be stirred up, either, as that does not enhance calm. Joe laughs about this, too, but by the time he leaves, my heartbeat is back to eighty.

January 1982

This is the weekend for Rob to come to dinner. Nikki first met him through a girlfriend. He lives in a western suburb. Nikki specifies pizza and tells me how nervous Rob is about coming over. But it goes well. Rob's a nice, tall, well-mannered kid who wants to be a radio announcer. He endeared himself to me by coming in, being introduced and saying, "This is a great way to make an entrance, but where's the bathroom?"

He drank a pot of coffee and ate a dozen pierogi before coming over, but he still seems able to eat some pizza. The first snows of the new year are blowing outside, but we are warm with a fire courtesy of Will.

I've been wondering what Nikki has told Rob about us—and about herself. She's been on the phone with him for hours on end. Has she said that we are her foster parents or has she just called us mom and dad? I have visions of Rob asking me questions about Nikki that I can't answer—was she a brat when she was little?

The next day, I see that she's brought all her books downstairs—the photo albums, the Life Book, etc. They're so important for her. What does someone like Rob think, seeing them all for the first time?

I only know how helpful they've been to me. When I get angry with her and out of patience, I often go up to her room and sit down on the floor with her books. When I see again the little girl growing up in all those different homes, I feel that I can stretch my love a little bit to try to understand the behaviors that annoy me.

January 1982

This past week there are separate conversations that really help sort out the irritation I've had with Nikki. My friend Wilbeth and I have lunch out one day, and we talk about raising a kid who has a different temperament from the mom's. Wilbeth has a lovely seven-year-old, and she says she gets on her daughter's case the way that I say I get on Nikki's case. She finds that her daughter is demanding and literal—unlike her own, more poetic, approach to the world.

Is it that simple, I ask myself? Are Nikki and I just two different temperaments? Peggy has told me that she's never run across a temperament more different from hers than Nikki's. And this week I get to talk to Peggy for the first time in ages.

I tell her how well I think things are going with Mara. "Mara keeps on Nikki. She tells Nikki when she's being rude. She tells Nikki that she's dumping a lot of anger on us that we have nothing to do with."

"My god. Paul never said anything like that to her. How great that would have been!"

Well, there are therapists and there are therapists. And even within that, there are different schools of thought. Paul's orientation is behavior modification, and I don't think that will work with Nikki. Nikki has real problems that should have been addressed by a good therapist with what's called a psychodynamic orientation at the time her mother died.

I keep thinking that if Nikki had someone like Mara then, she wouldn't have gone through two adoptive homes. I keep thinking back to the first home, where Kirsten feels she made a mistake. I often wonder if she did. I think Kirsten didn't really perceive how difficult Nikki is. So when Nikki complained that the family was trying to "make her over," Kirsten decided it was a bad placement.

Nikki told me once that the agency wouldn't give that family any more children. She was very smug about it, and I wanted to smack her. That mom sent her a Christmas card when no one in her own family did.

Peggy knows how difficult Nikki is and how difficult it is to articulate what makes her so difficult. Peggy says that sometimes what Nikki says doesn't make any sense. I don't think that's it. I could be wrong, but

I think what Peggy is seeing is the argumentativeness. Nikki will say anything for an argument, and often what she says doesn't make sense.

My problem is that if she wants a fight, I'll give her a fight. And I can argue better than she can, which is no surprise considering my age and my trade. I'm not proud of the fact that sometimes I steamroller her. When I'm feeling irritated, I just have to avoid conversation with her. The nice thing about talking with Peggy is that she knows what a toughie Nikki is. She helps by letting me ventilate.

The last conversation is with my friend Maureen, who has two biological children and two adopted children. Her first adopted child is Molly, and Maureen once said to me "When you first told me about Nikki, I was struck by the similarities." Molly's a talker, too. She doesn't give Maureen space, either figuratively or literally. She will stand one foot from Maureen and talk.

Molly must be even tougher than Nikki. When she came to Maureen and Dick, she was three. Now she's twelve. Maureen carried her around on her hip for six months, feeling at a gut level that Molly needed that contact for bonding. But Molly didn't bond, and Maureen knows now that age three was far too late.

"Bonding doesn't have to be in the first hour of life or maybe even in the first three months, but it's got to happen before a year. These kids who don't bond are a syndrome, a recognizable syndrome, and the professionals had better get with it," Maureen tells me. "You feel annoyed because you're stuck with a difficult kid, and nobody told you how difficult she'd be. You're annoyed with the situation in general, not Nikki in particular."

After that conversation, the irritation slipped away. It is Will's birthday. I go home to dinner. Nikki cooks onion rings and shrimp chips. She and Ben arrange the cake—with forty candles and a 65 for fun, using the big candles from Ben's last two birthdays, in the middle. We all have a good time, and I haven't felt the usual irritation since.

February 1982

This week at therapy I watch Nikki and Mara get into another one of those "You seem angry."/"No, I'm not." do-si-dos. Mara doesn't have any room left to maneuver. Finally she says, "You know, I'm not usually wrong about how people feel. It's my business. I perceive you as angry. How do you perceive Nikki, Anne?"

"Exactly the way you do. The anger is there like quills on a porcupine."

Mara sits for a moment. Then she says to Nikki, "You're only being dishonest with one person in this room about how you feel. It isn't Will or Anne you're being dishonest with. It isn't me. It's yourself."

That surprises me. I truly hadn't figured Nikki was conning herself. I'd been seeing her denial as stubbornness—that she knew damned well how she felt but she was damned if she was going to admit that someone else had her pegged. It never for one second occurred to me that she might not realize that she is angry.

I don't recall how we get from this to the death of Oreo Hamster and the fact that she was replaced immediately by Honky Guinea pig. Nikki is saying that she'd replaced Oreo right away because having Honky made her less sad. "Why be sad when you can be happy?"

That makes me wrinkle my brow. Is it that easy to lose sadness? Mara is intrigued by that, too. She probes. "Being sad is boring," says Nikki. Mara seems not to have considered that sadness can be boring. Me either. That is the last word I would have used to characterize sadness. Sadness to me is pain. Whatever pain may be, it is not boring. Boredom is neutral. Pain is not.

Mara tells Nikki that sadness is a very real part of life, that to understand happiness, you have to know sadness. She says that sadness is for consideration, for contemplation, the same way that happiness is. I think Mara is right. I think that sadness is to be experienced.

I felt that it was wrong to replace Oreo right away. I remember thinking that perhaps Nikki had acclimated to the short life-span of hamsters but that Ben needed to learn about death and sadness. "I miss Oreo, don't you?" I'd said to Ben a couple of times.

"That's good," said Mara. "You gave him permission to grieve. You encouraged him."

I am really sad about Orrie's death. Nikki thought that she was going into hibernation. We tried to warm her in our hands and with the hot water bottle the way the book said. From a gasp every thirty seconds, she started breathing every couple of seconds. I felt like a doctor who has brought a patient back. And then she died.

I miss her. Last spring in the midst of my struggle to accept my cousin's very early death from cancer, I thought of how easily we accept the deaths of animals. It seems to me that perhaps we should do that with humans. Why do we have to fight so hard to accept a person's death? We accept death as ordained for animals.

I know that I should bring up my awareness, when Nikki first came to live with us, that I had been her age when my mother died. Is Nikki a harbinger of fate? Is it time for me to die? Is Nikki here so that I can die? I know that this is legitimate material for therapy, and yet I cannot talk about it. There are perhaps only two people with whom I discussed those feelings. It was a very unsettling period, but it seems to have passed.

February 1982

Wednesday is a very nice evening this week. Nikki calls me at the office asking if there is anything I want her to do around the house after she puts the laundry in the dryer and takes a shower. Wow! Well, I say, there are pork chops defrosting in the sink. Would she like to work on dinner?

Yes, she would. We talk about various recipes. I tell her that I'll be stopping at Pam's on the way home to admire her wallpapering efforts, and Nikki can call me there if she has any questions.

It is so nice to sit at Pam's, contemplating the new wallpaper while having a drink. Nikki calls twice. I answer the first time, telling her to brown the pork chops in the electric skillet, then to put them in a glass baking dish covered with foil. Pam fields the next call about oven temperature.

I return to a house filled with good smells. Pork chops are baking, and stuffing is set out along with vegetables. There is no foil over the pork chops, and they seem a bit dry, so I cover them. It turns out that Nikki used a recipe for a marinade as a sauce.

She doesn't seem to know what a marinade is, so I tell her that it's usually used to tenderize meats for cooking. But, I assure her, it will make a good sauce. I do not want to discourage Nikki. She likes to cook, and she's good at it. Not only does she have a flair for seasoning food, but she's good at making food look attractive. I don't usually think of doing extras, but I remember once how she doctored up a hamburger pie with extra catsup, etc., on top. It really looked good!

I tell Nikki over and over how nice it is to have somebody do the cooking. I feel very mellow towards her all evening. I work on Ben's Christmas puzzle, and Will, Ben, and Nikki watch something on TV. It's funny how much less irritated I am because she has done something nice for me.

Probably that blends into the things that come up in this week's session with Mara. She says that I take too much work onto myself. She tells me to watch my feelings, watch how I feel when I'm doing the work. I'm trying to pay attention this week to what work it is I do and what feelings I have about it.

The pork chop dinner has one funny sequel. A few nights later, I turn on the broiler to cook some chicken. Having programmed myself (back when Ben was a toddler and tucked a dish towel in the broiler) to check the broiler, I find that something has cooked onto it. I was wondering when I last used it when I remember the pork chops.

Nikki must have browned them in the broiler before putting them in the oven. While they baked, the heat continued to cook the residue on the broiler pan. What a job! I mention to Nikki, as gently as I can, that browning things in the broiler isn't a good tactic for two reasons—it's hard not to dry out the food, and the broiler is tough to clean under the best of circumstances.

February 1982

Attention! Achtung! Here I am. I want to talk right now. I don't know what it is to wait, to test the waters to see if the other person is in the mood to chat. Maybe I really don't care. What I'm after is the audience for a monologue. I'm prepared to just plain flat-out talk!

We don't seem to be getting anywhere with putting a lid on Nikki's talking. Mara has told us that we have to program her the way that we programmed Ben when he was a toddler. We have to teach her not to interrupt, to respect other people's conversations and privacy. Mara said it would be hard, but she didn't say that it would be impossible!

If this weekend is any indication, it is impossible. Friday night Pam comes down for a drink. It is her birthday, and everything is going wrong. Her husband planned to cook her a birthday dinner but has the flu. All we want is a half-hour of time to collect ourselves before she goes off to cook her own birthday dinner.

No sooner does Pam arrive than Nikki appears in the middle of the kitchen. "Is there something you want?" I ask.

"No."

"Then clear out and let Pam and me have a drink in peace. You too, Ben."

"Did you see the dirty look she gave you?" asked Pam. Sorry to say, I missed it. However, at least we have some privacy.

Then on Sunday we are having company for dinner, and I am running a bit late. I come flying in from a workshop and am digging out clean placemats when the doorbell rings. Luckily I've known Mary since our first year of law school.

She and I are circulating through kitchen and dining room, getting things arranged, when Nikki appears. "Is there something you want?" I feel like a robot speaking my line.

"I've been cooped up in my room all day." The tone is definitely belligerent.

Pavlov would love you. You hear a doorbell, and you appear. But what I say is "I'm behind in starting dinner, and I don't need anybody else in the kitchen."

She goes as far as the junction of the dining room and living room and turns on the TV. "Can you turn down the TV?"

"I can't hear it."

"Are we making too much noise for you?"

"No." The sarcasm is lost on her.

"Is that show on cable?" I hope that it isn't so that she can watch the program in her room.

"Yes." She stays.

Eventually Mary's friend, Dale, arrives, and somehow I chase Nikki away. Dale has a twenty-year-old daughter. "Would your daughter have hung around like this when she was seventeen?"

"No," he says with a puzzled look.

"Well, Nikki isn't really seventeen, either, in lots of ways." But I feel helpless about changing this behavior.

February 1982

Nikki really does have a creative streak. She came down the other night with something she'd written. She was listening to her favorite radio station, and they were giving away a record to the person who could "beg" the best. She had a "beg" written out that was great. I thought it was really funny! Unfortunately, it had to be phoned in, and even with her speed dialing, she couldn't get her call through.

On a rainy day last fall, she came in saying, "Riding a bike out there is like walking through a bowl of corn flakes." That's a great way to describe the fat, yellow leaves on the ground. And once this winter, as we were riding along in the car at night, she took off her glasses and observed that the street lights looked like cotton balls.

From what she says, one of her junior high teachers encouraged her to write, and she does have a little cloth-covered book that she writes in.

I think the main topic of that book is Matt. So far as school goes, Nikki doesn't seem to like writing assignments.

February 1982

Sometimes I forget that I have another life. The Assignment Office at Juvenile Court called me last week with another assignment. "I don't know if you'll want to take this one," Lynn said. It's a sexual abuse case, and my assignment is to represent the father who is accused of sexually abusing two daughters.

When I talk with my children's services counterpart, she says that I am gutsy to take this on. My answer is "If you've got the case that you say you have, there's nothing I can do except be sure that you present the evidence correctly."

She asks me how I can deal with him. I can shut the feelings off. I can put them to one side. I learned that during my seventeenth year. I can almost hear the overhead gate clank down on the feelings.

I go to see the man at the county jail. Aside from the juvenile case involving the children, he's being prosecuted criminally in a separate adult case. It would be nice if I could say that he were a monster, because that would make things understandable. But he's not; he's just a sick, troubled person.

February 1982

A fair amount of stuff has been broken since Nikki came to live with us. The first casualty was a saucepan that we've had for years. It's one of the cheaper pans, with some type of molded plastic handle. You wouldn't cook rice in it; it's not that heavy, but it has served many a purpose.

One night after Nikki did dishes, I found the pan in the drainer with the handle broken off about two inches from the pan. Nikki's only response was "It broke while I was washing it."

Her double bed, which is a spool bed from Will's grandfather's house, is constantly losing slats, and finally she cracked one in half. Molly, Kate and Beth were all able to use that room without major disaster.

I brought the office pencil-sharpener home one day, determined to sharpen every pencil in the house. Nikki beat me to it, and the sharpener jammed on an ebony pencil left over from my drawing days. I was furious. Ellen gave me that pencil sharpener as a gift. It sat until Will's folks visited, and Mac repaired it. He said that one part was damaged beyond repair, but he fixed it so that it would turn on when plugged in.

There have been other things too. The entire FM band on my car radio is out. Every time Nikki would hop into the car, without even asking whether she could listen to the radio, she'd change from the AM country-western station that I always listen to to the loudest FM she could find. Now she can't do that.

I've heard that breakage is not an uncommon phenomenon with foster kids. In some ways Nikki doesn't treat her own things any better. Her bike is in constant need of repair, and much of it is just from a heavy hand. My father has worked on both her tape recorder and her tape deck thus far. Her camera didn't even last the summer before being dropped and broken. But since I mentioned in a session with Mara how angry all this breakage was making me, it seems to have stopped for the time being.

March 1982

There's a lot about Nikki that I've been thinking over. At our last session, I was in one of my moods of chronic and terminal irritation, and I said so. Mara began to probe—when did I feel most irritated, how long did it last, was it directed at Ben or Will or Nikki?

Well, I say, it's nothing in particular and everything in general. It's as Maureen said: it's the you've-got-a-difficult-kid-and-it's-hard syndrome. I can accept that. And, unexpectedly, Mara accepts it too. "I think your friend is wise," she says. "Sometimes we therapists get hung up on specific incidents."

Then we talk about plans for the summer. I bristle at the very thought of the coming summer. To me summer means everybody else first and me last. Ben's schedule changes. Nikki's schedule changes. And therefore, my schedule must change. I always lose work time.

Funny. Until now it suited me to cut back, to spend some time at home. Perhaps it would still suit me if it weren't for Nikki. Perhaps if it were just Ben and me, I'd enjoy the time. But if I'm home with Nikki, then we have friends and noise all day long.

But that's not all. I'm making the transition from a part-time working mom to a full-time working mom. While I used to relish time at home—neighboring, puttering—now my attention is on the office. The truth is, of course, that I'm nowhere near working full-time. There's still too much child care and house care. But I have more office time than ever before.

The surprising thing is that I don't really hate housework. Not only do I like the rhythm of household chores, but the house is a refuge to me. My office is a place to work. I don't go there to sit on the couch in the reception room and read magazines. I am programmed to go there to sit at my desk and work. When I'm weary and need a break, I can come home, maybe take a nap. I lose that refuge in the summer.

Nikki is here with her stereo, her tapes, her one-hundred decibel voice. I feel angry—and maybe criticized—because neither Mara nor Will seem to share my concern about how Nikki behaves when she's not at our house. I'm concerned about where she is and what she's doing, and I think that my concern is legitimate. I think that too many parents don't keep tabs on where their teenagers are. Those teens gather at homes where there's no supervision. I think of it not solely as an individual problem but as a community concern.

The bottom line to that is that while Nikki is relatively responsible by herself, that responsibility diminishes quickly in the company of other teens. My hard-earned wisdom of last summer is that when teenagers are in groups, the whole is definitely less than the sum of the parts.

Mara speaks to my feeling of irritation by saying that she perceives that Nikki and I have a sort of low-level personality clash. I don't really have any problems with that. But I wonder about some other factors. There are roles. The mom role in our society is not palatable to the average teenager. It's especially not palatable to a foster teenager when mom gets all the responsibility for "housebreaking" the teen into the routines of the biological family.

And there is yet another factor that we haven't explored yet. Perhaps Nikki has different patterns of relating to women than she has of relating to men. I recall that Peggy perceived Nikki in much the same way as I do. And I don't think that Peggy and I are that similar in temperament. What we do have in common is that we're both moms.

It seems that like Russ, Will has less trouble getting along with Nikki. Dads are rare in Nikki's life, and perhaps that makes them more valuable than we women who are always there. Will doesn't have to supervise Nikki as much as I do, and I don't hear her giving him the same lip that she gives me.

March 1982

When the therapy sessions started, they were to be family sessions, but as Mara began to perceive that the most conflict was between and Nikki and me, we began leaving Ben home. But there have been a few incidents recently when Ben has been upset, so we take him with us this week.

A couple of times in the last few weeks, Nikki has made some mildly disparaging comments directed at me that didn't really bother me as much as they seemed to bother Ben. He seemed eager to defend me and upset at Nikki. Even though we explain this to Mara, he isn't really communicative in the session. "I don't know" seems to be his standard response.

Ben seems unwilling to say anything negative out loud, though I've tried to tell him that I often get irritated at Nikki. At one point, Ben runs over to Will and begins whispering in his ear. We ask him if it has to do with the session. He says it does, but in spite of cajoling, he won't tell us what he'd said, and Will can't make out the whisper. Mara suggests that they talk out in the hall.

When they come back, Will looks at us, shrugs and says, "Men are different from women." Not bad coming from a six-year-old.

We wind around and about with many things, but basically we try to examine the Ben/Nikki relationship. Nikki says that it is like the relationship between her and her sister during the period when Nikki lived with her sister and her grandmother. Nikki sees Ben and me siding together, and she saw her sister and her grandmother siding together. I find myself wondering if Nikki tried to push her sister aside in order to get her grandmother's attention. Even though she has a blood relationship with her sister, she hadn't ever lived with her. Maybe the experience was like coming to a foster family.

Before we leave, we plan for the next two sessions. Mara needs to make a change next week, and the following week Nikki will be gone on choir tour. We decide that I'll come alone the next two weeks, and Mara will use that time to get some background information that her supervisor wants to see in the file.

March 1982

I am unsettled today. When I was finally beginning to feel that I could handle Nikki for two more years, Ben seems to be having serious difficulty. I get into a conversation with the Great Glynnis last Friday evening as I am walking her home after babysitting.

She says that Ben seems "ready to blow" about Nikki. Apparently every time Nikki appeared, Ben made sotto voce (or not-so-sotto) comments. "That's funny," I said. "We took him with us to therapy this week so that he could have a chance to get some things off his chest."

"He won't say anything while she's there," Glynnis assures me confidently.

I think about that on my way back. Glynnis is a super teenager. Her mom is also a lawyer, and 'way back, when Ben was three and our scheduled sitter called in sick at the last minute, I remembered that Kathryn said that her daughter babysat. I called and was lucky. I warned Glynnis that Ben was at the age when he cried with the sitters he knew. I didn't want her to get upset if he carried on for awhile.

Glynnis arrived with a backpack full of children's books. "Could you tell me if he's read any of these? They were my favorites when I was a kid." She sat down on the floor and opened the pack. Ben was there in a second, totally entranced. I shook my head no, that he hadn't read most of those, and Will and I went on our way. There wasn't a peep.

It was love at first sight for Ben. It's hard for me to believe that Glynnis and Nikki are the same age—they're both in choir even—because they're such worlds apart developmentally. Glynnis is truly mature, and therefore I take what she says seriously.

So I think about her words. I guess that perhaps it is asking a lot of a little kid to understand that you can say things in a therapy session that you can't say at home.

I decide to take him with me to the next appointment. I call his teacher to say we'll be going and that I'll bring him to school late. He is still on the quiet side, but Mara talks to him and to me about Kate and Beth.

She appears to be satisfied that he did indeed have a different sort of relationship with them. "If you were upset with anybody, no matter who, who came into your house, that would be another story," she tells Ben.

When Ben and I get to his school, the kids are just leaving for lunch. Mrs. Farr asks if I had a minute to talk. She expresses great concern that the happy little boy of last fall has been replaced by a tearful and aggressive little boy who can't take turns and who doesn't want to help clean up when asked. I am most struck by her comment that he has stopped learning and is busy playing all the time, as though he has to be busy to work off the energy.

Her picture is so bleak and so frightening that I ask her to please talk directly with Mara. Just that morning I told Mara that on a scale of one to ten, my concern about the Ben/Nikki relationship is about a five. Mara, too, said that she wasn't terribly worried, though she was aware that some things might be having a deeper impact than we thought. We decided that Will and I should come without the kids for the next session.

I feel terrible. The relationship between Ben and Nikki bothered me from the start. I should have trusted myself. I had a naive faith that things would work out, that a little time would help them both. But the problem runs so deep. Nikki's manner is virtually always hostile, unfriendly, and unkind with Ben. What have we done?

March 1982

I have a very helpful discussion with Emily about all of this. She's the woman who's taken care of Ben since he was eight weeks old. For his first three years, I only worked two days a week, then it was three. Now that he's in kindergarten, he goes to Emily's house during vacations from school.

What a beauty Emily is. She's sensitive to both Ben and Nikki. She spent her childhood in an institution, and she can feel for the Nikkis of this world. She understands my wish to keep Nikki, but she also understands Ben's needs. She told me earlier that it is a good thing that Ben is an only child—that his temperament is just suited to lots of attention. I didn't really hear her then. I thought she was just trying to make me feel better about not having a second child.

But she really means it. She feels that it could well be that Nikki is getting to him behind our backs. A look, even, she says, is enough to set a kid like Ben off. She says that her kids, now grown, tell her things that their siblings did to them that hurt, things she never knew about. Siblings. I like that word. It makes me think of a litter.

March 1982

I just hate this current situation. Now that Mara has talked with Mrs. Farr, she's very concerned herself. She seems to think that moving Nikki is probably the most reasonable alternative. She doesn't seem to put any faith in the "halfway" measures, such as finding her other places to stay for weekends. Yet I know that at least two local agencies have been involved in such programs.

At first I thought that Nikki could be "threatened" into better behavior simply by knowing that if she continued to pick on Ben, she'd have to move. But Mara says that threat has always been there, and I guess she's right. It was there even when it wasn't spoken. Around four this morning, I thought of a better way.

I'll say something like this: "Nikki, we're really worried about Ben. We seem to be in a crisis with him, and it's not clear whether it will pass or not. He's showing some disturbing signs in school, and his teacher and

Mara are trying to help us. So we have to make some decisions about how
to help him. One of these ways may be to move you. Lord knows, I don't
want to do that, but it may be the best solution."

That's not saying to her "You have to shape up." It's saying "There
are problems with Ben, and we have to work on solving them. If this
passes, that's one thing; if it doesn't, then we'll have to find a solution."
That doesn't make Nikki the focal point.

I tell you, I hate this. I'm not good at decision-making. I seesaw back
and forth. I tell myself that I shouldn't jump too quickly, that I should just
gather evidence. But we have to have a time frame, and that will be the
end of the school year.

March 1982

Well, I've done it. I am shaking, but I have the talk with Nikki. I think
it went exceptionally well. Will and Ben went upstairs to pillow fight,
leaving us alone at the dinner table. I work the conversation around to the
fact that I picked up Ben early and that we went to the church playground
before dinner.

"We're trying to spend a little extra time with Ben. We've gotten a
very disturbing report from his school. His teacher says that he just isn't
the same happy little boy that she saw in the fall. He seems about to
explode, he bursts into tears, he doesn't want to work in his workbook. He
just wants to play. I asked Mrs. Farr to talk directly with Mara, and Mara
is very concerned, too. We feel that if Ben's behavior doesn't turn around,
we'll have to make some changes."

"What changes?"

"Well, the most drastic one would be to move you. I don't want to do
that. You and I have been getting along much better."

"I've noticed that." She smiles for the first time.

"Well, none of us expected this problem with Ben, but it's serious,
and we have to deal with it."

"But nothing has changed at home." She seems genuinely perplexed.

"In some ways that's the problem. No, things haven't gotten worse,
but they haven't gotten better, either. Will and Mara both feel that the
effect on Ben has been adding up, and now he's showing signs of strain.
We're hoping that we can turn this around."

"Do you think I should spend more time with him?"

"Maybe not more time. It's more important to get the right quality of
time."

Nikki is very serious, very sober. There is no argument, no defensiveness. I wonder whether this means that she truly knows exactly what it is that she's been doing. This is a good point to end the conversation, because the pillow fighting is rocking the bed upstairs over us and scraping a broken caster on the floor. I say that I want to go look for an extra caster.

I recall an author saying that you should never fire anyone during the main course, because by the time you've gotten through dessert and coffee, you've reneged. I know that if I go on too long, I will dilute the effectiveness of what I have to say. I am still struck by the fact that Nikki did not argue. Perhaps it is that I didn't blame her. I didn't say "Ben is having problems, and it's all your fault." I just said that if we couldn't turn his behavior around, she'd have to move.

My heart goes out to her. She's blossoming so much now. Tuesday evening I picked up her floor-length gown for her. She's been asked to the prom by a boy named John. I've met him. He's a learning disabled kid with a residual speech problem. But he has a kind manner, and he was flattered that I wanted to meet him. And Nikki's getting ready for the choir tour, trying ahead of time to fit everything into the suitcase. Sometimes I get angry that she takes so much time with this, and I have to ask myself what form of the Puritan ethic it is that makes me feel that she should be studying. Fun is probably the one thing that she hasn't had in her life. Having fun now may be more important to her development than anything else.

I hate the thought of her going from here into a group home. Mara has said that she shouldn't go into another family home because she's so disruptive. In a group home she'd be away from her friends, and she'd be on a more rigid schedule. For sure she wouldn't have a phone.

The immediate effect is that Nikki gives Ben three lollipops and invites him into her room. But the real question is whether she can change over the long haul. Change is so hard. Mara and Will and I have talked about that. Mara knows that it's a lot of pressure to put on Nikki. But she also says that Nikki wants us to stop her behavior. I don't know. That's such a social work classic. But Mara has said all along that we've been too nice with Nikki, and perhaps she's right.

March 1982

Easter is over, and a new week begins. Nikki goes back to school, but Ben is out for vacation. I'll be staying home most of the week, and I'll try to spend some extra time with Ben.

I'm feeling some sadness over my sister's moving. The sadness is mixed up with the feeling of sole responsibility for Dad. I am angry with Alice for deserting me at this point. Dad is finally looking his age, seventy-four now. Until this decade of his 70s, he's always looked ten years younger than he is. Yet he seems to be in good health. His eyesight is poor, which might not mean that much if he were living in the city, but in the country where driving is essential, it's worrisome. It was last winter that Alice had started expressing concern about his health. And now she's moving. I don't think it's a coincidence.

Knowing that this was the last family celebration that Alice could easily join in made Easter a bit sad. Alice got on me once about my sniping at Nikki for something, but she hastened to say that she couldn't stand someone talking at her all the time, either.

April 1982

It's been a more quiet period. As Will points out to Mara, Nikki has been trying very hard to improve her relationship with Ben instead of "snapping and snarling" at him. "Nikki has given you the best possible response," Mara says. "She could have said 'Screw you guys, I'll find another home.' But she wants to stay."

And indeed Nikki says that she doesn't want to move again. "Is that all?" Mara asks.

"I feel rejected everytime I move," says Nikki. She adds that she's thought about where she might go and can't think of any place.

I fear that the "turnaround" won't last. It's too much pressure to put on Nikki. But I am happy for the short-term effects nonetheless.

April 1982

For awhile I didn't know what to do about the celebration I'd been planning for April 9th, the anniversary of Nikki's first year with us. I'd had the idea of ordering a cake saying "Hurray for Nikki," but I just couldn't swallow a bite if I thought she'd really be leaving. But after the last week, I see signs of hope. I had a wonderful conversation with Emily.

Some people can spend years going to all the right classes for a degree in social work or psychology, but they do not have the hearing ear. If that is lacking, they'll never be any good, and at this point, I'd say one is born with it. Emily has that third ear. I told her about my idea for the cake, and we had a conversation that went like this:

"May I make a suggestion? The Southworths need a cake too. You've all done something tremendous this year, and you deserve something too."

She's absolutely right. The celebration is for all of us. The cake is going to say "Hurray for Us."

Ben and I tell his aunt about the cake. "We've all worked hard," I said. "It's been a big job to make it for a year as a family."

Ben pipes up. "It's like a ladder with three hundred and sixty-five steps." We all break up.

Emily points out to me that including Ben in the celebration will involve him more. She also tells me that Ben will spit out what's bothering him eventually, but if he hasn't yet, it's because he's still feeling confused. I recall that when Ben and I were talking about the cake, he said, "When Nikki leaves, we can have the cake say 'Bye, bye Nikki.'"

"People say when you add another kid, your work doubles," says Emily." It more than doubles, and it's because of the relationships, not the physical work. It's the psychology that multiplies."

I think she's right. If Will were figuring this out, this is how he'd do it. "It's a factorial," he'd say. What I've always liked about factorials is the exclamation point. It's neat to see a number like 5! or 3!. A family of three would be 3!—or, three times two times one for a total of six. The family of four would be 4!—or, four times three times two times one for a total of twenty-four. That is quadruple the complexity of relationships.

April 1982

Ben and I go alone, through a snowstorm, to a session with Mara. We have his bag of blocks, and he proceeds to build a magnificent edifice. Even though it's completely white outside, we're talking about plans for summer, something that we've discussed before.

I tell Mara that I've had an insight into why summer is so rough for me. The house is my haven, and when Nikki is there, it isn't a haven. Mara says that makes her feel sad, that I shouldn't feel put out of my own home. Is she saying that I should enjoy having Nikki around? Perhaps she's not so in tune with foster parents as I thought. If foster parenting were such a stress-free thing, there would not be the shortage of foster homes that there is. No foster parent I've talked to feels "up" all the time. Just recently I talked to a foster mother who was involved with one of my juvenile court cases. She was talking about a fourth grader. "There's not one part good about that child. She lies, she cheats, she steals."

"How do you do it? How do you keep her with you?"

"I just pray and go on."

And Pennie, another foster parent, has been telling me about the six-year-old she's had for a couple of years. He's been sent home to mom, and Pennie thinks he gets beaten. "My life is easier without him, but I think he's better off with me."

Yes. That's how it is. My life would be easier without Nikki, but I think she's better off with me. She's been gone for five days now, on the choir tour, and it's been so peaceful. She'll be back, the ocean pounding on the beach. Oh, to be able to turn her into a quiet pond.

Mara asks how Ben's school is going, and I have to say that Mrs. Farr called recently to say that Ben had been awful the past Friday. "He marked in another kid's workbook and threw pencils. That's not Ben. He still seems ready to explode."

After dinner I tell Will about the discussion. "I just cannot fathom this. In November Ben was great. Now, four months later, he's a basket case!" Will thinks that Nikki's effect is cumulative, and Mara has supported him in that reasoning.

April 1982

I am sitting here with a cup of tea, feeling perfectly rotten about my behavior with Nikki. I knew that I had mixed feelings about her return from the choir trip. But I had righted myself emotionally, was even looking forward to seeing her until I picked up Ben yesterday. When I mentioned that we were going to stop back at my office to see if Nikki was there, he grew very quiet and looked sad.

When we discussed the logistics of the choir trip, I told her to take her things to my office when they returned. My office isn't even a block away from the high school, and they were getting in around 4:30 in the afternoon, which is usually when I'm out getting Ben.

When we don't find her at the office, we drive to the high school parking lot. We don't see her and are starting out when she gets out of a station wagon and starts waving.

My first words are "Why didn't you go over to the office?"

"I forgot. My suitcase is too heavy to carry over there anyway."

"You could do it," I say, opening up the back of the wagon, thinking You never pay any goddamn attention. The people in the station wagon had to wait for you, and they probably think I'm an insensitive parent. Plus, you always have two or three reasons why you can't do something.

I should have just kept my mouth shut. Instead, I am argumentative and outrageous in general. Nikki is chattering incessantly about what they had to eat, where they went, how cute the hockey players were. And I am just not in the mood for high school.

Mara certainly hit a raw nerve when she said that I shouldn't feel put out in my own home. "It is your home, and Nikki has to learn how to fit into it in a way that you can be comfortable with." But then, after all of my bad temper, Nikki gets out presents that she bought for us. Mine is a really lovely mug, with a curved shape and nice colors. Do I feel stupid.

April 1982

It's spring vacation for the kids. Yesterday morning I went to Juvenile Court for an 8:30 hearing, figuring to be out by 10:00. I made Nikki a deal that if she would stay home with Ben instead of leaving for Rob's on the 9:00 bus, I'd drive her over when I got home. As Will said, I had a lock on that deal. Ben is probably the only loser. When Nikki "sits" with him, she gets on the phone, etc. She doesn't give him the personalized attention that he gets from Glynnis.

I planned my schedule to stay home with Ben because of this vacation. But one of my delinquents is in County Jail, and when I am offered an arraignment at 8:30 on Thursday morning, I take it. I don't like kids sitting in the Detention Home, let alone County Jail.

Not only do I handle Carl's case, but during the usual and interminable wait, I am asked to handle a case in another courtroom where the assigned counsel hadn't shown. It is a busy morning with a lot of nervous energy, and when I walk out of court, all of the previous day's irritations are gone. Maybe that is just what I need—a place to blow off the nervous energy and the irritation. For that there is no better place than Juvenile Court.

We have a nice trip to the west side suburb where Rob lives. Ben and I meet Rob's mom, and she fills us full of pastry. I tell you, the west side is really not on the same planet as the east side. Somewhere on Pearl Road is a turn into the fourth dimension. You don't realize it until you're among the little box houses, with women all at home. That's the way it's supposed to be in a goodly portion of my own programming, and I do not put it down. It's just that I took that step into the world of women at work. Rob's mother and I get along very well while Nikki talks with Rob. This is the dimension where Nikki was raised. If she marries a guy like Rob, they will fit into the world she was born into and programmed for.

April 1982

Our celebration was nice. We had pizza and the "Hurray for Us" cake with one candle. After supper we watched TV, and Nikki worked on the macrame that Alice had given her in the cleanout for the move.

The clerk in the bakery remembered me when I picked up the cake. "It looks nice. When I saw it, I got tears in my eyes. It means something special to you, doesn't it?"

"Yes. Our foster daughter has been with us for a year now."

"Are you going to adopt her?"

"Probably not. She's seventeen. She was placed for adoption in the past, but not now."

It was a pretty cake, and one year with us does mean something, whether we're an adoptive home or not.

April 1982

When Beth was getting ready to move out, she asked me if I wanted her parka. It's a very nice parka, with a fur-trimmed hood. It's blue with yellow detail, well-made but with a few bad rips. "Don't you want it?" I asked. "It could be mended."

"No," said Beth, and I said I'd be glad to have it. I've worn it a few times to walk Taco. It's nice and warm; the hood fits so snugly that I don't have to wear a cap to protect my ears. It's a little snug in general, but then, Beth is smaller than I am. I worried a bit about the fact that the zipper had been ripped out about six inches, but I really didn't know how to fix it. I'm only good at hand-mending, and this clearly needed a machine.

When Mary and I made our Michigan run to Aunt Rosemary and Uncle John's in October, I pulled it out of the closet. All of a sudden winter had replaced fall, and the parka was the warmest thing I had. It was a lifesaver, and I wondered if my aunt, who sewed, could show me how it should be mended.

"Oh, let me do it," she said, and proceeded to make it look new. I'm sure that it seemed like such a little thing to Aunt Rosemary. But I don't have anybody to do those things for me. It's times like these when I realize just how much I lost when my mother died. At eighteen, of course, I thought I could handle the world.

I made it to about age thirty before I saw some of my friends develop very good relationships with their moms. Then, once in awhile it would strike me that perhaps I was missing something. When my friends had babies, their moms came to help them. They were mothered. When Aunt Rosemary mended that coat for me, I had been mothered.

The parka hung in the closet all mended. Then winter really came. I wore it to take out the trash, and it was gloriously warm. When the temperature fell below zero, I told Nikki that she could wear it on her paper route. Her warmest jacket was just that—a jacket. One day I noticed that the zipper was beginning to tear again. "Be careful. We need to mend that before it gets worse."

The next time I saw it, it was right back to six inches of rip. I was furious. "You are not to wear this again. You did not take care of it." I put it away in a garment bag in the basement. I was somewhat surprised at exactly how furious I was. It seemed to be out of all proportion to the damage. It was then that the meaning of mothering began to hit me.

One day recently, I struck a deal with Pam. She would sew up the parka on her machine, and I would write her a will. The parka is all right again, and so am I.

April 1982

We had a very stormy session with Mara yesterday. As a friend puts it, "Nikki work? Heaven forfend!" This past week I'd mentioned to Nikki that this summer she would have to have a job or perhaps go to a camp. Her response had been that she would rather be with her friends. But she didn't seem upset.

Not until this session with Mara did I really perceive how little Nikki was willing to do in the way of work. That angered me, and I said so. "It really makes me mad when I'm willing to take stress and put myself out to have Nikki with us and she's not willing to take on any burdens."

We were right back to the lip and the pout and the anger that rises from her body like mist from the grass on a damp summer morning. As Mara put it, Nikki had developed the expectation that she was going to have all summer long to do exactly as she pleased. Oh, she might take a babysitting job here or there. Or maybe she had a vague idea of taking a summer job if someone would call to offer her one. No, she hadn't put any ads in the paper herself.

First of all, she didn't want to work or do anything else on a regular basis. She wanted a vacation. Will says that he, beginning at age sixteen, had not had a "summer vacation." Instead he went five hundred miles away from home to work in his uncle's factory.

I said that I felt that Nikki had been having a continual vacation all year. She hadn't been working too hard at school, she'd had lots of invitations, she'd done lots of things. If she were one of those kids who really worked hard in school, then I'd feel differently about her summer vacation.

Tied to that is my perception that we've pretty much let Nikki run her own life this school year, that we've asked very little of her. It seems to be a real blow to her to be asked to do anything at all. She expressed feeling hurt, too, that I didn't seem to want her around the house much.

It looks as though we need to do more work with Mara on the issue of why having Nikki is stressful. I don't know that Nikki has any understanding of how she causes stress. The picture is such a perfect illustration, if I may be pardoned for the pun

In her photo albums and notebooks, Nikki has lots of pictures of herself as a baby. I would bet that her mother couldn't pass a photographer. I thought I'd seen all of the pictures, but recently I'd stepped over another one on her bedroom floor. Nikki must look at the pictures a lot, because they're always strewn around. This one is a black and white 5 x 7 in a beige cardboard folder. Nikki is probably between six and nine months old.

Not long after I first saw it, Nikki came flying downstairs one afternoon and plunked it in the center of the mantel, saying "This is the best picture we have of me. We need to put it out." She disappeared as fast as she'd come.

My immediate thought was that now, while there are tremors in the foundation, she especially needs to belong, to have her picture in the center. I knew that the mantel wasn't the right place for it, but for the moment I let it stay.

One day when Ben was home from school sick, I said to him, "Why don't we take your baby picture and Nikki's baby picture and put them over on the shelf?"

"Okay," he said, and I got his out.

"Put Nikki's higher." I was puzzled because there was no place for it any higher. Then I understood that this was Ben's way of telling me that he didn't want Nikki's picture there at all.

Ben and I had a chance to discuss this alone with Mara. To my memory, Ben hadn't been in the room when Nikki burst in with the picture, but as Mara talked to him, it was clear that he had been aware of it.

"Did it upset you to have Nikki's picture on the mantel?" Ben gave a nod.

"Did you tell your parents that it upset you?" Ben shook his head.

Then Mara turned to me. "How did it make you feel?"

"Bemused. It was saying so much so fast that I knew it would take me awhile to figure it out."

"But the picture didn't belong there," said Mara.

"No, of course not, but it didn't threaten me, if that's what you mean."

"This is the kind of thing that you need to work with Nikki on. She is a guest in your house. She needs to respect you and your feelings—Ben's feelings. She could say, 'Anne, I really like this picture of me. Could we put it out somewhere?'"

Of course that's what we need, but it will be a lifetime task. I chose not to revisit the picture with Nikki, but I began to think that this might be the time to give Nikki a copy of the story.

My first piece of writing had recently been published. It's on foster teens, and it's largely about Molly, Kate, Beth and the phenomenon of the short-term, informal placement. But there's a little about Nikki, too. When Mara saw it, she asked me if I'd shown it to Nikki. I hadn't. I'm really shy about my writing. I've changed all the names and have written under a pen name so people who know the kids casually won't identify them. But I know that I should show the story to Nikki

So that night I gave her the story with a card saying, "Yes, we do have our bad times. But for every time that I want to smack you, there is a time that I want to hug you. Writing is my way of doing all these things. Love, Anne."

April 1982

All of Alice's plants are over here now, on the nook table. I don't know where I'll find room for them. And the movers missed their first date so that she was over all this past week for dinner. Dragging out the goodbyes made them more difficult.

Not that we've ever been really close, but Alice has lived in this same suburb now for about ten years. We've had our ebbs and flows. Sometimes we've seen a lot of each other, and sometimes we haven't. She's a single, career person—systems analyst—and she's leaving for a new job.

I've been upset that I'll be the only child here to watch over Dad, but I haven't said anything about it. That's kind of the pattern in our family. I'd like to yell at her sometimes, but I don't. Friday night we said our final goodbyes, and Saturday morning Ben and Will left on their annual pilgrimage to the Boston Marathon. Ben waved good-bye to me, and I felt really lonely.

I went back in the house and went upstairs to put on some lipstick. I walked into the bathroom where Nikki had just finished a shower, found the usual water on the floor and went berserk. "Goddamn it," I yelled, "why can't you take a shower without getting water on the floor? And why can't you clean it up?" When I got no response, I yelled louder. Finally she appeared. She'd had her radio on.

"We'd get along better if you didn't always yell at me!"

"I don't always yell at you. This is one of the few times that you've heard decibels like these. Maybe I should yell more. Mara keeps telling me I'm too easy on you. Maybe if I yelled, you'd pay some goddamned attention."

I was really angry. I went off to haul four bags of junk over to a fund-raising flea market, telling myself that I wouldn't even have to be doing that if Nikki hadn't volunteered us to give stuff.

When I got back, she came down with her check book. She'd called the bank to find out how much she had in her account. I tried to explain that one keeps one's checkbook in sufficient order so that one doesn't have to call the bank. They don't appreciate these calls, I told her. I went over the book with her, and I think we got it straightened out. We were both under control.

When I drove her to her voice lesson, I told her that I thought I knew why I'd been so angry. Some of it was at her; water, water everywhere isn't right. But some of that anger was for Alice. I told Nikki that I had mixed feelings about Alice's moving—that I was sad that she was going but that I was also angry that she was leaving me with the full responsibility for my father.

Nikki seemed to understand that. "You're the only one that can visit him now."

When I left Nikki at the lesson, I felt weary, but the anger was gone.

April 1982

Along the way I've stumbled onto two programs that give breathing space to families. One is at The Place in our suburb. I've talked to a worker there who says that the agency has been trying to find homes where a teen can stay for weekends. They haven't exactly had a huge success rate in finding homes, but they believe that giving a family and a teen a weekend off from each other leaves each better able to cope. It's a time out.

The other program is a bit more formal and is run by a larger agency. Foster homes licensed by the state are used for temporary placements of no more than ninety days. At the end of ninety days, the teen either returns home or is placed in a long-term setting—institution, group home, etc.

I had talked with a staffer for material on the piece on foster teens, and I liked the sound of the program. I filed it away in my mind as something that I might like to do someday. I truly feel that the short-term stuff is more suited to my temperament than these long-term placements. I could muster the energy to deal with a kid for ninety days, knowing that then I'd have a rest for as long as I wanted before I agreed to take another child.

May 1982

Well, here I am at seven on a Sunday morning, yelling at Nikki instead of sleeping in my nice, quiet bed. I was really yelling about something that happened Saturday night. I still have a problem getting to feelings right away, but Mara would be proud that I'm making progress

We got home late Saturday night from a very nice evening with friends. The lights were on in Nikki's room as we pulled in the drive. I took Glynnis home and began tidying up a few items in the kitchen. At one o'clock Nikki came down, and I asked her what she was still doing up when she had a Sunday paper route breathing down her back.

She claimed that she'd just gotten home from her own babysitting job and that she had to know about a few other babysitting dates. It wasn't a long conversation, but later I found myself lying awake thinking about it. It finally came to me that I was bothered because I was reacting to the emotional content of the conversation, not the word content. Nikki's tone had again been defiant and snotty.

This is the heart of the Nikki-mystery. This is what bothers everybody who has dealt with her. Mara has said that it's the anger and hostility spilling over. "You're dumping things on these people that don't belong to them. You have legitimate reasons to be angry, but you have to put that anger where it belongs."

Mara has said that ideally Nikki should have individual therapy, but we all realize that she won't hear of that. And we also know that until she herself finds a need for it, it can't be forced. But Mara tells me that I should call Nikki on the anger when I observe it.

When I get up this morning, I can hear Nikki getting up for her paper route. I am still angry, so I go down to the kitchen, bent on carrying out Mara's instructions.

"Hi ," says she, again in that loaded tone.

"I am still angry with you for that conversation last night."

"What did I say?" Same tone, same snottiness. I tell her that it's the snottiness and the smart mouth that I dislike.

"It's like yelling at a dog for something he did before," she responds.

"I don't blow off when I should, but Mara has made me aware of that, and I'm trying. But I give you credit for one thing. You're smarter than a dog, and you can remember what went on the night before." So I come in to read the paper, and I am still angry enough to need to write. One thought about anger. The day that I yelled at Nikki about the water all over the bathroom floor, even though I felt that I was being unfair, there was a feeling of relief right beside it. "Do you know," I said to Pam, I feel that I acted badly, but, boy, does it feel good."

May 1982

We had a nice session with Mara yesterday about Ben. He took his workbook and did some tracings. I was spaced out on cold medication, so Will did the main part of the session. He was very articulate. He talked about being a perfectionist and about having resented, when Ben was a baby, the time given over to his care. I used to say then that Will didn't particularly like child care but that he was fair. He certainly did his share.

I told Mara that Will and I have differences in style about our work. Will will try to do two things at once. I used to wonder why Ben's baths were so long. Then I came upon Will reading the Journal of Organic Chemistry while Ben splashed. I'm surprised that Ben didn't turn into a prune or a submarine. I once told Will that if he wanted an evening each week to do professional reading, all he had to do was to let me know, and we'd schedule it. He could stay late at work and grab a hamburger for dinner.

Mara told Will that he's too tough on himself, that he beats himself up for what he considers mistakes, such as perhaps not giving Ben high quality time when Ben was a baby. She told us that we're both hard on ourselves. We are. A great example arose this morning when I was packing Ben's lunch. I filled the thermos too full, and then I had to pour some liquid off, which did not go too well. "Damn!" I said about four times.

"Why are you being so hard on yourself?" came a little voice from the dining room.

"You know, Ben, that's a good question. Remember how Mara says we're too hard on ourselves about mistakes? I made a mistake and filled the thermos too full, and then I was being hard on myself. It was just a mistake."

He was conversing this morning just like old times, fixing up his plastic airplane with tape over the windows for the effect of that thick plexiglass. Why do things fall out of the plane windows if they break? I wasn't sure—something about pressure. Too high or too low? I wasn't sure. A difference in pressure, that was all I knew. We'd told Mara yesterday that Ben is a real mixture of both of us. He's both humanist and scientist.

He seems better now. I remember when I was going through mental gymnastics in March thinking that we might have to give Nikki up. At that time I didn't want to let her go. Now I only feel tired, and I occasionally question whether I have the energy to get through another two years with her.

This is my forties decade, and I know that it brings me its own problems and tasks. I have to admit that I fear the magic of numbers. My mother died when she was forty-eight. Earlier I feared that Nikki was coming to take my place. Now I fear that the strain that she puts on me probably isn't good for me. Well, my forties will be tough with or without Nikki.

May 1982

Yesterday I made an appointment for Nikki with a really good hairdresser. I left the appointment card as a surprise for her. This will be my present for Prom Day. Nikki's so excited. She and John came in after school yesterday higher than kites on a windy day. John's uncle has some sort of limo that he's letting the kids use. The phone wires must have had heavy use last night as the three couples who are going in the limo called back and forth. It's time like these that Nikki is really enjoyable.

May 1982

"Two For the Seesaw" comes close to describing my relationship with Nikki. This is Sunday, and my end of the seesaw is down, but it was up last Friday. I was looking around at the view from up high and wondering how it was that I came to be there. I was just plain feeling good about Nikki.

I've been trying to develop same behavior mod type techniques for getting me out of the rut of irritation that I so often get stuck in with Nikki. I've been looking at her black and white six-month-old picture and imagining that I'm holding her. She smells sweet, she's cuddly. The picture does look enough like her so that the imagining isn't hard. What am I trying to do? Build a bond that can never be there for us? And yet it seems to work, at least for limited periods.

I was a little annoyed at her on Saturday when she missed the bus from the west side, and I had to go over at ten at night to pick her up. When she called, I hung up the phone in disgust, saying to Will, "That shithead missed the bus."

"She's not a shithead, she's my sister!" chimed in Ben, whom I'd thought was in bed.

When I told that to Nikki, she was pleased. When she next saw Ben, she said "Thanks for standing up for me, Ben, when Mom was mad at me."

As best as I can figure, I'm put out now, Sunday, because I asked her to turn down her stereo and got a sigh worthy of Moby Dick in return.

May 1982

For the first time I left a therapy session feeling angry and frustrated. I had business that I really wanted to deal with, and it just kept getting sidetracked.

I wanted to talk about the continuing static between Nikki and myself. I agree with Mara that some of it is just basic personality clash. But recently I've been more concerned than usual about it. It's been a drain, and I find myself wondering whether I want to be drained for the next two years.

But what Mara heard was that I had too much work to do. I had complained about having done the laundry that morning and noticing that Nikki's clothes smelled worse than ever. They ran downstairs by themselves and jumped into the washing machine, begging me to turn on the water and put in some soap.

This had made me realize that I couldn't finesse the personal hygiene issue any longer. I'd told Nikki that she had to get into the tub more often. This time I said that she'd have to take baths; I didn't want to have any more hassle over water on the floor. Nikki was maintaining that she preferred showers.

"How often would you bathe if you were left to your own devices?" Mara asks Nikki.

"I wouldn't rule it out," replies Nikki, causing all of us to laugh. But Nikki says that I have denied her the privilege of taking showers. I am impatient with that argument because she had twelve months of being able to take showers, and she still rarely took more than one a week. But Mara says, "Here's your chance to negotiate. Anne and Will are reasonable people."

No. I'm not a reasonable person where this issue is concerned. I've been a lot more comfortable with baths and no water on the floor in the last few weeks. But I want to be thought of as reasonable, so I say that I'm tired of the issue but Nikki and Will can negotiate it if Will is willing.

I try again to say that I've been mentally weary lately, but what Mara hears is that I'm doing too much, and she gives me a very hard time about my not asking for help. Damn it. That's not my issue today. When I leave, it is with the feeling that Nikki has often described—that counselling sessions are gripe sessions. I do not like the feeling at all, but it is probably fair that I get to experience it myself.

I reflect for a day or so on why it is that I, for whom words are usually no problem, cannot articulate what is making me upset. I'm even more puzzled, because in the midst of all this upset, I'm experiencing some really good times with Nikki—times when I feel that I have two neat kids, and I'm happy with that.

May 1982

I've been thinking on and off about that therapy session. It was really unusual for me to have come away feeling angry. These sessions have been such a safety valve for me. I'm learning so much about family interaction. Mara is really great. She's intelligent, and she's able to understand the dynamics of foster families.

I've often said to friends that it's easy for me to go to therapy with Nikki because I don't carry any baggage in with me. I didn't raise Nikki, and I'm not responsible for the problems and behaviors that she has now. That's very different from going in with your own teenager. I think I'd be really defensive about that and would have problems finding solutions.

I laugh to myself as I remember Mara's illustration of the tea. She was describing her own difficulties in letting someone else do something for her. When she was first married, if she was feeling sick, her husband would say, "I'll make you a cup of tea."

"Oh, no," she'd reply. "I'll get it myself." So he told her that she was robbing him of the experience of doing something for her. And now, if she's ill or tired, she'll say, "You know that cup of tea? I could use it."

Within two days, Nikki had drowned me in tea. It's funny, and it's a little sad, too, because she's so literal. But I know that she's trying to do something for me. The day after that last session, I was tired out of my mind. I fell asleep in my big chair after dinner and woke up around ten. As I stretched, I could hear Nikki puttering in the kitchen. "Would you like some tea?"

"I think I drank it all," I answered.

"I mean some hot tea."

"Thanks anyway, but I guess not."

The next morning I was still tired. I felt like lead all the way through. I lay in bed for an hour before I could engineer my body out. Nikki was already back from her paper route. I went downstairs, opened the kitchen door, and greeted Taco-dog, a ritual that takes a few minutes, intent as he is on licking the hell out of my face. It's an intricate series of moves, especially for someone who feels stiff. When Taco settled down and went on his way, Nikki handed me a cup of tea.

"Thank you," I said, and she told me that she put the paper on the table. I decided not to do the dishes from last night until after breakfast, and I sat there with my tea and my newspaper and a fine feeling

It's carried too—not just that feeling but extensions of it. I'm in one of my moods of "get off her case," and she recognizes a change and responds to it. She talks, and I listen, but when I eventually crave surcease, she seems to pick up my need.

May 1982

Have we thought about where we are now with regard to therapy? Mara asks us this question, rocking in her chair, obviously pregnant, and saying that as of July 1, she'll be on her maternity leave. She'll come back part-time in August and will probably keep a part-time schedule during the winter.

There are a number of options, she says. We can terminate, we can remain (though probably with another therapist at least part of the time) or we can come in now and then. She looks quizzically at us.

I have never thought of terminating, though it's clear from what Mara is saying that she believes that that is an option. She goes so far as to say that she has more faith in me than I probably have in myself. I think of the main character in *The Cracker Factory*, saying that the inmates of the Factory disappear into shrinks' offices, looking terrible, and emerge with stark terror in their eyes, clenching their release slips.

No, I don't feel terror, but I do feel that I'll need some future support in dealing with Nikki. As expected, Will really doesn't feel a strong need to continue. We do have the Ben issue, of course, and summer has always been my worst time, so finally I say that I'd like to schedule an appointment in late August to review how we've done over the summer. Then we can decide how to proceed during the fall. Maybe we won't need a weekly appointment during the fall but perhaps a monthly one.

Then we turn our attention to Ben, who's busily building with Mara's blocks. When I went to pick him up at school yesterday, he was sitting out in the hall. Mrs. Farr seemed rattled, unusual for her. She said that she'd gotten to the end of her rope with Ben and that she'd asked him whether he had thought about acting rude, silly and out-of-control. No, he'd said. She'd replied "Well, then you may be spending a lot more time out here in the next few weeks."

I told Mrs. Farr that the next day would be Ben's time with Mara and that perhaps we could talk about the behavior. We've been alternating recently, one week with Ben and the next week with Nikki.

Mara asks Ben what happened. "I fell out of my chair." None of us has the slightest doubt that this event was staged.

"And why do you suppose that upset Mrs. Farr?" asks Mara.

Ben claims not to know, but he does volunteer that it was a surprising thing to him to be asked to sit out in the hall. He won't really admit that he's done anything wrong, which Mara says is part of being a perfectionist. I would think that a perfectionist would want to act perfect and wouldn't be asked to sit out in the hall. Mara says that it's Ben's upset at having messed up that makes it hard to admit having messed up.

Ben is impatient when I ask him whether he made the other kids laugh or whether he said anything rude to Mrs. Farr. Mara asks him if he thinks we're picking on him. "Yes," he says. "No," says Mara. "Your parents are showing concern, but you're reading that wrong, and you're feeling criticized."

At the end of the session, we get back to talking about how we two adults are perfectionists and how Ben learns that from us. Afterward, we three perfectionists go out for dinner. We enjoy ourselves on this spring evening. I think of how I have seen the seasons change during this period of therapy. I've seen fall, I've seen the dark of winter when even halfway through the therapy hour it was black outside. Eight months. Perhaps we are ready to look ahead to functioning without therapy.

June 1982

Prom Day is here, and I have never seen more rain in my life. It rained all day, and when we left for the early afternoon hair appointment, there was no sign of let-up. I dropped Nikki off and went to run errands. When I picked her up, she dashed into the car. On the way home she mused, "I guess I'll take my bath now."

"You're kidding! The steam is going to wreck your hair!" It does look nice, even though I'm surprised that it seems a "younger" do than I expected. It's done up, with curls pulled over to the side on top.

"I'll be careful."

When Nikki started running the bath water, I went up to the third floor to work. Suddenly I heard a shriek. "I've got my T-shirt on!"

Neither of us had noticed what she was wearing. A blouse would have avoided this problem, but now she was going to have to get the T-shirt off over this hairdo. "Guess you'll have to cut if off," I said, knowing that she couldn't see my grin.

"It's my favorite T-shirt! I can't cut it!"

"Guess you'll just have to wear it under your gown." Judging by her next words, she'd found a way to get it off.

John came in the limo, and Pam and Ken came down to see how she looked. Ken took pictures with his decent camera, and I took some with my mediocre one. I'd planned to see them off in this huge car, but it was still raining too hard to do more than stand on the front porch and peer through the shrubbery.

Later Nikki said that it had been a nice evening, and she displayed a couple of souvenirs in the form of an "official" prom picture and a crystal goblet.

June 1982

The usual. Irritation and not-irritation are so closely entwined that they're like a rosebush and a suffocating vine. Nikki was gone yesterday for a Cedar Point trip. She got in very late last night and overslept her paper route this morning.

I had another interesting talk with Glynnis. As I was walking her home from babysitting with Ben, she was telling me that she knows lots of kids who are screwed up or who have had bad family experiences or have been on drugs or have slept around, but, says she, they're real people with feelings that show. They may not be likeable, but you know they're alive. She doesn't have that feeling about Nikki. If Glynnis were a psychologist, she'd say that Nikki has a flat affect.

I think I know what Glynnis means. Perhaps there are places where Nikki doesn't show her feelings. But then, as I walked home alone, I found that something doesn't fit. Nikki shows anger almost constantly. But I didn't know it for anger at first, either. It took me awhile to recognize that the abrasiveness, unkindness, roughness and brusqueness were anger. Maybe it's the struggle to put a lid on the anger that shows as those other things.

Even her walk is explosive, as though the anger would just like to blow her up into the sky like dynamite. It's what the little kids saw that day. But Nikki keeps a lid on that anger. So between the emotion and the control, what you see is the balance, dead center, and it looks as though nothing is there.

June 1982

I am having a hard time giving up therapy. I was really nasty to Nikki immediately after the last session. I can't quite figure it all out. I see, or think I see, what Mara is trying to do by pushing us out of the nest. If I don't have her to lean on, I may use the techniques she's taught me. And she's been right on the money almost every time so far. I'd like to trust her judgment. It's flattering to know that a professional thinks you're doing well. But...I don't think I'm doing that well.

Yet I feel that if I say that I want to return in the fall, Mara will feel that she's failed. Or would it be that I've failed? Aside from that, I don't like the message that this is giving to Nikki. No matter how much we say that leaving therapy isn't a sign of eternal health, she'll take it as such. She isn't interested in changing at all. Does she ever try? She brought me the tea. I find myself singing, "She brought me a little coffee, she brought me a little tea, she brought me damn near everything, except the jailhouse key." My own adaptation of "Midnight Special."

I feel much better about Ben and Nikki as a pair right now. Mrs. Farr feels that not all Ben's problems have been addressed, but it's hard for me to feel her concern because Ben is doing so much better at home. What do we have here? Is it a school problem or is it a family problem?

June 1982

It's grey and rainy, and our last therapy session was yesterday. Mara begins by asking Nikki and Will why we are terminating, and neither of them seems able to answer. Mara gets one of those oh-my-god-didn't-I-get-this-through? looks. She asks me what my understanding is. I say I think she' s figured that we've defined the problems pretty well and that we know how to deal with them. I add that I think that she wants me to start dealing myself without having her to lean on.

She seems satisfied with that, but I tell her that I have my own doubts about being able to get through another two years with Nikki. She understands that. She says that I should trust my feelings, that if I feel I need to call, then I do need to call.

I've gotten confused about this. At one point Mara said that we could set an appointment for the end of August. Now she's saying that we shouldn't set one because we might not need it. If we have one on the books, we may just come in out of habit. We can call in if we need to, but we can't schedule an appointment now. I leave feeling that an IV has been ripped out of my arm.

June 1982

Shirley Griffin at Cuyahoga Community College has offered me a free-lance writing job. My task is to put together a foster parent education handbook to illustrate the accomplishments of her foster parent training class. I said I'd love to do it, and now I'm knee-deep in course descriptions and parent comments. Shirley has written a great introduction, and I'll do the body of the book.

Pennie Riha is doing illustrations. The format will be an 8 1/2 by 11 sheet turned sideways to leave wide margins for Pennie's drawings and the parent comments.

The only argument that I have at all with Shirley is that these classes should be open to prospective foster parents. At the moment only active foster parents can enroll. I think it would be so great to know these things beforehand, to have some idea that the kids that will come to you are not going to be functioning like normal kids.

There are two course sequences. The first general sequence totals thirteen credit hours and covers child growth and development, social ecology, community resources and child-care techniques. The second sequence is directed toward special needs children and totals fifteen credit hours. Twelve of those hours are in community mental health principles and practices and the remaining three are in alternatives to institutional care.

Parents can use these credits toward an associate degree in community mental health, but most of them simply want to do a better job as foster parents. Shirley feels strongly that one of the foster parent's most important needs is to feel equal to social workers, psychologists, school officials etc., who often ignore the talents and knowledge of the foster parent.

How I wish I'd known about the program before we took Nikki!

June 1982

About the time that we end the therapy sessions, we take off on vacation. Will and I cannot really remember when we last had a vacation. I've tended to take long weekends to visit friends, etc., and Will's gone off for his mountain climbs. But now Will's professional association is meeting in San Francisco, and we decided to go.

His folks have been great about offering to take both kids. I think they understand at this point what a "foster grandchild" is. I've worried a little bit about Nikki's continuous talking, but I know that Mac can handle it. He teases her, and she seems to love it. Mom will just turn off her hearing aid.

For the four days that we're in San Francisco, I spend the bulk of my time at the desk in our hotel room, trying to get started on an article about the Guardian ad Litem project that I've been involved in at Juvenile Court for the past five years. I've brought lots of notes and my microcassette recorder, thinking that if I just talk out my memories, I'll have a place of beginning. Somehow the opportunity to do this just hasn't come up at home.

Will and I venture forth in the evenings to enjoy San Francisco, but my vacation really begins when we fly to Albuquerque to spend time with friends we met during our two years in New Mexico just after we married. Annie is someone I've really missed, the kind of person I'd love to have as a next-door neighbor. She and Fred have built a spectacular modern adobe in the hills above Albuquerque, and we revel in talk, country-western music, Mexican food, and more talk.

I pour out to Annie all of my angers and worries and fears about Nikki. She understands perfectly, having a daughter only a few years older than Nikki from whom she's been estranged for a year or so.

"Hell, none of them are grateful—your own or anybody else's." I hate to see Annie and Lorie apart. I can still remember opening the door to a pretty three-year-old in a starched dress and hearing Annie say, "Mother and daughter."

June 1982

Everyone has temporarily disappeared, and I'm writing. Sun is pouring through the narrow windows of the adobe, and I'm sitting at a table in the breakfast area. A number of beer bottles sit on the table, and a dog perches on a banco to my right.

This land is incredible. Its effect on me grows each time. There are hills and f-stop 22 camera distances, mountains and blue skies. To really experience it, I have to leave the cool house and stand outside in the bright sun. For short periods it's not bad, even though it's in the 90s. I'm a person who likes to sit in a bathtub and turn on the hot water. Standing outside in New Mexico is the same sensation without the dampness.

Last night and this morning I had a touch of homesickness. I tried to call Pam and couldn't get her. I told Will that they must all be down watching our house burn. Will said that of all the reasons for Pam not to be home, that was low on the list of averages. But I miss my home and my kids. We talked to Ben and Nikki last night. Ben has such a tiny voice. That cannot be said of Nikki. Space and time away from her is good for me. It'll prepare me for the next togetherness.

June 1982

We reached home one day before the kids were due, and that last day passed in a tangle of catch-up with both home and office chores. Then I took the rapid to the airport where Will met me with the car. We stood together at the gate, watching for our kids. Ben came out first, and when he saw Will, he just let everything fall from his arms and ran to him. Bystanders chuckled.

I hugged Nikki. To my immense surprise, I was genuinely glad to see her.

"Boy, am I glad to be home!" was her greeting.

Didn't she have a good time? It had been okay, but it was boring without her friends. Everybody talks at once on the way home, and for once I do not shush Nikki.

June 1982

Something came out of the mists while I was lying awake this morning. I was recalling one of the anecdotes that Will's mom tells. One day when Will and his sister were small, she'd noticed two little kids playing together in her yard. When she went out with her kids to go to an appointment, one of the little kids said, "Hey, you can't go anywhere! You're supposed to be watching us."

"Oh, you must be mistaken," she said and went on her way. It never happened again. My reaction was to be outraged that someone would do something like that. It reminds me of so many moms who take advantage by letting their kids wander around the neighborhood for someone else to watch over. But I also had a sense of anxiety, and I didn't know where that came from.

Then, this morning, I held it up to the light another way, and the question asked itself. When was I left with two little kids? When my mother died! It's so simple. Sometimes I feel like an absolute retard, a real slow learner. It shouldn't take Sigmund Freud to see that I might possibly have felt angry and put upon. But I didn't see it because I didn't recognize those scared and angry feelings.

I still don't, really. I still see only the feeling of pride in being able to run a house at that age. But now that the sun has shone through the prism, I'm aware that there may be other feelings as well, hiding, their own bold colors blended into one stream of light and only discernible when bent.

July 1982

Ben was drawing in the driveway today, and it wasn't until I was looking at the drawings the second time around, with a neighbor, that I said, "Sigmund is a little slow today. Does that remind you of a little boy who just spent ten days away from home?"

Patrick laughed and nodded. There were two big banners and some little sub-units. The largest banner said, "Come home, Dad, Ben is depending on you." Below the right banner were the words "Throw confetti." Below the left banner were some conversations: "Save some of this." "This what?" "He won't come." "Yes, he will come."

In front of all this were about four stop signs, and when Will drove over them, Ben was upset. But when he explained their importance to Will, Will gave him a big hug.

July 1982

I'm finding myself on a strange roller-coaster these days. I'm finding it more and more difficult to deal with Nikki. One evening she and I are in the kitchen when Will returns from a jog. He's pouring physical sweat, and I'm pouring emotional sweat from a go-round with Nikki. This continual emotional sauna just melts all of my reserves.

"I'm glad you're home. Nikki and I have just been hassling again. Maybe I should just admit defeat. I just can't get along with her."

Nikki appears not to understand. "But we've been getting along better lately."

She just does not notice the tension that she produces. It goes back to what we talked about so many times with Mara. She cannot "read" people, cannot tell their moods.

"Well, we have to do something. Right now I'm going to get dinner, and we can talk about this later."

As I get dinner, I try to calm myself down. I truly don't want to get into a discussion when I feel that I'm not in control. Is it the fact that I don't have Mara to lean on any more? Or is it the comparison of a few weeks without Nikki to this continual struggle now that she's back? Or is it both?

I keep thinking of what I'd said to Annie about Nikki and her concept of family. "It's as though she thinks that somewhere out there, there's a family for her, and when she finds that family, there will be immediate, unqualified acceptance. How else can you explain the disregard of those she lives with? It's as though she's learned nothing from all her moves. She still comes charging in, taking over, demanding attention and not seeming to have any understanding of anybody else whatsoever."

July 1982

I've been talking to a number of close friends, trying to come to some sort of resolution to my feelings. I think I know what somebody contemplating divorce must feel like. One minute I think I can make it; the next minute I think I can't.

I asked Maureen out for lunch, and I told her that I was virtually at my wits end with Nikki. "But I keep having this idea that if I could find someone to take her for the weekends, we might be able to make it through. I know that Mara didn't seem to think that this would work, but I know at least two agencies that are working with that type of program."

"I like the idea too," said Maureen. "Why don't you see what you can come up with?"

But the next morning I wake up in a horrible state. I feel anxious and depressed all at once. I decide to call the agency, even though I know that Mara's baby is due right around now. Sure enough, a daughter was born early this morning. "I've got to talk to someone," I tell the receptionist, and she connects me with Mara's supervisor .

I seem to recall talking to her somewhere along the line, probably when we were just getting started at the agency. I tell her that I really feel that we're in a crisis, and she suggests that we talk with another therapist, Karen. She'll have Karen get in touch with us.

I feel like such a failure. I haven't even made it a month without asking for help.

July 1982

Karen calls today, and I try to sort out for her what the problems are. I tell her my idea about respite care, and she is supportive of that. "I know one family that knows Nikki," she says. It turns out that both husband and wife are therapists who live on Nikki's paper route. "They like Nikki, and they never could figure out what happened with the adoptive family. They might be a possibility. Can you think of anyone else?"

"There are two families I've thought of. She's babysat for one. There's somebody else, too. There's a lady named Linda who met Nikki when she was living with the Yanceys. She's been really nice to Nikki. Linda told me once that Nikki reminded her of her niece. The husband has a child from his first marriage, but he and Linda don't have children.

"Talk to them. See whether any of them would be willing to help. You know, I'm really impressed by your commitment to this kid. You wouldn't believe the parents who have called me to tell me to come get a kid, his suitcase is packed."

"You're kidding!"

"I certainly am not. It happens all the time. But you're really trying to work something out."

We set an appointment for all of us to come in, and Karen gives me the names of the couple she's mentioned. I feel better than I have in a long time.

July 1982

Today I call Linda and find to my surprise that she dropped by last night while we were at the strawberry festival at a neighborhood church.

She'd found out about the problems and proceeded to give Nikki a lecture.

First Linda told Nikki that her room was a mess and that I no doubt thought she was a slob. Second, she told Nikki that if she'd had trouble with Peggy and was now having problems with me, then just maybe it was her fault. She wrapped up this glorious three-ringer by asking Nikki why she wasn't doing anything to try to stay. Why wasn't she getting her act together, in other words?

Linda tells me the story of a girl she once shared an apartment with. She advertised for a roommate and ultimately chose a girl who was planning to go to the local community college three nights a week. It fell out that the girl didn't go. Linda sat her down and said, "Look. I was counting on those three nights because I need the time to myself. It's not that I don't like you, but I need that time. Now you find something to do those three nights."

I ask Linda whether she and her husband would consider taking Nikki one weekend a month. She says she'll discuss it with him.

Bless Linda a thousand times. She understands my need for peace and quiet. She understands that Nikki needs to grow up. She understands that Nikki can be overwhelming. "I'm an adult. I do not want to hear about it every time we pass a Thunderbird," Linda told Nikki.

It is all I can do not to roll on the floor. If I had written Linda a script, she would still have gone it one better. I have heard about every T-bird on the road since Nikki's been enamoured of Rob.

July 1982

I'm waiting for three calls, one from each family that I've talked with about Nikki. Despite my trepidation, the initial contacts went well. I almost choked the first time, recalling the coughing fit I'd had at lunch with Maureen. She was imitating a television ad. "You don't know how hard it is for me to make this call. Will you pay my medical bills?"

What was I going to ask of these people? Would I say, "Will you let this unhousebroken teen into your home for one weekend a month so that she can rob you of whatever rest you were contemplating?" The first person I called was Kathy. She's Lia's mother. I told her that I was calling her because she'd been kind to Nikki and because I'd gotten to the point where I just couldn't look at another two years with this level of tension. I said that I was considering every alternative, from returning her to her home county to trying to find someone to keep her on the weekends to trying to find a group home to keep her during the week while I kept her on the weekends.

Would Kathy and her husband consider taking Nikki for one weekend a month? A silver lining would be a live-in babysitter. Kathy puts her husband on the line, and we have a companionable talk. "She's a little girl in a grown-up body," says Kathy, "and that could be trouble." Yes, I acknowledge, knowing that Kathy is a nurse who works with mothers and babies. This summer Nikki is volunteering some time at the hospital where Kathy works, and Kathy has been giving her rides.

"She talks a lot, doesn't she?" asks Kathy, in her sweet, small voice.

Yes, I say. Nikki is a compulsive talker, which is a large part of the problem.

"When she comes over to babysit, I'm usually trying to get Lia ready, and Nikki's talking about things, and now, when I'm driving to work with her, the traffic is heavy, I'm trying to merge on those ramps, and I just can't listen."

Oh yes. I know. I know.

"Listening to her is like picking up a book and beginning to read in the middle. It doesn't make any sense. I can never figure out which particular people a particular story is about."

Oh yes. A social worker neighbor told me once that that could mean same perceptual problems—that Nikki may not have a clear idea of what makes a story—that there's a beginning, a middle and an end. I know exactly what Kathy means. We talk a little bit about my missing the support that therapy gave me. Kathy, as a professional, expresses her feelings that Nikki should be getting individual therapy. We end on the note that they'll talk it over and call me back.

Then I called the family that Karen had mentioned. Helen is a social worker, and Alan is a psychologist. Helen and I had almost the same conversation that Kathy and I had had. One slight difference is that Helen specifically defines my feeling as a need for "respite." Respite care is big in the literature these days. Shirley Griffin at Tri-C has spoken of it as an immense need of foster parents.

"We like Nikki," Helen says, "and I can see what you mean, because sometimes after she's babysat, we sit and talk. When she leaves, I settle back in the chair and say 'Whew!' She's so needy. Why isn't she getting individual therapy?"

"It's certainly been suggested, but so far she's been resistant. Can you suggest anyone?"

Helen says that she'd like to talk with Alan about that. "She relates better to males," I say, "if that's a consideration in picking a therapist—which it might not be." Helen doesn't give me a yes or no on that question or the larger one but says that she and Alan will talk it over and get back to me.

I feel strangely excited by this endeavor. Perhaps its the theoretician in me. I can grasp the intellectual patterns and insights of dealing with these kids. Unfortunately it's the day-to-day practicalities that I don't have the patience for. I have the compassion for a kid who needs help, but I can't deal with the actuality of that kid taking up more than her share of the oxygen.

I have a vision. Let's say that each couple will take Nikki one weekend a month. Each of us would have her every fourth weekend. It would be unorthodox, but maybe it would work! We'd need to touch base with each other, so that we would be consistent in our handling of major things. We could give each other support, too. I certainly need support, and I can't believe that even a weekend parent wouldn't need support.

July 1982

We've had our sort-out session with Karen now, and she handled it very well. It's Karen's thinking that Nikki should be involved with a therapist that is hers alone, but for family therapy we should return to Mara. For Nikki, Karen suggests The Place, a local center that works with teens and includes involvement in music and art. I talked with a worker there when I was writing the article about foster teens, and I found their concept quite interesting. At that time, Place staff were looking for weekend homes for kids.

The more I thought about it, the more perfect it seemed. Maybe Nikki could get involved in some of the music groups. I hadn't been clear that The Place was engaged in individual therapy, but Karen assured me that it was. At this point I'm feeling that individual therapy is mandatory for Nikki.

Karen says that Nikki should be the one to initiate involvement with The Place—that she should make her own appointment. Karen tells me that The Place has a parent support group. That's something I'm definitely interested in. The Place may also be the solution to a possible monetary crunch.

Karen has raised the question of whether our insurance would cover Nikki if she weren't in family therapy. The Place has a sliding fee scale, which would mean that Nikki could still get help regardless of the insurance. At this point, Will's company has changed plans, and we don't even know if family therapy will still be covered.

I have my own ambivalence now about family therapy. I seem to be a bit hesitant to ask everybody to come in once a week when I seem to be the only one interested in that. I have a strange mixture of feelings about returning to Mara. I'm a bit embarrassed that I haven't been able to make it alone, and I don't like the feeling of failure. On the other hand, I'd maintained right from the start that I'd need to come back, and I just wasn't listened to. So I have angry feelings about being abandoned. Just like a foster child!

I end the session with a sense of having some direction. I hope that Nikki sees that we're trying to work things out.

July 1982

I had another phone conversation with Linda this week. She's really been trying to work with Nikki. She took Nikki to a mall on some errands earlier in the week, and Nikki had pulled her hostile, silent bit. "You won't get away with just not talking," Linda told her. "We will sit in this car and not get out until you talk."

I gather that Linda did some talking herself. She told Nikki that she was extremely self-centered, that she never thought of anyone else, and that she didn't always listen to what other people were saying. "You know how you just walk into our house, start talking to me and don't even say 'hello' to Terry? You know how I have to keep telling you to wait for the commercials if you want to talk when we're watching TV?"

Linda ended our conversation with the statement that she'd told Nikki that she would have to get involved with therapy before they could consider a weekend placement. Bless you, Linda.

July 1982

We are zero for two thus far. First Kathy called to say that she and Bill had talked it over and had decided that they just couldn't take on anything else. I told her that I understood. And I do. But I don't.

Helen and Alan were a little more artistic about saying no. Respite care might not be a good idea for Nikki, they say. She might give us a worse time all week because she'll feel rejected on the weekends. As I see it, it is simply reality that she is being rejected part of the time, and I don't know how she could be any harder to deal with than she already is. I think she needs to feel the reality of rejection if that's what her behavior brings. But at least their theory gives Helen and Alan a nice exit from the trick bag, to quote one of the Juvenile Court judges.

I understand. But I don't accept. I've had this child full time for fifteen months. Here are two couples who profess to like and care about her who can't take her one weekend a month. The next time Nikki asks me how the search is coming, I tell her no luck so far. "Am I that bad?" she asks, and despite myself, I crumble inside.

"You are difficult, I won't tell you that you're not. But I think that what you're seeing here is that very few people will put themselves out much. That's not you; that's just life."

In the meantime, since I haven't heard from Linda, the one ray of hope that I've been given comes from a private agency. I had heard about this agency's program while I was working on the foster teens article, so I called the woman that I interviewed. She was going off on maternity leave, but she gave me another name. It took me awhile to connect with the other person, and I was beginning to feel some frustration. Finally Judy called me, asked a few questions, listened intently and indicated that Nikki might be an appropriate referral for her agency's program.

Judy left me with one very interesting thought. I'd been giving my usual spiel of how, for a teenager, Nikki was such a good kid—no booze, drugs or sleeping around. "From what you say of her general behavior, she isn't old enough for the drugs, drinking and sleeping around yet. She's much younger than her years."

August 1982

Last night I was really in a strange state. I was worked up, strung out, whatever, about dealing with Nikki. Almost without thinking about it, I called Peggy. She must have realized intuitively how close I was to the edge—or perhaps I was that obvious. At any rate, she invited me over.

We sat in her backyard and had a glass of wine. "I know what you're going through," she said. "I have never seen anyone with a personality so different from mine as Nikki."

"I needed to hear you say that. It has been such a struggle to deal with that kid. I hear her coming in the back door, and I cringe!"

"I did too! It's like peace goes to the winds!"

We laughed and drank some wine, and I felt better. We didn't solve anything, we didn't unravel any mysteries. It was just one person saying to another, "Yes, I had the same experience. I felt the same. You're not crazy."

As I left, I asked Peggy whether she thinks that Nikki gets along better with men. Her answer is yes. As I walked home, I remembered my past thoughts that men are more valuable to Nikki. There certainly have been fewer of them in her life.

August 1982

I've taken a long weekend break with Aunt Rosemary and Uncle John at their summer home on a lake in Michigan. We visited an outdoor fair where there were some perfectly lovely stained glass pieces. I got a blue anchor for Ben and a rainbow for Nikki. The pieces look so nice in their windows.

While I was gone, Nikki decided to upgrade her phone service. When she'd talked about adding call forwarding and conference calling, I'd told her to forget it. I also told her that her umbilical cord must have been blue and curly like her phone cord, and she seemed to get a kick out of that. While I was gone, she ordered the two disputed services. However, the phone company called me before processing the order. "It sounded like a teenager, so I thought I'd check," said the lady.

"I'm glad you did. Don't go ahead with it."

This is the first time that I've questioned Nikki's spending of her own money. I think she picks up more trinkets than she needs—stuffed animals, etc.—but basically I've felt that she was sane in her spending. Now I'm not so sure. Nikki was clearly unhappy with my decision.

I told her to start keeping a ledger—to write down everything that comes in and everything that goes out. She continually hedges about how much the paper route brings in. I told Nikki to save some money for The Place, although it was an unbelievable surprise to find that their top charge for all services would be $10.00 per week. They were willing to forgive that in Nikki's case, but I said that it was extremely reasonable and that we'd share it.

September 1982

While dinner was in the oven last night, I sat out on the back porch with Ben and Nikki. I felt completely virtuous, spending "high quality time" with the kids. Ben was watering his garden, which was in sore distress, like the grass. The carrots are so tiny that I've been calling it the fourteen carrot garden. Nikki didn't get that at first, which is unusual for her.

She gave me another sociology lesson, this one about lunch in the cafeteria. This is the first of the "no hot lunch" at the high school years. There are machines with "sandwidges," as she calls them, and apparently there's yogurt. There is also a jukebox this year. She said that when white kids go over to it, the blacks yell "We don't want none of that white music!"

"You're going to be surprised," she told them. She said she played a song the blacks all like. The black music is easier to dance to, she said. My God, in the 1980's do we still have race records? Blues have always been my favorite, and I know that most of the great bluesmen are black. I don't usually think of blacks and whites listening to completely different music. But now that I think of it, there are two radio stations in town that are black stations.

"The black kids go over and kick the jukebox when you play white music. If one of the teachers sees them, we'll lose it. That's going to hurt all of us. It's really nice to have the jukebox in the cafeteria." You can't do better than music and food, I guess.

Nikki spent dinner trying to convince Will that she needed to take a shower because she couldn't stand sitting in a hot tub on a hot day.

"Put cold water in the tub," said he.

"I need to wash my hair, and the shampoo won't dissolve."

"You're crazy," Will replied, and after dinner Nikki got into the tub.

While she bathed, I found a good show on TV—a true rarity. She got out of the tub and dragged the phone to the landing, a towel wrapped around her head. "Larry has to hear this. I found a soup can on the stove the other day, all dirty. If I'd left that, I'd have gotten it!" I fail to see the point. I don't even remember a soup can.

"Larry says you're a trip," she said, going back upstairs. I heard her telling him that she threw away the can. Virtue needs to be rewarded, I guess. That must be the point.

September 1982

We've had a rocky moment or two with Nikki, but the positive thing is that she geared up amazingly well for the start of school. I'd been a little disconcerted by the evaluations she'd received at the end of the prior year. One teacher had written, "I have the feeling that I am not listened to when I am talking with Nikki."

That was no surprise, nor were the evaluations as a whole, but it was hard to see so many negative comments all in one place. Poor test scores, lack of comprehension, lack of attention, lack of background work. There were a few nice remarks, thank heavens, but the overall picture was of a kid who's not particularly talented academically and who doesn't try very hard.

I think that I will propose to her that her next two years will be a real challenge in school and probably difficult. We'll talk about deferred gratification and how she'll have more fun after these last two years of high school are over. I find that I have a real conflict, though, about pushing her to work harder in school. As Mara said a year ago, making Nikki study is not my job. But it's more than that. I was raised by two parents who kept their hands off most of the daily routines of their children's lives, and those are the parenting tapes that keep running in my head.

And this fall Nikki's been doing well on her own. The very first weekend, without even having been assigned history homework, she outlined a number of pages. Perhaps "outline" is too technical a word. In effect, she rewrote each section, claiming that she has trouble outlining. I figure that this is one of her bursts of enthusiasm that will stop in two weeks.

Her affair with the piano has those same earmarks. Her piano teacher and I have had a few conversations recently, and in one, the teacher wondered out loud why Nikki was taking piano lessons, her lack of practice being quite obvious. "After a winter of family therapy," I said, "I think I may have the answer. Attention. She gets one half-hour of your undivided attention every Saturday morning."

"Hmmm," said her teacher. She's just told me that Nikki doesn't seem to be able to memorize, repeat a tune, fit four quarter notes into a measure or transfer the note "A" from the sheet of music onto the keyboard. "But she knows it's a 'A' if you ask, and if you ask her where 'A' is on the keyboard, she knows. But she can't relate the two. Repetition, repetition, repetition, I tell her."

But now at least, she's on a fall study program. She told us that she planned to unplug her phone each evening until the homework is done. She and I carried the old dinette table from the basement to her room so that she could use it for a desk. I let her have my portable typewriter for her dental assisting notes. The first week she pronounced Homework as though it were Holy.

September 1982

For once Will is the one who got angry with Nikki. Susan and I went out for dinner, and I put the TV dinners in for everyone. We didn't leave the restaurant until almost eleven. "Safe to go home," I joked. "Nikki's lights have to be off at eleven." Her lights were still on when she dropped me off, and as I was getting out of the car, Will ambled outside, looking up at the windows.

"Going to throw the breakers?"

"Yep."

I talked to Susan for a few minutes, and by the time I reached the front door, all the lights were off. Nikki came ripping out of her room and down the stairs. "I've got three more pages to outline!"

"Tell it to the man," I said, nodding toward the kitchen. She went back to encounter Will emerging from the basement, whereupon she repeated her sentence.

He walked right past her. "Yeah, and you were on the phone from eight until ten." By now we're all back in the living room.

"Well, Larry called, and then Vicki called." But she doesn't look or sound very sure of herself.

Will looked at me. "Eight o'clock. She wasn't off until ten."

I chipped in. "You don't have to take a call because the phone rings. You told us you were going to take the phone off the hook. You'll have to give us the phone every night, and we'll give it back to you when you finish your homework. If that doesn't work, we'll have the phone company take it out."

She went upstairs. Maybe we shouldn't have even let her have a phone. I'm angry at myself, though, that I laid down the law so fast. I should have backed off. I should have let Will follow through. I could tell by the sound of his voice that he was really angry with her. That's good for her to see and experience, but when I came in, he turned it over to me. And I took it. I shouldn't have.

September 1982

Somehow I've been putting off going to The Place, though I kept saying that the parent support group was just what I wanted. The first few weeks after school started, I was just tired out of my mind. But now I'm in a revved-up phase. I tore through the day yesterday, started a big batch of spaghetti sauce so that everybody else could eat, and simply made up my mind to go.

We've had a couple of contacts with The Place by now. Will and I went over one night to talk to Tonya, Nikki's worker. I was a little disappointed in what seemed to me to be a real lack of intake information. But maybe some of that had come with the referral from Mara's agency. I was also a bit concerned that Tonya's being just out of school would be a real drawback. A social worker friend had once told me, "New social workers are all breast. They're still in that stage where they perceive their roles as befriending people, drawing out confidences, etc."

At one point I, myself, thought that was what a good social worker did—made people feel comfortable. Now I see that it is just the opposite. The good social wo rker hits the pressure points, makes a dient uncomfortable, but knows when to let up. Nikki has been rattling around about how much she likes Tonya, as opposed to Mara, who, of course, made her uncomfortable.

But on the sunnier side, Tonya follows up if Nikki doesn't show, which doesn't seem to be general Place philosophy. Nikki told me that this week's appointment was on Thursday. Tuesday Tonya called to see why Nikki had missed Tuesday's appointment. So Tonya is on to the fact that Nikki's recall is a bit selective.

We all went to the big, fall open house at The Place. "I signed up to bring a taco casserole," said Nikki. We had asked Peggy for the recipe for taco casserole, since it had been one of Nikki's favorite dishes. We all piled into the car with our taco casserole. The Place was packed with folding chairs, and we could barely move. The food was fabulous. We couldn't have done better at a high-priced buffet. I sat on the floor, although Nikki managed to find herself a chair from which she moved only to load up on desserts.

The staff band performed. They were very good, and Tonya was one of the vocalists. There was word of a slide show in the promotional material, but when the band finished and the lights came on, there was no mention of that. I turned to the bored-looking teenager beside me, wearing sequined black slippers and hair to match. "Is this it?"

"I most certainly hope so," she said in a languid manner. She's probably a court referral, ordered into involvement with this agency as a condition of probation.

When I returned later in the week for the parent group, I was the first one there. Sam, one of the leaders, introduced himself and told me to make myself at home. I got a cup of tea and wandered around. The Place's ambience is grass-rootsy, with a lot of weeds in between. The furniture is old, and the decor is somewhat tacky. The parent support group meets in what I suppose you'd call a conversation area. There are big blocks to sit on or lean on, and they're carpeted in orange shag. There are a few huge pillows thrown around. No one has vacuumed for awhile, so I felt right at home.

There are a number of books on a ledge near the conversation area, and I looked through them while people started drifting in. Finally there are enough for a group. I'm asked to introduce myself and to tell why I'm there. I give a brief sketch of our experiences as a foster family and some of the difficulties that we're facing right now.

The first person to talk is Betsy. She's the mother of a kindergartner, a second-grader, and a sixteen-year-old girl. She's just that day discovered that she may be cyclothymic. She stumbles over the word, and I supply it, saying "A social worker friend of mine has always said that's what I am. She says it's like being a miniature manic-depressive."

Betsy says that she may have to take lithium, and she seems to be afraid. "I would find that a relief," I say. "You know that it's not your mind; it's your body."

She seems comforted by that, but I find my attention drifting away from the group as I recall the mood swings. I haven't had real ups and downs for six or seven years, yet I remember vividly how horrible they were. I do still seem to have ebbs and flows of energy. Sometimes I really have trouble slowing myself down. I'll just keep going. Then I get to a point of being almost catatonic for awhile before the energy returns. It's a two-edged sword. Having that kind of energy lets me get a lot accomplished, but I'm not so sure that being revved up is good for the body. I feel for Betsy, because it appears that she's having a rough time right now.

My attention focuses on the group again as a woman who's come in a bit late wants to speak. Her name is Les. She's heavy, with a pleasant face. She has glasses with very large frames and hair braided tight down the sides of her head. "I had a horrible row with my kids just as I was leaving. That's why I'm late." She has a son about ten who's already spent two months in a psychiatric hospital, another son about twelve, and a fifteen-year-old daughter.

Apparently the boys had been fighting all day, with an occasional friendship break of five or ten minutes. Just as Les had her hand on the front door, she heard an upstairs door being banged back and forth. Then she heard it splinter. She raced upstairs to find the door cracked in half. She was furious, and she ordered one son into bed. He got into bed and ripped the sheet in half.

"I lost it. I really lost it. I got the biggest, fattest belt I could find, and I beat him." Everybody is serious. Sam seems concerned that if the boy goes to school with bruises, a teacher will report abuse. Les says that she is sorry that she hit him and told him so, but at the moment she does not feel guilty. She plans to talk with the boy's Place worker, and then she will talk with the school. She does not feel that the situation will escalate. "I lost control this once. That doesn't mean I'll do it again."

There's a lot of personal conversation from group members to Les. They're very supportive. When the conversation trails off, Sam says we'll wind up by having a slideshow. The projector doesn't work. Everyone swarms over it, but no one can fix it. "Can we all gather again for a final word'?" asks Sam.

Just then another woman who has come in late says she'd like to share something. Her adopted fifteen-year-old daughter has "bolted." Carol is the mom. She looks drawn and worried, making her seem older than she probably is. "I wanted Darcy to come here with me tonight. She said she wouldn't. I grabbed her and tried to make her come. When Les was talking tonight, I kept thinking of myself. But Darcy wouldn't come. She ran into her room and jumped on the bed. She looked up at me and said 'I hate you.' Then she ran out of the house." The pain on Carol's face is so real.

Why does it seem worse when an adopted child tells you that? Is it because you started out in a special way—with the joy of giving as well as getting? Is this the same bind that a foster parent gets in when she expects gratitude from a kid who can't give it?

We all talk about runaway behaviors. Darcy has run before, to friends. "You wouldn't find her if she didn't want to be found," I say. The lawyer in me is clear about some aspects of runaways, but Carol has to deal with her personal worry. We sit and talk until Sam throws us out at 9:40.

I come home and call a mother from one of my juvenile court cases. "I think you'll like this group. Please come." I hope that she does. Her son is one of "my kids," and he's been having a stormy time. What it seems to boil down to is a family situation that deteriorated after a divorce. The mother is left with three teenagers—or near teenagers—and doesn't seem to get much emotional support. We've talked about that, and I've been trying to get her involved with some group where she can find help. I think this may be the one.

The boy might get some involvement here, too. There are a number of kids who are referred by the court. He desperately needs a male model. I like him. To me he's the most mannerly kid in the world. I find it hard to believe the litany of aggravation that I see in the complaints that land on my desk. So far he's been locked up in the Detention Home and in the County Jail, and I very much don't want him to get sent away.

September 1982

Nikki and I have been doing pretty well, but the equilibrium was disturbed by an argument involving Larry, her latest flame. She invited him to come with us on a trip to my dad's farm, and apparently his mother is worried about this. "Tell her I won't even let you sit next to him in the car," I said.

Somehow that ticked her off, and I'm not sure why. She may have thought that I was siding with Larry's mother and thought she needed chaperoning. I swear I was trying to be funny. Even though I should know by now what Nikki is up to, I got sucked into one of those arguments that didn't really go anywhere. I finally just told her to leave me alone. So she went upstairs and began playing her chord organ, a little keyboard thing of three octaves. I told her to shut that off, too. I'm angry. She's angry.

The next day I bought a card with two beasts on the front. The outside says "You and I are very different." The inside says, "But we belong together." I left it by her phone. However, I'm still annoyed at this game, and I'm looking forward to the next parent group.

For this week's meeting I take my time getting there and am still first. Tonya greeted me with "Just the person I wanted to talk to." She and Nikki must have beepers. Apparently Nikki had told Tonya all about the Larry issue. She'd also told her about the card. "That card was really a nice idea. She liked the flower that you drew on the envelope. But you need to follow it up with some discussion. Nikki's concerned that she be able to show you how mature she can be with Larry, and she wants to negotiate a compromise."

Lord, I think. This little penny-ante thing has escalated into something world class. What kind of compromise can I make? There's really no issue. But maybe this is the other side of the mountain. Maybe this is how Nikki felt when I was getting to set all the agendas. Each of us had the opportunity to tell Mara what we wanted to talk about, but mostly I was the one to put a problem on the table.

I remember Will, one evening with friends, saying "Mara's on our side." She really isn't on anybody's side, of course, but since she's a rational person and we're treating Nikki as rationally and as fairly as we can, she hasn't found too much fault with us. That may have left Nikki with the feeling that we had total control.

Tonya is giving me a long lecture about how Nikki and I should stop each other when we see that a discussion is turning into an argument. If it gets too hot, we should walk away from it. Somehow I don't find this very helpful beyond a superficial level. With Mara there seemed to be more genuinely helpful suggestions.

I find my mind wandering during the parent group. If we're going to do family therapy, let's do it as a family. When we were working with Mara, we were all there together, and everything that was said was said openly. But here we have: (a) Nikki and Tonya talk; (b) Anne and Tonya talk; (c) Nikki is supposed to talk with Anne and Will but usually doesn't; (d) who knows how long this ball can bounce? In family therapy we all tackled issues together and resolved them. This way it just goes on and on. If this keeps up, I want to go back to Mara for family therapy. That won't mean that Nikki can't continue with Tonya for individual therapy.

I try to turn my attention back to the group. We have co-leaders, one male, one female. Tonight they're both here, and they're trying to get commitments from the parents as to our participation in the group. All of a sudden people are getting very cagy.

"We have another commitment on this weeknight, but we can come half the time."

"Both of us can't come every time. One has to watch the kids."

"Suppose I'm sick?"

It shakes down that no one will be expected to come absolutely, virtually, every single time, but a firm commitment to be part of the group is expected. Most of us seem to have that, and a few take it even further and ask that we list our phone numbers so that we can call and be called on in times of stress.

"I'll give my business number," I say, "because I can take calls in the daytime, since I work for myself. But I do so much business on the phone that sometimes at night I don't really want to talk." That's true. So many nights I have to make business calls that can't be made during the day.

October 1982

As it turns out, Larry isn't going with us to the farm after all, but I find that I still want to discuss the issue with Nikki. On the way out, I ask her to tell us what it is she wanted to talk about. "It doesn't matter now that Larry's not coming."

"Yes, it does. Tonya was saying that you wanted to talk to us about how mature you could be, and that's still relevant."

"Well, after I got the card, I didn't want to piss you off again."

I didn't really understand that, so I ignored it and brought up the family therapy question.

"I didn't know that I was only supposed to talk with Tonya about certain things."

"That's not the point. But this seems to be turning into family therapy, and if we're going to need that, then I'd like to go back to Mara."

"I don't want to go back to Mara."

"Well, we certainly can't do family therapy with Tonya."

Will, in his usual calm way, points out that it might take awhile to see whether it is family issues that keep coming up with Tonya. In my calmer moments, I'd said the same thing. Nikki seems to feel that she doesn't need to get into anything deep with Tonya. "I talk about what's bothering me now. The old stuff doesn't bother me." I tell her that it does so bother her and that's what's spilling over all the time. I stop because I can feel my own anger.

October 1982

One of the parents at group this week said, "I feel like an abused parent." She'd said it before, so it's obviously a feeling that's on her mind. I can certainly relate to that. We'd been listening to one of the leaders talk about confidentiality between a child and a child's counselor. It isn't clear that a parent with a Place counselor would enjoy the same confidentiality. I've begun to perceive that at The Place the child is king. I've even heard the group leaders say that kids don't have problems unless they're in a family where the parents have problems.

I've also heard the statement that where there is change in parent/child relationships, it's due to the parent becoming more relaxed in dealing with the child. Maybe that's not totally accurate, but it's very close to what's been said. So I asked about confidentiality. I said that I felt that Nikki had an advocate and that I had none. I said that I thought we'd set up our family therapy to be non-aligned. I had one intake session with Mara, and from then on we all met as a family. There was no information given behind anyone's back. But Nikki didn't like the family therapy, and at times I don't give a damn what she likes or doesn't like.

I don't recall getting a response to my statements. Nikki isn't even following through with her Place schedule. She missed another appointment with Tonya yesterday. A rehearsal at the high school ran late, but she was here at the house by halfway through her hour. The Place is closer to the high school than this house. I hope that Tonya can handle this.

October 1982

I don't know exactly why, but I've been feeling better about Nikki. There was an interesting incident on Saturday. Friday evening we had friends over for Chinese food, and Nikki went to a football game. She promised to phone me if she decided to go somewhere after the game. But she didn't phone, and she didn't come home until after midnight when I'd gone to bed. So when she got up Saturday morning—afternoon, really—I trotted her out onto the front porch so that we could discuss this in the presence of Will, who was torching paint.

"I forgot," said Nikki, with one of her stony looks. I was leaning towards a punishment myself, like losing the phone for twenty-four hours or not being able to go to the evening's Homecoming dance. But Will seemed to be inclined to let it go, so I contented myself with telling her that if it happened again, the phone would be yanked for a day.

Later that evening Will said that he saw Nikki's saying that she forgot as tantamount to an apology. I said that I didn't think so. To me an apology is saying "Gee, I'm sorry that I forgot to call and that you worried about me needlessly." No, says Will, it's so hard for her to admit a mistake—and forgetting to call was a mistake—that to her it was an apology.

I'm still not sure, but maybe her lack of argument is tantamount to an admission of being wrong.

October 1982

Just when things were going calmly, I had a phenomenal blowout at Nikki's latest flame, Jack. Nikki and I had really been having a good weekend. We had laughed about the brownies that just didn't harden. We kept sneaking in to observe them, but they were forever gooey.

But when I was cooking dinner Sunday evening and talking on the phone—a semi-business call—Nikki and Jack came in the back door. She heard her phone and raced off upstairs, leaving him in the breakfast nook. He stood there for about five minutes, then streaked across the kitchen behind my back and hit the stairs.

"Jack, come back here!" I yelled. There was no response. I repeated the sentence as I went to the living room. Jack was standing on the stairs looking at me.

"You do not go upstairs in this house. You sit in the living room and wait for Nikki to come down."

"I wasn't going upstairs."

"Get down here!" I stated in the authoritative manner that my father used to use with us.

Jack came down, sat on the sofa, and I went back to the kitchen. I was shaking. That kind of amassing of anger pumps enough adrenaline into my system for two weeks. I tried to finish my phone conversation, but I was not concentrating on it. I was aware down to my nerve endings of that kid sitting in the living room. When Nikki came down, I told her that it was time for him to leave.

She walked out the back door with him and didn't return. I wished that Will weren't outside working on the house. I needed him with me while I discussed Jack's behavior with Nikki. I planned to be very relaxed. "Gosh, Nikki, I'm really having a problem with Jack's behavior. I don't feel at ease with him. Do you think we could talk about it?"

But she didn't come in, and Will didn't come in. Finally Taco solved my problem by barking to go out, which gave me an excuse to go to the back door. I heard voices, but I didn't see anyone. "Get out of the basement!" I yelled, turning on the lights.

"Ha, ha, ha," came Nikki's voice from around the corner. This was a mistake. If she had any idea how angry I was, she would not do this. Her behavior has not been great either, ignoring a guest while talking to someone on the phone. For the moment I simply slammed the hell out of the door when I closed it.

Nikki and Will came in at the same time, and I forgot all about my relaxed speech. "I'm really pissed off at Jack. Where does he get off?" I attempted to tell Will about the race through the kitchen and up the stairs.

"He wasn't coming upstairs. He was just going to sit on the stairs and wait for me."

"Then why didn't he come back the first time I yelled? I don't want to see him around for a month."

Now Nikki was looking upset. I gather this guy is looming larger in her legend. I don't know what's happened to the "going together" she was doing with Alan.

"You scared the shit out of him. We were talking about it outside." Her tone is accusing.

"You bet I did, and I hope it impressed him. What do you think, Will?"

"I wish I'd been here."

Swell. Thanks for the support. I went back to the kitchen, where I realized that I'd done the recipe wrong and that it will take longer to cook. Damn. And what happened to my reasonable discussion? I didn't have a relaxed note in my repertoire. I was overstating, the way I so often do.

Why do I need to overstate? Is it just my native flamboyance? Or is it anxiety? Do I figure that people are going to walk over me unless I get to them first? Damn. How do I change my behavior?

Will came into the kitchen, and we both had a drink. "Taking the offensive is what I learned from my father," I said. "That's what he used to do—scare the shit out of us. It's a handy technique to know once in a while, if you don't make a habit out of it. I don't know, with Dad we always had the feeling that he was on the hairy edge, that he might just flip out and go absolutely bonkers. I don't think that I have that quality."

Will really didn't have much to say, but his presence was calming. I puttered around the kitchen, and he went into the living room. Nikki came down with her character sketch for English to share with me. I was touched. She was using this to say that she understood that I wasn't angry at her. At least I thought that was what she was saying, but I wanted to make it clear. I hugged her. "I'm not really angry at you, but I've got so much adrenalin in my system that I'd be rich if there were a market for it."

She laughed and told me about her sketch. Her character is named Brenda Bach. Brenda is twenty-one years old, 5'11" tall, 130 pounds, and a concert pianist. Nikki said that Brenda comes from a wealthy family. I said that was good, because then Brenda doesn't have to worry about making a living from music.

"I think I'll have the mom be a fashion designer."

"Sounds interesting. What is the dad going to be?"

"Oh." She stops. "I'd forgotten about him."

The next day I have an opportunity to discuss the Brenda Bach incident with Ellen. It happened that one of her clients didn't show, so I got the therapy time. It is a gorgeous fall afternoon, with sunlight streaming into Ellen's office, I sit in the rocking chair and tell Ellen how it had really stunned me when Nikki said she'd forgotten about Brenda's dad in the sketch she was creating.

"Wow," says Ellen, "That means you are it for her. The mom is really the only parent!" Ellen talks to me about what she calls provocative behavior. As I understand it, it means that when Nikki does something over and over again that she's been told not to do, it's a deliberate provocation on her part. It's a passive-aggressive thing, says Ellen, which makes it hard to deal with. "The hostility just oozes out."

There are a couple of behaviors that definitely belong in that category. One is Nikki's hand scrubbing each morning, that gets off the ink print from the newspapers but splatters all over. I've told her to use the lav off the kitchen. That faucet has a narrower stream of water, but she keeps coming back to the sink and splattering water all over the place.

Then there's the teakettle bit. For one cup of tea, the kid fills the teakettle to the brim, thereby wasting energy. No matter how many times I mention it, she just doesn't seem to get the point. Finally I walked out to the kitchen and demonstrated to her that she had put five and one-half cups worth of water in the kettle. Perhaps I do her an injustice in using this example because she's poor enough at conceptual things so that it could truly be that she doesn't realize how much extra water she's using.

"Do you sometimes get the feeling that you're just being picky?" asks Ellen.

"Yes!" My amazement shows.

"Well, that's part of it. She sets you up to tell her the same thing time after time. That's hostility."

We also talk about the requests Nikki makes that she knows will be turned down. She's often called one of her past flames to drive her somewhere. "Why does she do that?" asks Ellen. "Why does she need to be rejected? It's like her hassling you about driving until you said, fine, be my guest, and then she dropped the issue. As long as you'll turn her down, she'll ask. It's just to hassle you."

Ellen is certainly on to something about the car. I've been very puzzled about that. I don't understand why she dropped the driving. I thought it was a Very Big Deal to her. Is it really that simple? If we let Nikki do something, she doesn't want to do it?

We also talk a bit about how the hostility relates to Nikki's view of her mother. I don't know that I follow Ellen's hypothesis correctly, but I think it goes like this. Nikki has a deep anger against her mother for many things. Until Nikki deals with that anger, she will continue to provoke whatever mother figure is in her life. "But of course we know that she doesn't have any problems from the past," Will has said. "She's told us so!"

I ask Ellen if another hypothesis might also explain the hostile behavior. It would go something like this. If I am Nikki, I don't want to admit that maybe my mother was a failure, because maybe then I'm a failure by inheritance, so to speak. If I can show that all mothers are bad, then mine is just as good as anybody else's. Therefore I'll drive any mom to screaming fits with these provocative behaviors. Could be, says Ellen, but she feels the other is probably closer. I don't know. I sort of like my reasoning.

As we conclude our talk, Ellen expresses something she's said before—that she doesn't understand why Nikki can't see how helpful and ingratiating it would be if she were to try to do little things for us. "She's into unconditional acceptance," I say. "She feels that somewhere there's a family who will just plain accept her. She's not old enough emotionally to look out for someone else's needs. She' s probably thirteen or fourteen."

"I'd put her younger than that," says Ellen. "She's still in that stage of pirouetting and twirling and saying 'Look at me!' That's about two or three!"

I feel so much better after talking with Ellen. She's been great about asking me how things are going and listening to my tirades. I think she feels personally responsible for getting us into all this. And sometimes I capitalize on that!

October 1982

I have just had a terrible time with Nikki. This week there were school open houses for both kids. Nikki stayed with Ben while we went to his, and they stayed together again while we went to hers.

I was well-impressed with Mrs. Simmons, Nikki's dental assisting instructor. She said that Nikki isn't giving her any trouble, and I am very thankful for that. Nikki needs to pay attention and do well in this course. We've all been very straight with her about her need to be self-supporting after high school. This vocational course is an excellent means to that end.

At dinner the evening following her open house, Nikki said, in front of Ben, that Ben had been upset that we went to her open house. Very smugly she said, "I told him that fair is fair."

I really don't know at this moment how something this simple got out of hand. Will wasn't there, which is certainly a factor. I'd had a couple of glasses of wine, which was probably a factor, and I'd been annoyed at returning the evening before to find Ben sitting alone in the living room, exactly as he was when Will and I had left.

Will and I have talked many times about the minimal care and attention that Nikki gives Ben when she babysits. Our solution for a full evening out has been to hire a sitter, but that's silly for one to two hours.

I guess that Nikki figures that if she gets Ben out in case of fire, that's enough. Her idea of quality child care is to talk to her friends on the phone, hanging up only in case of fire or flood or some other disaster to the telephone lines. Will and I had both noticed that Ben was alone last night, but we'd decided to say nothing about it.

Yet here she is, knowing that he felt bad, rubbing it in that she's exactly equal to him. I did not behave well. I told her that she needs to pay a little attention to how hard it is for other kids in a family to adjust to a new baby. It's even harder to acquire an older sibling. Having a new baby in the house may be hard, but when there's somebody new who can out-maneuver you and out-talk you, then that's really hard.

Nikki began arguing with me, and pretty soon we were both yelling at one another. All of a sudden she burst into tears and started yelling that she didn't know I'd get mad. She took her plate to the kitchen and headed upstairs, yelling and crying all the way. I yelled too. Then I picked up the phone and called Tonya. I told her the call was against my principles, but I felt I had to call because I couldn't remember Nikki's having been this upset before.

Tonya said that it related to some of the things they had been getting at in their private sessions, and that she'd handle it with Nikki first and then perhaps with both of us. She had just been told that Nikki was calling in on another line.

I really had a bad evening. I was angry and upset that I had lost control. I decided that there were some things I needed to say to Nikki but that I couldn't trust myself to handle it verbally. So I wrote a letter that I left out for her.

October 1982

There was an interesting incident recently. Nikki loves Garfield, the cat. To my surprise, I don't mind the comic strip, though I think she has better things to do with her money than to buy a stuffed Garfield. She has no shortage of stuffed animals. But last week there was a Garfield special on TV.

Nikki passed up a Halloween party at The Place to watch Garfield. She and Ben were glued to the screen. Their remarks were so alike that I was amazed. Nikki relates to this cartoon character in the manner of a little kid. Her "kidness" overwhelmed me as she sat watching and reacting almost in tandem with Ben. Her "kidness" and her enthusiasm. Are they inextricably linked?

November 1982

Halloween has passed. I think there is some change in Nikki. Last year she was really involved in her costume. She went as a witch, and she really worked on her garb, getting completely into the spirit. She sprayed her hair red and glued on horns with spirit gum.

Sometime recently I read a piece by teens about teens, specifically discussing Halloweening. When a teen goes out with just a sack for the candy, he's saying that he's about ready to give up the holiday. But if he gets involved in a costume, then it's still fun to him. So last year it was still fun to Nikki.

This year she really didn't think much about it until the last minute and then said that she didn't want to go through all the mess of the witch costume. She talked about trick-or-treating for an hour or so, but ultimately didn't go out at all—possibly because of the weather, which was mild but more than a bit damp. Then she put on a karate outfit and went with Jack to a haunted house at the church.

November 1982

After the parent support group tonight, Tonya tells me that she's asked Nikki to write down five problem areas for the joint session that we have scheduled for Saturday morning. "I'm calling it a bitch session," says Tonya.

"I don't know that I like that designation," I say. But, after all, what is the purpose of these sessions if not to identify problems? Perhaps what you call the session isn't too important.

"There's one thing that I would like to ask you, Tonya. I would really like you to tell us how you perceived that event that led both of us to call you. There are some meanings there that I think I've figured out, but I'm not sure that I've got them all."

Does that count as one out of five? For the other four, I think that I can refer to what I call "foster parent issues." First, there's the continual lack of appreciation. I think we can put our "event" in that category.

Second, there is the continual "It's not my fault." Instead of "Those assholes scheduled another rehearsal," I'd like to hear Nikki say, "You were probably worried when I wasn't home earlier. I'm sorry I didn't call." I'd like her to accept the blame when it's hers.

Also, third, I'd like Nikki to accept responsibility. It's hard running this house. Nikki knows what she can do to help. She shouldn't make us continually ask her about doing things she's supposed to do. We don't give her that much to do to begin with. Let her clean up her own messes in the kitchen. Let her take out the trash Monday nights. Let her open her curtains and make her bed in the mornings. Let her take two baths a week. Let her not leave things around downstairs.

Fourth, there is the interruption issue. That's been constant, but I really think there has been some improvement. However it still comes up—like the coming in when we're watching TV and talking without regard to that fact. Is this part of the provocative behavior syndrome? I'll add argumentativeness in case the event doesn't count as one. That one word sums up an entire area of behavior.

November 1982

Yesterday morning we had our session with Tonya. First of all, I have been in better shape. My attorney friend Mary came over for supper on Friday evening, and we had a very good time. We went through a couple of bottles of wine, and we did some fine steps to B.B. King, including Ben and Taco in the dancing. I crashed on the bed and didn't come to until the middle of the night, when I went downstairs, cleaned up the kitchen, took some aspirin and went back to bed.

I got up Saturday morning, woke Nikki and got her started on her paper route and came downstairs. I was congratulating myself on being able to walk, and I started doing dishes. Midway through, I began to feel weak. My heart was pounding, and I was perspiring. I sat down in my chair and played at reading the paper. It was becoming a definite possibility that I wouldn't make it to The Place.

When Nikki returned, I was sitting in the living room with a cup of tea, watching Writer's Workshop on TV. "I don't know if I'm going to make it over there. I do not feel real sharp this morning."

"You guys were really funny," said Nikki. "I was talking to Jack on the phone and giving him a play by play. It was more fun than a party."

But we sallied forth and reached The Place in one piece. I find that I can usually mobilize myself under adverse conditions. I was also motivated by the consideration that Place staff might decide that I had a problem with alcohol if I couldn't came to a session due to a hangover.

As it turned out, my leveling with Nikki brought forth the confidence from her that she had tried beer at a couple of parties last summer. At the first party, she had half a beer, and at the second she had two beers. The two had made her feel weightless, she'd said. I tell her that two beers is all that I can really handle. She had confirmed with Rob the amount of beer she should consume. No more than two, he'd told her. By the time we reached The Place, we were talking companionably.

The session with Tonya confirmed my guess that Tonya has nowhere near Mara's ability. Nikki had "forgotten" to write down her list. Tonya rebuked her and told her to work on it right there. I had written mine, and I gave the list to Tonya.

While Nikki was writing, I reiterated to Tonya that I would like to have her tell us how she perceived our "event." She began talking about anger and "conflictions." She told me that I need to control my temper, which is probably the equivalent of noting that the sun sets in the west. She says that I need to think first and that Nikki needs to get the anger out first. That doesn't make any sense, and eventually Tonya seems to realize that.

But she doesn't seem to see any meanings in the content of the event itself. The only revelation I get at all is that Nikki apparently didn't understand that it was not good to bring up these things in front of Ben. We leave without any helpful input so far as I'm concerned. I need to control my temper, and we need to discuss things and communicate. So what else is new? Actually, we were doing a good job of communicating on the way over. If we adults can really share part of ourselves with our kids, it makes a big difference.

November 1982

After all the companionability, I got up this morning to find that the wastebasket was overflowing with the refuse from Nikki's midnight snack, the shopping cart that she borrowed for her papers was parked in the mud, there were extra dirty dishes that she hadn't cleaned up, she'd left for a day-long trip without doing her Saturday chores, and my brand new marker set was missing the purple marker, Nikki's favorite color. I found it on the floor of her room.

If I can, I will try to convey to Nikki that these things contribute to my "foster mom mood" that I was trying to explain in the session with Tonya. The question is whether this is normal teenage behavior or whether it's provocative behavior. Could another foster parent answer that for me? Maybe. I left The Place this past Thursday evening feeling again that this particular group just isn't meeting enough of my needs. I'm getting some useful information, but the fact is that most parents who are there have kids who are involved in drug abuse. The back and forth among the parents is really great.

"Get with it, man," says Dana to Bill, who's speaking of the need to "correct" his daughter. "When we were growing up, we respected our parents just because they were parents. It's not that way anymore. We have to listen to our kids. I used to lose my temper all the time. I don't anymore. I listen, and we work things out together."

The next day I call Roberta, a foster parent who has expressed interest in a foster parent support group. I'd seen her notice in the association newsletter. We talk and talk. She knows right away what I mean by the lack of appreciation. One of her responses sticks in my mind. "The community doesn't understand. People say, 'You can always get rid of the kid.' They don't understand that that's not what you want to do. You just need help."

We agree to talk some more about getting a group together. I can see some logistical problems. She, Pennie and I live in three different communities. Maybe we just need to set a time and place and try to make it. She'll put the note in the newsletter again.

November 1982

It gets so boring to realize that I'm just feeling more of the same. There's been one bright spot. Since I hadn't gotten any of the insight that I needed from Tonya, I asked Ellen what the "event" was all about. Permission, she says. When Will and I went to Nikki's open house, it made her feel good, secure. She began to feel bold, that she had permission to speak out. But she wasn't "reading" us, and she didn't know when to stop.

I feel better. I think Ellen is right. I do miss Mara. She would not necessarily have said that she had an absolute answer, but she would have proposed some possible explanations.

Thanksgiving 1982

This is a strange period with a lot of ups and downs. An up is that on the first day of vacation from school, Nikki comes in asking what I would think about her joining the Air Force. I am hard put to contain my enthusiasm. I fear that if I jump up and down and cry out about what a great idea I think it is, she'll cool down on it.

She says that she's stopped in at the recruiting office near the high school, and she has lots of information. It sounds great. The pay is beautiful, and it would give her a few extra years to grow up.

"Well," I say cautiously, "It could be a good move. Why don't you check around with people and see what you learn?"

It sounds especially good because I'm finally reaching the end of my rope with Nikki. I'm tired of telling her the same things over and over again, and I'm tired of the "one-way" attitude. The thing about Ben's birthday was really the last straw. She began planning her January 2nd birthday party last July; there's no doubt that she thinks that her birthday is important. She'd talked to me once or twice about what she was going to get Ben—maybe a little toy car—but when his birthday came, there was nothing, not even a card. I'm tired of living on her one-way street.

Over the vacation she was supposed to dog-sit for some people on her paper route. The agreement was that she was supposed to go over three times a day, because this animal is really a puppy. But she didn't do that, and whenever I'd mention it, she'd get hostile. Thanksgiving itself, we went out to my father's farm, and we didn't get back until late. "We'll just drop you over there," I said, "and then you won't have to walk."

No, she wanted to stop at the house and change her shoes or boots or something. It was fine with me if she wanted to walk back and forth. In all the confusion of unloading the car and getting Ben into bed, I didn't realize that Nikki had simply gone to bed without going over to see the puppy. It didn't register until I had gone to bed. For a kid who professes to love animals, her irresponsibility with them is shocking.

My annoyance at that certainly adds to my mood, and I think my frustration over the lack of help from The Place has led me to the point where I am going to turn around my act with Nikki. I talk to Will about it. "I've been really working on myself, trying to acclimate to Nikki, trying to be understanding. Well, I'm tired of it, and I want to see something from her."

"Doesn't sound unfair," he said. We agreed to talk to her after her paper route on Sunday.

We ask her to come up to the third floor so that we can have some privacy. Then I let her have it. "Nikki, there are going to be some major changes in the way that we run things. You've been here a year and a half, and there's another year and a half before you finish high school. For this first year and a half, you've been priority. We've all tried to put your needs first.

"If the next year and a half is going to come off, you are going to have to put out some effort. You're going to have to try to be one of the family. That means getting Ben presents, that means doing your share of the work. I'm tired of picking up your junk, doing your dishes, etc., without any help.

"I'm starting a demerit system. Every time I have to do something that I've asked you to do, I'm giving you a demerit. When it comes time each month to give you your clothing money, I'll subtract fifty cents for each demerit."

Thus far Nikki has been sitting on the floor in her characteristic pose with legs and lower lip stretched out. "You're going to take away the money the county gives me for clothes?" Her tone is heartrending.

I almost laugh, but I catch myself. "Tell this mathematical illiterate," I say to Will, "that it makes no difference whether I subtract it from the clothing money or whether she pays me directly from her paper route money." And Will does indeed explain that to her.

"Okay," I wind up. "From now on the ball is in your court. And just so we're clear on what got said here, I've written it all down for you. That way there won't be any misunderstanding." I give her the envelope with the letter, and we end the meeting.

November 1982

I am still sore as hell over one of my court cases last week. I've gone to the wall for a young black mother of two children. She's had some rough times, and children's services has temporary custody of the kids, but this lady is a fighter. She lined up an apartment in a white, redneck neighborhood, almost causing me to have a coronary. But she's moved in, she seems to be doing okay, and we're asking that the kids be placed back with her.

The caseworker is a real pain. She kept us both waiting for an hour on an appointment and then said various things including that her department didn't care what kind of priority Juvenile Court was giving to getting these children back in the home. She wrapped it all up by pretending to joke that "We don't really care about Sara. She can sleep on the floor. But the kids have to have beds."

It is clear that this worker won't help find an extra bed. Sara has bought twin beds for the kids, but she has none for herself. The caseworker won't approve the apartment until the heat is turned on—a reasonable request—and there is floor covering over the plywood floor in the living room, an unreasonable request. Further, she refuses to do anything about my client's Catch-22. Children's services has taken the children out of the home. The mother is now on General Relief instead of Aid to Dependent Children. But somehow she's supposed to find and furnish an apartment for a family on GR funds, which are a couple hundred dollars less a month than she was receiving on ADC.

When my counterpart in the legal department at children's services couldn't do anything with the caseworker either, he suggested that I file a contempt motion against her. So I did. I figured that Judge Robbins would give us a fair hearing if anybody would. To my absolute astonishment, Judge Robbins gave my client a hell of a rough time. She was clutching a red tag that had just that week been put on the space heater by the gas company men who said that it was unsafe and refused to connect it.

"You've got to figure it out, sweetheart," the judge told her. "So what if you only get $108 a month in GR. So what if your rent is $130 plus utility payments. You've got to figure it out. That's survival, sweetheart. Now I'm talking to you this way because we're both blood."

At this point he looked at me, and I must have looked perturbed, because he asked, "You're having a problem with this, counsel?"

I completely lost any shred of poise that I might have had. I got up and said, "Yes, I do have a problem with this. I'm not blood, and I don't understand how she's supposed to set up an apartment for herself and two children on the money that she gets as a single person."

Judge Robbins has been known to put people in jail for contempt of court. My colleague from the children's services must have felt that I might be adding my name to the list, so he jumped up and said, "I'm serious, Your Honor, I may need an order on my own department." This defused the situation, and we came to some sort of solution that kept me out of jail. But we didn't solve my client's problem, and I'm still pissed off.

November 1982

Again I find myself writing fiction. Some of the anecdotes and remembrances that Pennie has been telling me about foster kids are so vivid that I've turned to fiction to try to get a handle on them. Fiction is not my usual mode; I only end up writing fiction when something is too difficult to handle any other way.

I'm really overwhelmed by the insight and understanding that Pennie has for foster kids and foster parents. Her own life history has some pretty grim details. One of the most striking things she's told me had to do with a young child she'd taken who had been abused. She found a very creative way to deal with that child, and his response was fantastic.

But when someone asked her how she had hit upon that way of handling him, she couldn't answer. When she really thought about it, the pain of her own childhood began coming back, and she couldn't put it out of her mind as she had for years. Looking inside caused her to enter a very difficult period in her life.

The one thing she says that stays with me constantly is that foster parenting is "do-able" but only with supports that foster parents usually don't have. Agency support. Community support. Therapeutic support. Our experience has borne her out. I did far better with Nikki when I had regular therapeutic intervention.

December 1982

There's a nice smell in the house again—oranges, tangelos and grapefruits. Sixty-two cartons are stacked in the basement. It's the Big Fruit Weekend. It was during this weekend, one year ago, that I first came close to giving Nikki back to her agency.

We've came through the year, but how many times have there been when it's been close? There was that time in March when we thought she might have to go for Ben's sake. Then there was my vesuvius of last July. Then there was this Thanksgiving's ultimatum. It seems that about every six months something blows.

But we're in a new era now, the Anne first and Nikki second era, and it may change things. Not that the hassles have stopped. With all of this fruit to deliver, Nikki's been planning to go to the west side with one lone carton for Rob. She is not going. Will is available this afternoon, not tonight or any night this week. She'll just have to go to Rob's some other time.

After busting both physical and mental guts on this fruit project last year, Pam and I abandoned it, and Will took over. He's much better. He just goes about his routine instead of trying to get Nikki organized. He forces her to come to him.

Nikki's other problem of the moment is Christmas vacation. As a result of the Thanksgiving Ambush, she's been told that we will follow up on the weekends away, which had just not materialized. The time with Linda never worked out because Linda and her husband separated, and she went back to the west side. And the private agency has put me off because Nikki "belongs" to another county. "You really need to ask them for help. They don't want to lose you. But get back to us."

I cannot say how angry this makes me. This "turf" business between and among agencies drives me right up the wall. My friend Jean is the only person who seems to respond without asking whether an individual is in some way "eligible." Maybe church people are distinguished by that fact. I don't know.

Eventually, however, I call the supervisor at Nikki's agency, since we are without a caseworker again. To my surprise, her immediate response is "Sure. There are some families here that she's stayed with that might be possibilities, and we've also licensed other families in your county. Let me talk to Kirsten, and maybe we can set up a meeting so they'll get to know Nikki." I am amazed. Perhaps it's been very clear to Nikki's agency all along just how difficult she is.

And then there's the matter of Christmas vacation. Back last summer, Nikki's sister Laura asked her to come during Christmas because she was expecting a new baby. Nikki was planning to go, although there was a fair amount of talk as to how boring it was going to be and how she wanted to be with her friends. But then the baby arrived prematurely in early November, so Nikki has a little more leeway in planning this vacation.

She waltzed to the table one evening this week with the plan of a three-day vacation. "Wrong ," I told her. Then the agony started. She got out paper and pencil for one of her famous lists. The 24th, 25th, 30th and 1st she wanted to be here. "You've got a problem," I told her. I was sure that she wanted to be here on the 24th and 25th not so much because we're family and she wants to be with family at Christmas but because Laura and Grandma are Jehovah's Witnesses and don't celebrate Christmas. A Christmas without presents is pretty bad news to Nikki. The 30th is a party at one of Nikki's friends, and the 1st is a concert. "You can't have them all," I told her.

Finally she decided to bite the bullet and go to Laura's over Christmas. She'll be gone about a week and a half. In the meantime, Roberta, Pennie and I have started getting together for lunch once every month. "Foster parents are people who will do everything for somebody else, but they won't do anything for themselves," says Pennie. Needless to say, this fits my current philosophy like bacon fits eggs. I have so many questions to ask Roberta and Pennie, and they have so much to share. Roberta currently has two biological teens and two foster four-year-olds. Pennie and Vince adopted their last foster son and have two biological sons.

They seem to have a lot of questions to ask me, too. They ask the questions you'd ask of a lawyer who works in Juvenile Court and sees the precursors to foster care—the neglect, dependency and abuse cases. Why has it taken four years to get one of Roberta's foster daughters free for adoption? Saying that it was a notoriously difficult case that was appealed twice doesn't help. Both the child and Roberta have had a sense of impermanence. Roberta has been willing to adopt, and at one point the worker told her that everything was clear, Roberta could tell the little girl she'd be adopted. Then it was no, there's another appeal, tell her you take it back. Is this caseworker for real?

A Christmas card came from a special friend the other day. She's an obstinate, willful lady, who's blind and has taught educable mentally retarded kids. In my card I had told her of Nikki, and her response to me is "As for mixed-up kids, my only advice is to be firm and consistent and to only notice what you can do something about."

December 1982

Last Friday I had the brilliant idea of walking in the snow to school to pick up Ben and Mike, a neighbor whose family was having dinner with us. All day I'd watched the first good snow of the winter from inside the Juvenile Court library, and I felt the boys would like to be out in the flakes.

But Mike didn't have his boots, and Ben said he was tired and he wished I'd brought the car. We trudged homeward in the street, dodging cars. People in our neighborhood have forgotten what it is to shovel sidewalks.

Ben speaks up. "Did you get a call from school today?"

"No, honey, but I was at court all day. What happened?"

"I threw an iceball. Here's my friend Kevin," and he reaches out an arm's length, "and here's where the snowball landed," and he reaches out half an arm's length. "I can't go out for recess. I have to sit in the principal's office."

"For how long?"

"I don't know."

A few steps later he adds, "Matt and I had to stand out in the hall during the music class."

"Why?" The snowfilled evening is beginning to feel dismally cold.

"We were barking instead of singing," the little voice announced happily. "Mr. Johnson came along and saw us there."

"What did he have to say?"

"He was disappointed." The happy voice turned grave. Mr. Johnson is indeed talented.

Later I have a few minutes to talk with Nikki as I am making soup and salad in the warm, cozy kitchen. Our friends will bring the garlic bread. The boys are happy with Nikki's PacMan. "Ben threw an iceball in school today. He asked me if I got a call."

"He narced on himself?" Nikki's eyes were bright and laughing. "I have to talk to him!"

"You'll do no such thing! I want to know what he's up to."

December 1982

It wasn't until early Monday morning that the call came. Could I please come up after school to talk with Mrs. Barrett? Surely.

I am five minutes late and feeling like a guilty first-grader myself. I had left work with time to throw the day's mail into the chute at the post office and make it to school. But there is a jam-up. Some little old lady who can barely see over the hood has dumped all her Christmas cards on the ground because she can't reach the sleeve on the box. She climbs out of her car and picks up each card with all the alacrity of age.

Mrs. Barrett is waiting for me, sitting at one of those little tables, grading papers. She must be in her fifties or more and in great shape to be sitting on that little chair instead of her adult-sized desk chair. I sit down on another little chair and look at her expectantly. I see that she has a list.

"Benjamin has just not been able to settle down. I've moved him from one of the tables to a desk."

Why all these kids don't have desks, I don't know. A school is supposed to have classrooms, walls, doors, and desks organized in orderly rows. When I was in elementary school, we had those back-to-front desks, and those suckers were all nailed down. Nobody was going anywhere. But this is an open school built in the 1970's, not the 1890's-built school of my childhood. I'm glad that Ben has gotten himself a desk, although I do not say that.

"Benjamin always has his hands on the other kids. He grabs genitals. He hugs. He's even grabbed other kids' throats." She pauses. "I worry about that."

"I do, too." I am genuinely shocked.

"The other day one of the little boys had built a snow house. Benjamin knocked it down. The other little boy was terribly upset. But Ben didn't seem to be sorry. I asked him if he knew how the other little boy felt. He said, very flip, 'Sure I know. I was there.'"

"I get that flipness too, sometimes," I say.

"The other day at sharing, he wouldn't share, but he was making fun of the kids who did share."

Sharing. We'd already been told at his first conference that he wasn't sharing. I've urged him to share, and he'd taken the picture that came in the kit for the gingerbread house. But he hadn't shared. That's what we have trouble with at our house, isn't it? Sharing. Ben doesn't want to share with Nikki, and Nikki doesn't know what the word "share" means.

"I think the other kids are waiting for Ben to settle down. I've talked to Mrs. Moore. She's the attitude adjustment teacher, but she won't have any openings until February."

Attitude adjustment? Was that the phrase? Is Mrs. Moore a social worker, a special-ed teacher or a psychologist, I ask. Mrs. Barrett seems unsure. I sigh inwardly, but then I launch into my canned speech. I have it all down pat now. Ben was in nursery school when we got Nikki. The following fall he began kindergarten. The fall conference is just what every parent dreams of. He's bright, sweet, sensitive. I leave on air. Then in March, there is disaster.

I tell Mrs. Barrett about Nikki's first-grade year, knowing that will help her understand. When Nikki was the right size for these little tables and chairs, she was taken from her mother and lived in two different foster homes.

Mrs. Barrett does understand. She sucks in her breath. "The poor thing. I really take my hat off to what you're doing."

Part of me wants and needs that response, but I've gotten beyond that now. "Do not remove your hat. If I had truly known what I was doing, I wouldn't have taken her. But whatever damage has been done is done. Now we need to decide what to do about it." I tell her about our work with Mara and suggest that we should return.

Mrs. Barrett seems to agree that the best solution is to return to someone we've found helpful. I will contact Mara to see if we can set up a conference to determine how to handle this.

December 1982

I have a long talk with Will the next morning about Ben's school disaster. We've fallen into a pattern of sitting down with a second cup of coffee after both the kids are gone in order to have some time to go over whatever issues are on the table. I find myself saying, "I don't think Ben's showing his nice side to Mrs. Barrett at all. I told her that, too, and she said 'His little eyes snap.' I know what she means, and yet he can be so sweet."

Will agrees that Mara is our first resource, and I say that I'll call her. Later, feeling really weighed down by all of this, I call my friend Liz. Liz has had some serious problems with her own kids, so she's a comfort both as a person and as a professional. "So what if Ben doesn't share? Big deal. Who says that everybody has to share?"

Immediately I laugh. "I never thought about it that way. I just bought into 'Sharing Is GOOD.'"

"Sometimes I think that teachers just love to tell parents that they've done a rotten job." Liz is serious.

"I don't know if that's the case or not, but I sure left feeling that way. I really felt that I'd done a rotten job, except that I really do blame Nikki for a lot of this. I used her as sort of a tap dance, a shuck, but there's a lot of truth in it, too. Ben didn't have these problems until after she came. I'm feeling bad about a lot of this. I think I asked too much of all of us when it came to taking Nikki."

"You said something about sexual acting out. Do you have any reason to believe that Nikki might have molested Ben?"

"No!" I say, again genuinely shocked. "What she does do, though, is to talk about sex in front of Ben. Her conversation is really something else. Sometimes I just plain tell her to shut up."

"That could be it then. Also, teachers go ape when they're confronted with sexuality. That's the worst thing that can happen in most classrooms. If I were you, I wouldn't worry about that so much." I feel so much better after that conversation.

December 1982

All that I can say at the moment is that it's as hard to kick ass as it is not to kick ass. I've been on Nikki, making her do chores, calling her on hostility, but I haven't yelled or screamed. When she's neglected to do things, I've simply put a demerit on the chart, along with a little note as to why. Occasionally I've put up a "merit"—a new invention of mine—when she's done something nice that I think she should be rewarded for. A merit cancels out a demerit. But overall, this seems to create as much stress as there was when I used to just stifle the anger.

December 1982

It's been very nice with Nikki gone. I've been resting, wandering around in my bathrobe until late in the morning. In a way, these holiday vacations are enforced because of school vacations, and sometimes they're more welcome than others. It all depends on what's happening in my work life. Law is unpredictable, with real feasts and famines. But this vacation seems to be relatively smooth.

Nikki has given me a purely diabolical jigsaw puzzle for Christmas, and I am determined to finish it before she returns. She gave me such a grin when she handed me the box, insisting that I open it before she left.

Our present to her is money toward her high school jacket, so there's no real present to unwrap. Part of my relaxation during this vacation has been working on the puzzle.

But slowly it dawns on me that Nikki didn't leave a present for Ben. My heart sank. Will and I talk it over, and the best that we can figure was that Nikki's plan to take Ben to the Nutcracker is her present. "But a little kid needs something under the tree!" I say.

Will agrees. He also points out that Nikki asked him to provide transportation for this event as well as to let her charge the tickets to his charge card, so that she could phone in the order. Although she did pay him back, she doesn't seem to realize that if this event is a present, it isn't totally hers.

Over the next few days, I find myself wrestling with anger. Is this provocative behavior? But by the time I pick Nikki up at the bus station, I find myself genuinely glad to see her. I hug her hello, and we decide to play a few games of Ms. PacMan. However, the burly fellow at the machine seems to be getting a large number of free boards, so we go on our way.

We stop by my office so that I can run in to check mail and messages. I come back to the car saying, "Jesus. One of my juveniles is in the County Jail. I'm supposed to call the court. I wonder which kid it is. Come on, we'll see if we can find that bizarre house on the way home, that blue job." I'd been telling Nikki about an outrageous electric blue paint job I'd seen. Nikki and I collect these.

We found it, which was not hard to do, given the fact that the blue is deep, bright and shiny. Even Nikki is impressed. That street will not need plowing this winter because the reflected light will melt all the snow on its way to the ground. "You could shoot that house with black and white film and get a color print," I tell Nikki.

We are really enjoying ourselves. Once in awhile we get on a roll. We've been like that about our "collection" of outrageously painted houses. These are the times when Nikki is really fun, and I treasure them.

New Year's Eve 1983

Mary and I decided to have one of our big open houses. We asked some lawyers but plenty of others that we like. At the party one of my good friends asks me what is going to be new for me in 1983. Meanness, I say. I am going to look out for number one for a change. I'm going to put Nikki in her place, and there's one other agenda item.

I've been involved in a group for some time. It's just a group of friends, and we read some and discuss some. But recently I got into something unusual. I was hell-bent on a certain topic that others didn't want to talk about. Death. It isn't a pleasant topic. But I'm tired of just pleasant topics. There are areas inside me that haven't been charted and mapped yet, and I have the feeling that they are the lands of anger.

I've picked up a piece of fiction that I began writing years ago and set aside. It's a novel, and I don't know that it will ever be publishable, but I have to write it. Somehow now that I've stirred up some of those old materials, I have to find a way to live with them.

New Year's Day 1983

What a failure I am as a parent. Here's Ben hitting himself in the head and saying "I'd like to kill myself," and here I am telling Nikki to get out of my sight. I'd been looking forward to going to an open house at a neighbor's, even though Ben had been obnoxious there last year. I'd put it down to the presence of a neighborhood kid that Ben dislikes.

This year he'd said he wanted to go. Since he'd been up late New Year's Eve, he said he'd take a little nap—very unusual. That meant that he was really tired, but he asked me to promise to wake him when it was time to go. I probably should have just let him sleep, but then I would have broken my promise.

I awakened him, we went over, and he went upstairs to play with the kids. But he returned right away, saying that he was sick. I was really annoyed, and I told him so. Then he started with the "I feel like killing myself." It really frightens me.

Some friends are coming for an adult supper, and I tried to make plans to have at least one of Pam's children came down to watch a movie on cable with Ben. At the open house I learned that her kids weren't coming; they'd already seen the movie. I feel let down.

On top of it all, there's a school strike looming ahead, and Nikki will be clattering around the house with nothing to occupy her during the day. Happy New Year.

January 1983

Yesterday was Nikki's eighteenth birthday. Even though she had waived the family party in favor of having us drive kids to a pizza and movie party on a future Friday night, I didn't really feel that the day should pass unmarked. It was a beautiful day, cold but refreshing, and sunny. I planned out a shopping route that would get cake, ice cream and a card as efficiently as possible.

But my trusty, reliable neighborhood bakery had closed as of December 24th, so the sign said. I proceeded to the drugstore a few doors away for the card and ice cream and fell into a conversation with the lady at the cash register about the demise of the bakery. "Oh yes, they closed at Christmas. You say there's a birthday in your family?"

"Yes. Our foster daughter is turning eighteen."

"Those kids are hard kids. There's always something wrong with them. Moving around, it does something to them. They all have problems."

"Indeed they do," I acknowledge. "But your own kids, they'll give you trouble too, especially when they're teenagers."

"So my friends with teens tell me, yes. You must be a special person to take in a foster child."

"Crazy, not special. I don't know if I'll ever do it again." Did she see the article in the Sunday paper about the foster parents in a rural township? No, she didn't, so I proceed to tell her about it. In September these parents were given a citation by their county for ten years of foster parenting. In October the county revoked their license. The couple lives on a farm, in a remodeled house, with a bedroom on the first floor where they sleep. They have three kids of their own—fifteen, fourteen and eleven—and had taken foster kids younger than theirs.

But it seems that children's services has a rule that parents have to sleep on the same floor as foster kids age ten and under so they'll hear them if there's a problem and to "prevent sexual contact" between the kids. Funny, said the foster father, for seven years the department never even mentioned this rule. Now they bring it up.

The family can have a child older than ten, the department says. But the family feels it's got enough kids over ten, and they've always found that having the foster kids younger than their biological kids was best. The way that I see it, the department is just twisting these parents' arms to get them to take an older child. Those kids are hard to place."

"Don't you think there's more to it than that? Don't you think there's something underneath?"

"Not for one moment. Children's services departments often treat foster parents like dirt. I'm a lawyer, and I do a lot of work in juvenile court. I know a lot of people from this county's children's services department. Some are fine, but others are just plain lousy. No, I don't have any doubt in my mind that this couple is getting a raw deal."

"Oh, then you know, if you're in court with them. How do you work at such a beautiful profession and take a foster child too?"

"Because I'm crazy, and because I have some control over my work hours. But I'll never do it again. The beautiful people are the ones who take kids for ten years and then get jacked around by children's services." I go on my way to buy the cake.

I told Nikki we'd have rigatoni for her birthday, but I hadn't told her about the cake. I found a card that shows a garage mechanic with a pump. The front says "Your family hired me to work part-time on your birthday." The inside says "You blow out all the candles, and I'll pump the air back into you."

That night when I'm driving home with Ben, I say "Ben, I need your advice. Do you think we can fit eighteen candles on a smallish cake?"

"Sure."

"I'll need your help." He's great. When we get home, he wants to look at the cake. We take it to the third floor, peek at it, and we sign the card. I decorate the envelope with one of my special flowers. I want to involve Ben, and yet I don't want to make too big a deal over this party.

It is fun. Nikki roars with laughter over the card and blows out the candles in one gust. We both get out our cameras. She wants to use my flash, and we spend a lot of time trying to figure out what setting she needs for the electronic flash. We read the booklet for her new Canon (disastrously written) and the booklet for my old flash and make a choice. I hope the pictures turn out.

Later I tell her that I've talked to her agency supervisor and that we need to start thinking about these weekends. Is there anything on for the immediate future? Nothing is. Nikki says that we owe The Place fifty dollars. She doesn't seem clear as to whether the fifty dollars is the total or just our share. I ask Nikki whether she feels that she's getting anything out of going to The Place.

Yes, she says. She likes talking to Tonya, but she'll do anything about these weekends that will help. I say that I've made an appointment with Mara next Friday to discuss how we should proceed. At this point I don't know if Mara will just work with Ben or whether we'll do some family stuff.

Whatever will help, she reiterates. She seems calm, in control, not hostile. I find this response novel, and later Will confirms that what he overheard of this exchange seemed somehow different to him, too. We continue talking. Nikki says that she and Tonya usually talk about the relationship between herself and me. She feels bad about getting more demerits than merits and about our putting some down while she was away over vacation.

I tell her that we didn't do that to be sneaky but that some things she left undone didn't come to light until she was gone. I also say that I can see that it must be difficult for her to have to deal with Tonya about problems she has getting along with me. Dealing together is one of the strengths of family therapy, I say. But then, I add, my own mood for family therapy has probably been destroyed by my non-negotiation stance.

She laughs. She says that sometimes Tonya tells her to make a chart for me and give me merits and demerits. No way, Nikki tells her. I wouldn't touch that with my mom.

Later I think about this, and I know that what I'm doing now seems right to me. The entire Place philosophy, as I see it, is to negotiate. But that's not where I am. And I don't know whether that has to do with foster parenting or just parenting. In truth, a foster parent doesn't have the motivation to negotiate that a natural parent has, but I don't know that natural parents should have to negotiate everything, either. All I know for certain is that in this particular relationship between Nikki and me, non-negotiation is necessary and important.

The only other thought I have at the moment is that no matter what the relationship is between Nikki and me, that particular relationship is not the crux here. The relationship between Nikki and Ben is the larger problem. I could decide as an individual to take the flack of Nikki for another year and a half. But the crucial decision is what's best for Ben.

January 1983

Yesterday was a very busy day, starting with a 9:30 appointment with Mara to talk about Ben's school problems. Will and I sit for a minute in the living room with coffee after breakfast, and I ask him if he has any observations that he wants me to convey to Mara. We both seem to feel that basically we're the same family that Mara saw a year ago. Probably the only exception is my current non-negotiation stance with Nikki.

I arrive right on time at Mara's new office. She did not return to the agency after her maternity leave but entered private practice with her husband (who is a psychologist) and some others. Their space is very nice, and we chat for a few minutes about the available office locations in the area. Ellen and I looked last fall, too. We discover that all of us favored one particular building where the rent was simply too high.

I decided to read Mara the entry from this journal about my meeting with Mrs. Barrett. I knew that the writing would be more accurate than my memory, now, a month later. It was a good decision. It brought back some of the mood of the events, the feelings and worries that I am having.

Mara thinks that Ben does need individual therapy. She agrees with Liz that schools get extremely uptight about anything sexual, but she herself doesn't seem too concerned. She surprises me by saying that she feels that Ben's problems may not be related to Nikki. Personally I doubt that, although that may be a rationalization. If my own biological child has problems, it's so much easier to blame them on Nikki's presence than to admit that I screwed up as a parent.

Maybe it's just the damned temperament. Mara says that Ben and I are two peas in a pod. Yes, I know that. So many times I look at Ben and think "Why couldn't he have been like his father, who is calm?" But he is like Will, too, says Mara. Will keeps things in, she says. The calmness may be misleading. But I know that I keep certain things in, too.

Mara asks me if I think I need support. Yes and no seems to be my answer. I tell her that I have a network of friends, all of whom help me with the Nikki puzzle. In some ways, I say, Ellen has been able to give me some of the insights that I used to get from you. Tonya is no help at all in that regard.

Mara says that she asks because if she were to work with me, she'd refer Ben to somebody else. No, I say. I want Mara to deal with Ben. I trust Mara. If for some reason, she and Ben don't work well together, I could consider working with her, but I want him to have the first choice.

As usual, I find myself being secretive. I don't tell Mara about the big anxiety attack of Tuesday night. I woke up with my heart pounding and feeling afraid. I took two Valium but didn't fall asleep—I just lay there listening to my heart behaving like a jackhammer. Finally I woke Will and asked him to rub my back. I said I wanted to hold his hand and drain off some of his peace and quiet.

I finally fell asleep, but I was groggy the next day, and I worried about a recurrence. That episode was like one three years ago when I really thought I was having a heart attack and had Will take me to the emergency room. They were monumentally unimpressed, and I just felt very foolish. The strange part of this is that I am certainly no stranger to anxiety, but in my past it's always had a definite mental component. I was always aware of specific fears. But these attacks are basically just the physical half.

I really puzzled over the latest one. Then I had a picture of an evening the week before when one of my lawyer friends came over for dinner. Ben was absolutely great. He loves my friend and even got out the napkin rings for her. He often gets out the candles, but I didn't know that he even knew we had napkin rings. Nikki was being okay, and Will was having a great time with his new computer. My friend must think that we have everything, I remember thinking. And that's dangerous, isn't it? That's when you've got the most to lose.

I am not going to share this. That is typical of me, but I feel okay about it. I do talk to Mara about the "I'm going to kill myself" that worried me so much on New Year's Day.

"I don't think he's suicidal," says she. "It's just a sign of how much anger is inside that when it spills out, it's so great."

After I leave Mara's office, I make a brief stop at my own, then I meet Pennie for lunch. We hoped to have a few other foster parents this time too, but Roberta had a bad cold, and Pennie couldn't reach some of the others. We certainly had plenty to talk about, however.

I told Pennie that I had written The Place a letter "resigning" from the parent group. "Most of the parents who go there have kids whose problem is drug abuse. That's not our problem. And I don't think the staff there understands foster families. Sometimes what I need is another foster parent to talk to so that I don't call up Nikki's agency and tell them to come to get her. But I don't have to negotiate with her, I'm not going to negotiate with her, and they just don't work that way."

Pennie asks me whether we've made any progress on the weekends away. No, I have to say. As we are leaving, Pennie tells me to send Nikki to her house for a weekend. She'd have to sleep on the couch, but they're willing to have her. What a friend!

When I pick Ben up that evening at school, I chat a little with him about going to see Mara. I emphasize the elevator in her new building, figuring that he'll enjoy that. Then we gear up for the evening's activities. First we take Nikki and her friends to a shopping center where they're having the big birthday pizza dinner and movie event.

Will, Ben and I go to a Mexican place, and Ben cracks us up by ordering a New York strip steak. We tell him that is too expensive, so he orders a fruit plate. I don't believe that he really wants it, but he does. He eats every bit.

After dinner we go home, watch TV and play PacMan until it is time to pick up Nikki and her friends. Nikki bought a tabletop PacMan after Christmas, and we've all gotten into it. We take both cars to pick up and deliver kids, and it really isn't that bad. They're kind of fun. By 12:45 we're home, and Nikki remembers to thank us. It was a long and profitable day.

January 1983

Pac-Attack! I get up Sunday morning at eight ready to write, work on a case and read tons of newsprint. But my eyes fall on Nikki's little PacMan, and I can't resist. Then I go out for a walk. It is absolutely beautiful—sunny, blue skies, brisk. I line up my thoughts for an opening statement and closing argument as I go. I put this case out of my mind until this weekend because it's so tough.

Almost four years ago I was the assigned counsel for Montana when children's services was asking for permanent custody of her three daughters. It was my first permanent custody case, and I took losing very hard, although even then I had a sense that children's services always wins in juvenile court. Aside from that general principle, in this specific case their evidence was good. When I explained the judge's decision to her, Montana threw herself on the floor in hysterics.

The bailiff picked her up, put her in his office, and left me to deal with her. I took her hand, and I told her that she had one child left, that she should go home, love that child, and do whatever children's services asked of her, including standing on her head if that should please them.

And here we are, with children's services asking for permanent custody of the little boy. I've had some doubts about Montana's mental competence, and children's services' complaint included allegations of her psychological problems, so I'd asked for a Guardian ad Litem for her case. In the project that I participate in, one attorney can serve as both Guardian ad Litem and Counsel, but sometimes the two roles conflict.

A GAL represents a ward's best interests and makes an independent determination about what those interests are. Counsel's job is to advocate for the wishes of the client. In this case the assigned GAL for Montana is a new attorney who is great. She's just short of a master's in social work in addition to her law degree. We talked with a clinical psychologist who's examined our client, and we saw the client in her home.

We feel that children's services has treated her cavalierly and has not tried very hard to work with her, but we feel that the department will still make its case. As counsel, my job is to advocate Montana's wishes to have her son back. It is Susan's job as GAL to advocate for Montana's best interests, and Susan feels that those are not incompatible with the return of her son.

Even though we expect children's services to prevail, we need to give this woman her day in court, and we're going to do the best job we can. It has to be horrendously hard to lose a child to the permanent custody of the department and know that you will never see that child again.

I get very worked up practicing my opening statement. Children's services sometimes does absolutely outrageous things. In this case the little boy was removed from Montana's care in July of 1981. She was allowed to visit him until fall, when the caseworker told her that visits would be halted because the agency was going to file for permanent custody.

First, it is against the law to withhold visitation until the agency has obtained permanent custody, and second, the agency didn't even file for permanent custody until the fall of 1982, one year later. By the time I get home, I am feeling very righteous about our case on these grounds alone. Not that I expect it to make a difference. Nonetheless, I have occupied my mind with something other than Nikki's issues, and that is good for me.

January 1983

All of a sudden things are back on between Nikki and Matt. Nikki invited him to her birthday party, and he came. She walked home with him and started to kiss him goodnight on the cheek. But, says she, he turned his lips to her. I think she floated home. The next day she came running downstairs. "Guess who called me? Matt wants to go to the movies Friday night."

And it was the movies on Friday night, church on Sunday morning and another movie on Sunday afternoon. I went in to take a bath Sunday morning after having read part of the paper. Nikki's bedroom door was closed. When I came out, her door was open and her dulcet tones could not be heard. Therefore, she must be out of the house. "Did Nikki go to church?" I asked Will, who was still up to his eyeballs in newsprint.

"I guess so."

"Well, well. Ain't love grand?" He looked up inquiringly. "The child has not gotten religion. She merely went back to church after a year's absence on the chance that Matt will be there."

The Sunday afternoon movie safari included Ben, probably as a pretext on somebody's part—I'm not sure whose. I had a workshop that afternoon, and when I came home it was six o'clock, dark and cold. Will was running the snowblower in the drive. "When will they be home?"

"Sometime," he shrugged.

Damn. Does nobody ever plan? Luckily I had put a kettle of soup on the stove, and it was simmering all afternoon. When an hour went by, I call Nancy. "Was there any better planning on your end?"

"No. By the way, what's going on?"

"Well, whatever it is, this time it's Matt who's making the calls."

"That's what we thought. Dan and I were talking about it yesterday. Did Nikki tell you that she wants to invite Matt over to your house for his birthday dinner?"

"Yes. She asked me, and I said it would be okay. I suggested that she ask you and Dan, too."

"That was nice of you, but I think we shouldn't come. It's okay if Matt goes, but I think he'd think we were encouraging this if we went. We've decided not to forbid Matt to see Nikki this time, but we don't want to encourage this. I just wish he'd see other girls too. But Nikki is so available."

"I think I know what you mean, but I'm not sure. Nikki does make a nuisance of herself by being around all the time, if that's what you mean. But if you mean sexually available, I don't think so."

"Remember before when I said that Matt didn't have any hormones? Well, I think he's got them now. I can tell a difference in the way he walks around the house. I'm just afraid they'll get too involved."

"I don't really think so. I like Matt. He's a nice kid, and in general, I think Nikki picks nice guys. She's dated a lot this past year, and there was only one guy that I just didn't like. And I think there's some genuine caring between Nikki and Matt."

I continue, "Do you know, Nikki once said the nicest thing about Matt. We were coming back from therapy one evening, and she said that if anything ever happened to Matt, she just didn't think she could stand it."

I can tell that Nancy is touched by this, so I continue. "But I think I can see your concern. Down the road Nikki and Matt are just very different kids. They come from different backgrounds."

"Oh, I think that Nikki is a lovely person. I just think that they shouldn't see so much of each other."

We end the conversation with pleasantries, but I think I have recognized where the jugular is. The next day I tell Nikki that I've gotten the word on the birthday party. Nikki says she's confused.

"First Nancy didn't like my calling Matt, but now Matt is calling me, and she still doesn't like it."

"It looks to me that it is the involvement she doesn't like, and I don't know whether it's you or whether she'd be like this if Matt was seeing a lot of any one girl. I just don't know Nancy well enough to know, but I'm guessing that if Matt saw a lot of any girl, she'd have a fit. She's just a worrier."

Nikki looks upset, but she says that at least it is a small step that Nancy won't forbid Matt to see her. Well, perhaps now Nikki will have another topic besides me to discuss with Tonya.

January 1983

What a day. Susan and I spend virtually all of it in court with Montana, and, of course, children's services got permanent custody. Montana began to scream and sob at the courtroom table. I put my hands on her shoulders. Susan looks at me and says, dumbfounded, "He didn't even listen!"

"Welcome to Juvenile Court," I reply. The judge has left the courtroom very fast, and somewhere in the background a call is made for the deputies. Montana bolts from the courtroom, and Susan and I gather our things. We walk down the stairs, from the third floor to the lobby, looking for Montana, and we see her by the front doors, surrounded by a knot of three or four friends who have come to court with her.

When she sees me, she runs over, sobbing, and throws her arms around me. I hug her. "I'm sorry, Montana, he just didn't listen." I have tears in my eyes, too. I know that Perry Mason could not have won that case, but I am holding an anguished person. At last Montana pulls away and rejoins her friends.

Susan and I go down to the snack bar. Both of us are thirsty. We have been there since ten in the morning, and it is after four. The snack bar is closed, but we get pop from the machine. We could certainly use a martini, but those are not on the menu. I can barely talk, and I have tears on my cheeks. Susan says, "The only thing that's keeping me from tears is that I know the make-up will be gone in a minute."

We go up to the law library and sit for awhile, collecting ourselves and our thoughts. Two of children's services' major witnesses absolutely contradicted one another. We saw the two of them having lunch when we went down for a sandwich.

When the hearing resumed in the afternoon, we were surprised to see children's services recall one of the witnesses to the stand. She'd had an amazing recall of memory, and her testimony was no longer contradictory. It wasn't too hard on cross-examination to show that she'd had lunch with the other witness, who'd reminded her of something she'd forgotten.

"They just didn't make their case," Susan said.

"You're right. The record is going to be horrible against children's services. Not only was there the business with the two witnesses, but there was all that hearsay testimony that I objected to." I sit for a few minutes. "As much as I do not want to go to the Court of Appeals, we may have to go there."

"I was thinking the same thing."

"Well, let's not decide now. Let's let this thing sit for a week. We've got thirty days to file the notice of appeal. If we still feel this way when the emotion has settled down, we'll do it." I sit for awhile longer. "If the judge had just kicked the department's ass a bit, it wouldn't be this hard. But they pull their outrageous policies—like the denial of visitation—and they don't even get a slap on the wrist."

January 1983

Nikki's newest caseworker, Lee, has been working on the respite care question. She calls to say that thus far she has no "finds" but some possibilities. I'm sure she's trying extra hard because I told her of the school difficulties that Ben had been showing and said that if we couldn't get a handle on those, we'd have to ask the agency to move Nikki. I told her that Ben brought home one of his school projects, a little book titled "A Book About Me." Inside the book is the interesting statement: "I have no brothers. I have no 1 sister."

I ask Lee whether there were any foster placements for Nikki that seemed to go especially well. If there were, I could talk to the parents for their advice. No, said Lee, no placement was ever really good for a long period of time.

Although the overall impact of that information is sad, it actually strikes me as being good news because it takes a load off my shoulders. Here I had a mental picture of Mrs. A or Mrs. B or whoever getting along well with Nikki. I guess that's the foster mom myth rising up again, and I wasn't measuring up.

February 1983

Pennie has followed up on her statement that she'd take Nikki for a weekend. Since nothing has been forthcoming from the agency, I took her up on it. Friday after supper, Nikki and I drive to Pennie's. A young face peeks out from behind the curtains as we get out of the car.

Pennie offers me some coffee, and one of the boys shows Nikki around the house. Pennie, Vince and I talk for two hours in the kitchen, and when I leave, Nikki and the three boys are sitting in the living room watching TV and eating popcorn. What a remarkable person Pennie is. Our conversation gives me two things to think about. One is to try to see what the particular foster child's reality is. Is her reality one of constant moves? Is no place ever safe?

Another is the power that Ben has over her. A little kid has the power to make her move. I tell Pennie that Nikki sees Ben somewhat as she saw her sister Laura. "Laura had the power to make her move. Now Ben has it."

"That's big power," says Pennie.

But Nikki does nothing to help herself. She doesn't try to please. She doesn't observe, watch, pick up the signals that are going on. I would think that self-preservation would require that.

"I don't believe that child will put herself out for anybody," said an elderly lady on Nikki's paper route yesterday. I had been fielding calls from irate customers on Saturday, and on Sunday I'd unplugged the phone until one o'clock. The minute it was plugged in, another angry customer called. Even though Nikki gave the customers her private number, some of them always call us.

Will decides that Nikki should receive a demerit for poorly planning the weekend insofar as the paper route went. And she should. At least one. She knew for two weeks that she was going to be gone on this particular weekend. As far as I know, she didn't even try to get a sub until Thursday evening. When she went, she left a note for the route man taped to the front door, saying that she hadn't been able to get anyone to do the paper route.

It is such a quiet weekend that I hate to pick Nikki up. I also have the fear that Pennie will tell me that Nikki is a great kid, and I shouldn't be having any problems with her. I do hope that Pennie, with her experience and understanding, can help me figure out how to handle Nikki.

February 1983

I have been simply outrageous these past few days with Nikki. I've been angry, resentful, and I've dumped it all. It didn't help that I returned home from a meeting to find that nobody had cleaned up after supper. I'd left the house feeling good, having put together a special spaghetti sauce. Nikki was to start the water boiling at ten to seven and put in the spaghetti when Will came home. He could help her figure the amount. However, when he got home, she was talking on her phone, so he cooked the spaghetti.

Yesterday morning and this morning I actually said prayers for me to be gracious. I am not a praying person. I'm not a religious person in the traditional sense, either. I don't go to church, but I figure that something's out there somewhere. So once in awhile I engage in early morning prayer.

Yesterday it did not seem to have any effect. I was outrageous and ferocious, and one fed on the other until I was a real shrew. But I tried prayer again this morning, and I feel helped or answered or touched or whatever.

February 1983

I've still been on Nikki's case, and I'm bothered by it. Yet the last time I talked to Pennie, she told me that I wasn't being tough enough on Nikki, that I wasn't asking enough of her, that I wasn't preparing her sufficiently for a life on her own. "She's gotten used to a Cadillac lifestyle. How's she going to maintain that? When she was here, I told her 'Poor Nikki. Next week I'll come to your house and sit in your room and use your phone and your lav and watch your TV.'"

Cadillac lifestyle? In ways. Nikki is living an upper middle class life that she wasn't born into. She's living in a nice house with nice things around her. But let's be realistic. Most of us know, when we leave home, that our first apartment isn't going to be in the style of our parents' homes. I don't know that that worries me too much.

But Pennie believes that Nikki should be on her own sooner rather than later. I'd been thinking about the possibility of moving Nikki out during the next school year. I've envisioned a small, third-floor apartment. She could still came here for meals. That would be a halfway measure.

No, says Pennie. Put her in a place for a month, make her cook, make her find a way to do her own laundry. Make her do that while the safety net is still there. "Because she's going to fall flat on her face, lady. She doesn't even know how much money she gets from her paper route. Get her into accounting for that."

I respect Pennie. I think she walks on the water. But even people that walk on the water are wrong once in awhile. I think my plan for Nikki is tough enough. I think I see her fear now, behind the bravado of "I'm looking forward to moving out." And why shouldn't she be afraid? It's a big step.

February 1983

Something that Mara said almost a year ago keeps coming back to me. When Ben fell apart last spring, in kindergarten, Mara felt that he was showing his reaction to the strain of Nikki. "But everything was fine at the November conference," I kept saying. "I don't understand how it could have turned around so fast."

"It's cumulative," Mara kept replying. Maybe it is. Maybe what I'm feeling now is simply the accumulation of a lot of hassles. Maybe I've finally disintegrated.

But this morning, a bright and mild February morning, I'm feeling better. Nikki cooked supper last night, which always helps. She likes to cook, and I feel good when she's doing something for me

Matt. Nancy's latest is to tell Matt that he can date Nikki but that he has to date other girls too. Literally. If he takes Nikki out this weekend, he has to take out another girl before he can date Nikki again. I don't have to try to imagine the hustles that this is going to lead to. Double dates? Lying?

Apartments. Nikki now seems interested in getting herself an apartment. I feel good about that, too. Summer would be a good start. If it works, she could continue in the fall. We sat last night reading the classifieds. Maybe she's more ready than I thought. Maybe my meanness has served a purpose.

Ben. While Nikki and I were looking at the paper, after dinner, Ben was saying that he was going to have a party. I saw him drag the vacuum to the sunroom, hose hanging around his neck. He vacuumed and then came downstairs in his best shirt and pants, telling me that if I wanted to come to the party, I needed to put on a skirt.

So I put on a skirt and high heels, and we talked Will into putting on his new suit. He tried to get away with no shirt, but Ben sent him back upstairs for one. While Will was upstairs, Ben asked what we could serve for the party. "Popcorn?" I suggested.

"No," said he. "That's too movies."

We looked in the cupboard and found a big box of vanilla pudding. We made it up, poured it into the Japanese teacups, put a maraschino cherry on top of each and ate in fine style.

We danced to B.B. King, including Taco in the dancing. Ben let Nikki into the party without a demand that she dress up. All in all it was a very nice affair.

February 1983

"There seems to be something different about Nikki," says Pam as we sit at the nook table one afternoon. "I'm not sure what it is, but it looks as though she's combed her hair, for one thing. And she didn't stomp through here, the way she usually does."

"You were asking what had happened to the Air Force idea. You were thinking that maybe Matt would be encouraging about that? I asked Nikki yesterday afternoon what Matt thought about the Air Force idea. 'Why?' was his response."

"Damn," says Pam. "That's no help."

February 1983

Lee comes up Tuesday. By some stroke of fortune, Will is working at home on the computer, so he is here for the interview. Lee is a large person, very heavy, but personable. She has a nice voice. "Can you tell me what the problem is with Nikki? Kirsten says she just can't put her finger on it, but there's always been a problem."

I remember, then, Kirsten's saying "Nikki's just a square peg in a round hole somehow."

Even after two years, I don't know that I can be much more articulate than that, but I try. "It is subtle. It's awfully hard to define, but I think there are two points. I think the person who's been right on the money about Nikki is Mara. Mara is the one who described and pointed out the anger. She told all of us that Nikki has many legitimate reasons for being angry but that Nikki is dumping the anger on the wrong people.

"Ellen, my office mate, picked up on the same thing. She explained provocative behavior to me and explained how Nikki sets people up to be angry. I miss Mara. I feel that I dealt much better with Nikki when we were seeing Mara. If something happened, and I got angry at Nikki, I could just put that incident aside until we had a session with Mara.

I laugh. "Of course, part of what Mara was telling me was that I should go ahead and deal with things while the anger was fresh. Whatever. All I know is that I seem to work better by putting things aside. If I know that they're going to be dealt with, then I don't feel angry about them during the interim."

I turn to Will. "I think that I've been harder on Nikki this winter than last, don't you?"

"Yes," he says in his quiet way with his quiet smile.

I don't remember which of us mentions the renaissance of Nikki's romance with Matt, but I remember saying "Matt's a nice kid. Both of us like him, and there really seems to be some depth of human feeling between those two—more than just the boy/girl thing. There seems to be a real friendship there."

I go on to tell Lee about my worry that any boy/girl relationship with Nikki seems to have more than the usual weight. "She has all her emotional eggs in one basket," I say. "She puts all the love and caring she has into those relationships. If she showed any of that side of herself to her families, it might have made a real difference. But I guess I should be glad that she shows caring somewhere. Those relationships are everything to her. That's a lot to put on a boyfriend, though. I fear for the day they break up.

"The other thing," I continue, "that makes Nikki so difficult is that she's demands attention every waking moment. It's just very, very wearing. Mara used to tell us that we had to reprogram Nikki, go through the same steps with her that we'd go through with any little kid. 'Please don't interrupt. Mommy will be free in a moment.' I know what Mara means, but I just can't do it. I don't know that anybody can. No one can be a live-in therapist all the time."

Lee seems to understand. "That reminds me about our weekend plan. We haven't found anything yet, but if we do, that would ease that problem."

We talk for awhile about the prospect of moving Nikki out into her own apartment. I'm a bit surprised that Lee has no objections. Then Nikki comes in from school and joins us. Her main topic, not surprisingly, is

Matt. In a little bit, Will and I excuse ourselves so that Lee and Nikki can talk in private.

"I like Lee," says Nikki later. "Boy, is she fat! She makes me seem thin!"

February 1983

Thursday evening Mary comes over for dinner. When we are in the kitchen, cooking, Ben is in the living room. At the particular moment that Nikki comes downstairs, he is sitting in the armchair with her big Raggedy Ann doll and a few stuffed animals. I hear her say to him "I'm going to kick your butt! This is an old doll."

She comes into the kitchen carrying a strand of red yarn. "My doll lost some hair," she says, sounding deliberately childlike and sad.

"Oh dear," I say, though I feel nowhere so benign. She said that Ben could play with Raggedy Ann. But I don't want to get into a hassle with Mary there, so I put the matter out of my mind until the next morning.

Then I say to Will, "I think that's worth two demerits. When she told Ben she was going to kick his butt, that was abusive. That's what Mara's said we have to watch. I can appreciate her feelings about her doll, but she needs to deal with them differently."

Will agrees with me, and I add the demerits to the chart. But I find that I am oddly angry about the incident and that I really don't trust myself to discuss it. So I put the Raggedy Ann back on Nikki's bed with a note saying that maybe Ben is too young to play with Raggedy and that Raggedy should stay in her room. I say that I don't like the way that she talked to Ben about it and that I don't want to hear "I'm going to kick your butt" again. I end by saying that I miss having Mara to help us with some of these things. "Let's look toward your having your own place."

I still feel angry at work, but somewhere during the day, the key turns in the lock. I'm not sure why, although I do remember that at one point I recalled her note of long ago, about some change of plans, ending with "Love, I really mean it." How had we left that so far behind?

When I come in that night, I bring something from the bakery—the fabulous Hungarian Delights. When Nikki comes in, she sees them and decides to have one before dinner. We chat, and both of us seem to be feeling comfortable. There is definitely a better feeling.

After dinner we watch TV, and Ben makes more interruptions than Nikki! At one point her phone rings, she goes upstairs to answer it and returns, dragging the phone to the landing. "No," I say. "You can either watch TV or talk on the phone, but not both."

I feel comfortable pointing that out to her. I don't feel angry or put upon. It is one of the few times that I really feel like a therapist handling immature behavior without getting angered by it. I smile recalling an earlier time with the phone. One Sunday evening she went to the church youth group. The house was quiet. She hadn't been back five minutes when she was sitting on the landing talking on her phone with the TV turned way up. I handled that with anger. My behavior this time is better.

February 1983

I remember telling Lee that I feared Nikki's reaction if Matt were to break up with her. We seem to be living through that. I get up at five-thirty to go to the bathroom, and Nikki has already left for her paper route. It is Saturday, and although she is doing an adjoining route, she said she didn't expect it to take long. Usually on Saturday she doesn't even get up until seven-thirty or later.

I go back to bed, and by the time I get up, she's come back and is in her room. I hear her phone a number of times, but she doesn't come downstairs. I go shopping for a few items, and shortly after I get home, one of her friends appears and joins her in her room. I hear laughter and singing from time to time, and then Sandy leaves. Nikki comes down once or twice but doesn't stay.

We have an early supper because Nikki has a babysitting job. Afterwards Will and Ben go out to get some wood for a fire. Nikki says "I guess I'll fast."

I don't understand that. She ate most of her dinner, although she didn't have the usual seconds. "For Lent? That's pretty drastic!"

"I was depressed this morning. Something's going on with Matt." She looks miserable. "Last night he said that he feels that he's keeping me back. He says there are places I've got to go and things I've got to do. He doesn't know what the feeling is. It's just intangible."

Oh. Many novels have been written around this exact theme.

"Sandy says that's the way it started when she broke up with Ed. He didn't know what was wrong. It was just a feeling. I asked Matt if we still love each other. He said 'Yes.'"

Nikki shows me a letter that she's written to Matt. It's about five pages of "I love you, it can work out, please don't leave me." I expected this some day, but somehow not now. There are certainly about two dozen eggs in this one basket. Sometimes it's no fun to be right.

Nikki talks about the Air Force. I'm not clear as to whether Matt thinks that Nikki changed her mind about it too fast or became interested in it too fast.

"I did make the decision really fast. As soon as the recruiter began talking about the money I made up my mind. It seemed to solve all the problems. Maybe it was too easy."

"Maybe not. It seemed like a good idea by itself."

"Maybe sometime, but not now. Matt and I really have to talk. I thought he was going to call me earlier, and he didn't. Then when I called him, his mother said he was sleeping. Then I called again, and he was gone. Now if he calls tonight, I'll be babysitting."

I rub her back. "I'll answer your phone," I say. I feel for her. I'm so glad that key turned in the lock the other day.

March 1983

I've been thinking a bit about our April "anniversary," if you will. Last year we had the cake with "Hurray for Us." The theme was integration, making a family of us. But now the theme is separation. I keep going over this again and again, because I almost can't believe that the end is in sight. Is it really true that as of this summer Nikki will no longer be living here?

Yes, it is. Go over it again. She's applying to work at Cedar Point this summer—something she's planned to do for years when she reached eighteen. If she gets a job there, she'll live there. If she doesn't, she will move into a separate apartment.

Is the prospect of relief in sight too good to be true? Once there is the absence of hostility in our daily atmosphere, will we all blossom? And with an eye for the promise of the future, can I enjoy the present? What is it that I fear? That we will never truly be free of the difficulties of dealing with Nikki? I do not know.

March 1983

Last night on PBS there was a documentary called "Children of Pride" about the eighteen children adopted by Kojo Odo of Harlem. I missed half of it, but in the second half, he came across as a strong, beautiful person. It's hard on the rest of us to have a model like that!

March 1983

A group of foster mothers and a few others gather at Pennie's. There is a real spread—ham, cake, pie, devilled eggs, potato salad. We eat and talk. My friend Barbara, a Montessori teacher, has come with me. She's a quiet and thoughtful woman who has an exceptional talent in working with children. She's had the good and unusual fortune to have been able to adopt two white infants. She's been wondering if she could take foster children, if that would be a good outlet for the mothering need and ability that she has. I wanted her to talk to women who are foster-parenting younger children.

There are many here. Mary Fran has two-year-old Katie with her. Katie is a real chunk, with blond, curly hair. She weighs fifty pounds, Mary Fran says. Lord, Ben weighs that! Katie runs back and forth on occasion but is not a bother. Mary Fran will be adopting her.

Pennie tells Barbara that she'll have a 90% chance of adopting any particular foster child that comes to her. Betty says that of eight kids that have come to her, seven have stayed. She now has kids from pre-school to twenty. She recounts the story of her problem with her suburb's zoning laws when the oldest foster child turned eighteen and became "an unrelated adult" living in the family's home. "I hated to tell him," she says, wrinkling up her nose. "It sounded perverted."

She laughs. She has a sly sense of humor that peeks out from behind a serious facade. There is a timidity that surfaces when she tells of going to therapy with one kid and feeling that the kid kept setting her up. But she never said so. "One day the kid kept rubbing his leg. Finally the therapist asked why. 'It must be from the spring that's poking through my mattress.'"

Betty laughs now. "That was the first time I ever heard of that. Boy, the therapist must have wondered about me!"

Betty has two pre-schoolers with her, dressed in green outfits. She's firm with them in a nice way. "Don't you hop through this room again," she says quietly to one. That's the one that comes to kiss Barbara and myself good-bye when we leave.

Marsha is a heavy woman with three or four kids, one of whom is a foster child she's had since he was four. He's now a teenager. "He's your child!" I say.

"Of course," she replies matter-of-factly.

Marilyn is from the county ombudsman's office. She has four kids of her own and has worked with the foster care association to try to unravel the hooks and pin pricks of bureaucracy. She's the sophisticated type—tall, thin, with straight, shoulder-length dark hair, dressed in slacks and hiking boots. Pennie equates the work that Marilyn and I do in standing off the system. I tell her of my recent triumph at Juvenile Court. Children's services began moving for permanent custody of older children in a case where I'd gone to the Court of Appeals over the youngest child. And lost. But then the department withdrew its motion. "You're notorious," the attorney told me with a grin. Maybe it's been worth the six years in the trenches if I'm getting the reputation that I want. But some days I get very tired.

On our way home, Barbara observes that these people have really made a lifetime commitment. Yes, these specific people have, for whatever reason. I, too, think that most of them walk on the water.

But a much more limited commitment can be made, and I talk to Barbara about that. She's also interested in the religious ramifications that she sees. She talks about how hard it is to make a Christian commitment. "I'm seeing what a difference there is between this and a Junior League white gloves approach, where you go out and put in a couple of hours. Then you take the gloves off and walk away. Here you're involved every moment of your life."

Yes. Not that what the Junior Leaguers do isn't important. Most people don't even do that much. But yes, foster parenting does take more. I don't know that I look at it in religious terms as a general rule, but that element hasn't escaped me. I see an irony. Here I am, an agnostic, behaving more like a Christian than most people who go to church every Sunday. And a further irony is that it's been this experience with Nikki that's sometimes moved me to "early morning prayer." Sometimes when I've been particularly outrageous to Nikki, I've awakened saying, "Please God, give me grace. I am not dealing well. I need your help. I can't do it alone." The true irony is that sometimes it seems to work.

March 1983

While I was getting supper last night, Nikki talked to me about Matt. "Something's really wrong. He says we can't even go together. He doesn't seem happy about anything—school, even the trip to France. Something's really wrong."

I am puzzled myself. This does seen to be a total reversal. Who knows, it could be as simple as his putting his arms around her and getting a whiff of a kid who really needs a shower. Nikki's personal hygiene has not improved in the least.

March 1983

Two times now I should have spoken up in public and didn't. For instance, I should have gotten up yesterday at the Community Federation and said, "I'd just like to add a few words as a practicing foster parent. You've developed a model for specialized foster care, and now you're gathering a group of agencies to deal with the proposed model. Please. Put at least one foster parent on the committee so that you'll know what the view is like from the other side of your model. Perhaps a foster parent could tell you how to recruit more foster parents. This entire model is not going to work unless you have the parents. How are you going to find them, and what are they going to need in the way of support? It's crucial for you to know."

What would I need if I were to do this again? I, personally, would need the support of one weekly session with a good therapist. It may be that that's just my particular personality, but I don't think it's only that. As Pennie has said, a foster parent has to be a live-in therapist. I think she's right, and so we need on-the-job training that only another therapist can give us.

I don't think I'd take another teenager. I don't think that I can take the selfishness of that age along with the intrusiveness. Little kids are selfish, too, but they don't have the ability to control the total environment the way older kids do—with stereos, TVs, friends, phone calls. Also, you can put little kids to bed.

My sister-in-law made an interesting observation on the intrusiveness. She and my brother teach in a boarding school, and they live on campus. One spring vacation, they took in a fourteen-year-old girl who was left with no place to go. Mary said of that week's experience, "She had the facility of being everywhere in the house at once."

Aside from the question of whether my personality would better suit a teen or a younger child, there's the consideration of the ages of biological children. Bringing in a child older than the biological child can lead to exactly the problems that we've had. I wonder what the experience would have been with a boy younger than Ben.

March 1983

More of the same. I get on Nikki and later cry on Pennie's shoulder. "Don't beat yourself up," says Pennie. "You're doing a fine job. She has a full set of claws."

Yes, she does, but I have a full set of mouth. I am exasperated by her projected summer plan three hundred and one that maybe she'd just visit friends all summer in the town where she was first placed for adoption. This is really a scared kid, who talked bravely at first about hardly being able to wait until she was on her own. Then came these other plans that show fear of being independent.

I think that Lee, and perhaps Tonya, should be the ones to handle this with Nikki. I'm too personally involved. If you will, I have a conflict of interest, where I want her out badly but also seem to have my own idea of where she should be. I can't have it both ways. I can't let go and still hang on.

Nikki has a great weekend mapped out—a big musical at the high school tonight, singing in a choir group tomorrow night, and then going to a movie with still another boyfriend. I keep having to remind myself that she must be feeling very bad about the breakup with Matt. She isn't showing it, but it is strange to walk into her room and not see Matt's picture there. It's just one more in a long series of rejections, and I've got to try to listen more closely to that.

March 1983

Last night the Nova science program on PBS did a piece about fat. "This is for you," says Will to Nikki.

"Stick it," she says, but without real anger.

To my surprise, I come to her aid. "He called me flabby the other day."

Do I remember calling her "fatty" the last time we had popcorn, she wants to know? I really do not remember that, but she says that I did. She is enrolled in one of those health clubs and has even been trying their special diet with the packet of stuff to be dissolved in water for one meal a day. I never can remember the name of it, so I just call it "Fatstuff." As usual, Nikki is very up and down about the program, but if she wants to pursue the idea of joining the service, she has to lose the weight.

Now that she's getting ready for the choir tour, I am keeping my mouth shut about all the cookies, chips, etc., that she and Sandy are buying. My favorite is the three boxes of pop-tarts that they plan to heat with hair dryers.

March 1983

A few days ago I got a phone call from a woman who has a little girl in Ben's class and who is on Nikki's paper route. "A few of my neighbors were wondering why Nikki has left us notes to make our checks payable to her instead of the paper."

"I think I know what's up. She's leaving on choir tour, and she'll be having a sub. Once or twice before, so she says, money has disappeared. But I did tell her that people might wonder about making the checks payable to her."

"Yes, that's what we were wondering about."

"It seems to be okay. A lot of people already do that. Then she writes the route man a check when he gives her the bill."

"Oh."

"I know that Nikki's a disaster on her paper route."

"She is?"

"She isn't?"

"Oh no. We think she's very conscientious. The paper is always there. It's where it's supposed to be. We've never been missed."

I am stunned into silence. "That is so nice to hear. I get so many complaints, especially about how late the paper gets there."

"Oh, we don't read it until evening anyway."

That explains a lot. The woman continues, "But I like to be positive when I can. So many people are negative. There's something else I would like to share with you about your son. He's been so nice to my daughter. I don't know, maybe I overprotected her, being with her until she was seven. But I'm working again in the afternoon, and in January she started the after-school program. It was really hard for her, and Ben sensed that. He told her that he was always there, and he'd help her out."

"That is really nice to hear." My mind spins back to Robin, coming to nursery school two weeks late into the fall term and being lonely. Her mother told me that Ben had said, "I'll stick with you, Robin."

I go on to add, "I think that the after-school program is very rough and tumble. That's okay for Ben, who loves to run and jump and fly across the floor, but I can see that it would be hard for others."

"Oh, yes!"

We get off into a discussion of some of our concerns about after-school and that leads into some of the concerns about the first grade. She seems to feel that there are some kids who are having problems learning. "Our problem seems to be the opposite," I say. "Ben seems to be doing okay on the learning end of things, but the teacher seems displeased with his behavior. That's why it's especially nice to have you give him this compliment. We've even started him up with the therapist we were all seeing last year with Nikki. We wouldn't have lasted sixth months if we hadn't gotten that therapy."

"For heaven's sakes, you did all that with her?"

"All that and more."

"Well, I want to tell you something else about Ben. Do you remember when the kids had that play?"

"Jerome," I laugh. Ben apparently played the title role, that of a frog. "About all that he'd ever told us was that he needed to dress in green on the day of the play."

"My daughter was so scared. And Ben helped her with that. The teacher said to me, about your son, 'Ben is a little boy who's very sensitive to feelings.'"

"I'm so glad you've told me this. For so long I've been very concerned about bringing Nikki in."

"Is she mean to him?"

"Oh yes. It doesn't make any sense to me. But just this past weekend a social worker told me that she'd even seen hostility between a teenage foster child and an infant. Instead of learning to like the infant, the teenager was jealous."

"For heaven's sakes!"

"That's what I thought. But it's worth Ben's having some difficult times if it's helped him be sensitive to feelings."

We chat a bit more, then ring off. I feel so good the rest of the day.

April 1983

There was a wonderful movie on cable this week. It's *The Great Gilly Hopkins*, the story of a foster child. I'd asked a librarian friend whose specialty is young adult work if she could recommend any fiction involving foster families. She told me about Gilly, and I took it out. I loved it, and I began reading it to Ben after dinner one night.

"That must be about a foster kid," came Nikki's comment from the other room.

"How did you know?"

"Most kids don't have a social worker."

Somehow I don't think Ben ever got the entire book read to him, but then Will noticed that the movie was going to be on cable, a short show, less than an hour. I told Ben and Nikki, and we all made a date to watch. It was on late in the afternoon, and I hurried from a Juvenile Court hearing to pick Ben up and get home in time.

Both of the kids were entranced, as I was. Gilly is a twelve-year-old girl who lands in a foster home with an older single mother who also has an eight-year-old foster son. W.E., the son, has been kicked around, and he's very shy, hiding behind Maime Trotter's skirts. Gilly picks on him at first, and Nikki immediately comments on her meanness. I wonder if there's even a glimmer of identification.

April 1983

This is one of those weekends where I have no desire to do anything. I've been mentally working on Carl's case, which is due for an important hearing. I've also been re-reading my favorite psychiatrist, William Glasser. I'm reading about involvement and the need for a therapist to get involved. Nikki came here with a need to get involved. I must have some of those needs too.

I have a fantasy of a big, old house with lots of kids. How do I square that with my need for privacy and my over-sensitivity to other people? Just another one of those images gone wrong, I guess. We just have to realize what we are as opposed to what we'd like to be. I'd like to be Kojo Odo, but I'm not.

Lee came up last week, and she, Nikki and I talked about moving. I'm planning to have Nikki come over three times a week for dinner, and she can do her laundry here. I know that's not what Pennie projected, but I feel comfortable with it.

Later that night, when we were all sorting out our calendars, I said "Pennie and Vince are coming on the ninth. We're going to try to get together our presentation for the Psychological Association."

"There's something about the ninth," said Nikki.

"I think I know what it is," I said lightly. She didn't add anything, and we continued our conversation.

April 1983

Carl's case has been taking lots of time and energy. The story is too long to set out here, but suffice it to say that this boy's problems are more the result of a scrambled home situation than any native meanness. In the past he has assaulted police officers, and now he is taking the rap on a purse snatching. I go to the Detention Home to see him, and although he refuses to budge on the rap, we have a very nice talk.

At one point, in trying to explain to him why his dad might put so much time and energy into his second family, I said, "Look, a little kid just comes up to you and gives you a big hug. But your teenager comes up and gives you a lot of lip."

"I never thought of it that way." He laughed.

I knew that there wasn't a whole lot that I could do in court if Carl wouldn't change his plea. He would get sent away. I was prepared for that, but I wasn't prepared for the range of disaster that befell us. When the psychologist who had examined him touched on a past suicide attempt, Judge Robbins ordered Carl on a tour of the morgue.

I went berserk. He ran that on one of my kids the very first time I was ever in his courtroom. In that case, however, there had been at least some sort of connection, however tenuous, between the kid's actions and violence. But to order Carl there for having once made a suicide attempt made absolutely no sense at all. I stood up, entered an objection and said that I would appeal. Carl's mother was crying, Carl had tears running down his face, but he hugged me and said that he'd go.

I had another case back-to-back in that courtroom, and after the second case, Judge Robbins invited me into his chambers so that we could discuss this. He certainly doesn't want me to appeal, because that will get publicity. He offered me his rationale for the order—that if a teen thinks he'll be handled with kid gloves because of a suicide attempt, you've lost control.

I understand that in some contexts, but Carl didn't hustle me to bring that up. I was the one who asked the psychologist the question. I finally said that I am going out to the morgue with the kid. Judge Robbins said that I can do that, but I can't take the tour. That's fine by me.

I went back to the DH to see Carl, and I told him that I wasn't arguing over the order because I felt he wasn't up to the trip. I was arguing because I felt that it was an inhumane order. I further said that Judge Robbins had sent one of my kids there before and that I'd let the doctor scare me off when I showed up. Not this time.

I put in a bad three days waiting for the appointment. I met Carl and his probation officer at the morgue, and I had Carl tell the doctor in charge just exactly why we were there. I almost fell over when he said, "I don't think the coroner would approve. I'm not taking him through." I damned near kissed the man.

I went back to my office and put my head in to tell the lawyer in the next office what had happened. "Girl," he said, "you better lay low. Those judges can put out an order and get you picked up out of your office!"

I intend to keep a very low profile around Judge Robbins' courtroom for the foreseeable future.

April 1983

The ninth was a Saturday, and not only was Nikki going out somewhere, Pennie and Vince were coming over. So I'd decided to have our second anniversary party on Monday. We had so much to talk about on Saturday evening that we barely touched on our presentations.

A psychologist who's well-respected in dealing with foster kids and foster families asked the three of us to put together a presentation for the May meeting of the local professional association. "Lots of professionals haven't been made aware of the special issues of foster care, so if you three could cover the waterfront, we'd be grateful."

At least we get some broad divisions worked out. Vince is going to talk about the Foster Care Association—how it came to be organized, what it has accomplished and what is still to be done. I am going to talk about the role of the Juvenile Court. In all cases where children's services has temporary custody, state law mandates that a comprehensive reunification plan be drafted, showing the goals to be reached by the natural parents so that the children can be returned. Often the children are placed with the parents while the department has temporary custody, but often they're placed in foster homes.

Like much legislation, this is well-intentioned. It is meant to force departments to review cases and plan for families to be reunited. It is meant to end the impermanency for children who'd otherwise spend a lifetime in foster care.

In practice it's often just one more layer of paperwork (the written plan) and bureaucracy (the custody review board). But. But if the parent has a strong advocate, the advocate can follow up on children's services' written requests of the parents. I tell my clients that if they follow their part of the plan, we will return to court to see that the department keeps its part of the bargain. If the parents don't meet the goals that are set for them, then the department is supposed to move for permanent custody and adoptive placement.

Pennie is going to talk about the actual experience of foster parenting, and I know she'll be spectacular. All of her humanity, humor and caring come through. She's quite animated, and her observations are original. She'll be the icing on the cake.

April 1983

We have our party on Monday. I get steaks and a birthday cake with a "2" candle to put on it. Pam tells me later that she gave Nikki a ride to school that morning and that Nikki told her about the steaks. "She seemed real pleased. You know, when you see that, see her being pleased that she's been with you for two years, then maybe you think, oh well, what's one more year." Then she looks at me and adds, "I know, I know. It's three hundred and sixty-five big ones."

"You bet."

"It's nice that you've done it, though."

I am surprised. Pam's never said that before. She's really been a shoulder for me to cry on, and she's commiserated with me. But I always figured that she thought I was stark raving mad to do this. She always maintained that she and Nikki wouldn't have lasted a week.

When Ben sees the cake, he asks me when Nikki is going to another foster home. "She's going to have her own home, honey."

Again I wonder. Ben gets all the "honeys" and the hugs and the rhymes and the praise. I really don't have that much of it for Nikki. Part of that is the shy streak that I've been able to overcome with Ben.

April 1983

Will and Nikki went to look at a third-floor apartment and took it! May 1st will be Liberation Day. Will says that the landlady told them that she'd been a foster child herself and that she'd take good care of Nikki. What good fortune!

Ben cuddles up in bed the next morning with Will and me, and I tell him that Nikki has gotten her own apartment. "Ben," I say to him, "I bet that you don't remember this, but when we first heard about Nikki, you said 'Let's get that girl!'

"You liked Beth so much," I go on, "you probably thought that Nikki would be like Beth. So did I!"

"I used to come upstairs and call 'Beth!'"

"Yes, you did. Beth really liked little kids. You don't remember Molly, but she's been having bad troubles."

"With drugs." So he had paid attention to the conversation that night a month ago when Franny and Jean were here.

"That's right. Jean said that the only time that Molly smiled was when she mentioned you."

"Mom, do you think that you would ever take another foster person?"

"I don't know, Ben. How about you?"

"I might. Especially if she were like Beth."

"You know, you were saying the other day how you'd like to be the older brother to a kid at your school. Maybe someday we could think of a boy foster person—a little boy, younger than you."

Ben seems to be thinking about this. "Of course," I add, "we have to remember that being a foster kid is tough, and foster kids usually have lots of troubles."

April 1983

Last night Will and I are at a huge wedding reception, very casual, for two old friends who found each other the second time around. One of the guests is Paul, the therapist who worked with Nikki and the Yancey family. I introduce myself to him, reminding him that we met just one time two years before, with Nikki.

The party is really flowing by that time—both units of a duplex are being used, and we are in the upstairs kitchen. Paul is a short, bear-like man, with curly, grey hair and a short beard. He seems genuinely interested in hearing how things have gone, and we get into a very helpful conversation.

He has a theory that there are two kinds of kids—apples and onions. The apples are sweet, no matter what life has done to them. They have a core, and they have seeds for growth. The onions have no core. You can peel off layer after layer without reaching a core, and they make you cry. Nikki is definitely an onion, he says.

And yet he observes that Nikki might be classified as a success of the child welfare system. "She started out life about six lengths behind, with her natural mother. Although she's still six lengths behind—or maybe a tiny bit less—she's no further behind than when she started. That's a success. You can tell yourselves that you've done well."

"I really need to hear that," I say. "I've been feeling ambivalence about getting her out on her own. I feel some real conflicts."

Paul goes on to say that a Nikki just doesn't have the core of security and trust that an apple has. He believes that that was lost very early, perhaps in her first year with her own mother. "The thing to remember is that what makes a crucial difference is how severe the early deprivation is. If it's been severe enough, it doesn't matter how strong a family unit you place the kid in later."

I sigh. "Yes," he continues, "Nikki's the kind of kid for whom you give and give and give. And one day you reach into your bucket of warm fuzzies, and there's nothing left. Yet you still think that maybe if you'd tried harder..."

"Yes! That's exactly the way that I feel!" I can't believe that I'm hearing this.

"Most people who work with kids like this have the same experience that you're having. It isn't you."

"Thanks," I say, holding out my hand. "I really appreciate having had this chance to talk to you. Now I'll let you join the party."

On the way home I tell Will that I couldn't have run into Paul at a better time. I think that maybe the theory about the apples and onions is a bit simplistic. I really think that Nikki has lots of strengths and potential for growth. Yet it's so good to hear that those of us who work with these difficult kids are constantly thinking that we could be trying a little harder.

April 1983

Daylight savings time has done us in. I shut off the alarm and then fall back to sleep. I awake at 7:40 and rush downstairs saying "Give me caffeine."

Nikki had made a pot of tea. "Caffeine is the eighth wonder of the world," says she.

April 1983

Yesterday Mrs. Evans, Nikki's dental assisting teacher, calls. She wants to be sure that Nikki made it back from the conference downtown. We get into an interesting conversation. "Remember last fall, at the open house, you asked me if I had seen the other side of Nikki? And I hadn't? Well, now I have. You know, the other girls, they're really trying to help her, and she just takes offense.

"They tried to encourage her to wear something nice for the first day of the conference, and all she'd say was 'I don't know what I'm going to wear,' and she'd say it through clenched teeth."

I can't help laughing. "Oh yes, living with that kid is like living with a piece of sandpaper."

"She even got mad at me other day."

"At you? I'm surprised. She really respects you. She's always bitching about the choir director, but she speaks well of you."

Mrs. Evans laughs at the mention of the choir director. "She and I were talking the other day, and she said that she wished I wouldn't...I can't remember the exact word...correct her in front of the class. 'Nikki,' I said, 'we're the only ones with our voices raised. That's why everyone can hear us.'"

She goes on to say that she feels that Nikki sees slights in things that aren't even directed at her. "That's very familiar," I say. "She has very little sensitivity for anyone else, but let someone say something to her... What really worries me is that this attitude is going to hurt her on the job."

Mrs. Evans agrees, and I add, "I have something to suggest. Nikki is seeing a counselor at The Place, and it might be helpful to involve you in one of the sessions. If Tonya and Nikki can work on some of these things that are going to affect her job life, it might help. And since we're not doing family therapy now, Tonya only knows what Nikki brings her."

Mrs. Evans seems to think that this would be a good idea, so I'll talk to both Tonya and Lee.

May 1983

This is Moving Day. Will is out of town on a mountain-climbing expedition and won't be back until late afternoon. That leaves me to haul Nikki and her things to the new apartment. By the time we've gone up and down to the third floor ten times, I feel that I could probably handle a mountain myself. Most of her things are in shopping bags or cardboard boxes. The only really bulky thing we have to handle is the dresser, but we unload the drawers and carry them separately.

I've decided to just let her keep the dresser. It's an unfinished wooden one that we bought when Kate came. It's really nice, and I wouldn't mind keeping it, but Nikki needs it. She's bought a double bed frame and mattress, and she's picked up a few chairs from a friend.

She and I got on a roll one night and went through the cabinets and shelves in search of kitchen items that could be parted with. We did the same for curtains, and we actually turned up a fair amount of stuff. I'll let her keep the two-drawer file, too, and the portable typewriter.

To add to the mountain-climbing effect, it is raining out—not hard, but steadily. By the time we finish, her new beau, Ralph, shows up in his van with the chairs, and it's time for me to take Ben to a soccer game. Soccer seems to be something that doesn't get called on account of rain.

I, however, am not sitting in the rain. I have plenty to do. Susan and I are on deadline with our appellate brief, and we've planned to work this Sunday afternoon. I'll take a break to pick up Ben, and he and I will run to the rapid to get Will. Then Susan and I will finish the brief.

By ten at night, we've just gotten rolling. Susan had tried to get her section of the brief typed at her weekend court clerk's office job, but those typewriters didn't like the godawful erasable paper we're using. So she's typing, and I'm sitting at the desk, feeling a bit low. It is hard to have Nikki leave home. I call her to see if the rest of the day had gone okay. "Yep," says she, sounding fine.

"See you for dinner tomorrow then. G'night!"

This is a strange new world. I remember the discussion we had last Friday evening that wavered between being hostile and being friendly. We ended up talking about how well she's done considering her history. I kept feeling like hugging her, and finally, I just did it. "I love you, kid. I know we have our differences, but I really love you."

May 1983

"Wait until you have a foster kid some day," I say to Nikki.

"Foster kid?" Sneer. "I plan to have my own"

When I recount that recent exchange to Pam, her response is "How could you not have hit her right in the mouth?"

"Lots of practice. Something told me that if I let myself react, I'd beat her up. Now that she's living on her own, those things are easier to take. And when you think about it, if the idea of taking a foster child is so repugnant, then being a foster child must be horrible."

May 1983

Yesterday was Mother's Day. Ben's present is a book made by his class. What interesting stories these kids come up with! A friend and I were talking about how easy a novel is to write as opposed to a poem. All you do is tell a story—no matter that you have to create it. Telling a story is easy. We all know how to do that. But wait! Here are the first graders, who tell partial stories and are content. Ben's had no resolution. "I got mad and went home." Or is that the way it really is, and novelists crap things up with phony resolutions?

We hadn't seen Nikki for three nights. I am checking the stew when she comes in. She hugs me, gives me a kiss and says "Happy Mother's Day!" I wondered if it would even occur to her that it was Mother's Day. I really feel the thank you I say, and I show her the women's group ad in the paper with both her name and Ben's. I think she is pleased.

On Saturday night, as we are having dinner with neighbors, Patrick asks "How do you like your freedom?" He repeats it because I look so puzzled. Finally he asks "Didn't Nikki move out?"

"Oh yeah, that freedom. Yes, it is nice."

Patrick laughs. "I guess you must have lots of other things to do."

"I do. More than enough. But it's easier every day."

I realize this morning, getting breakfast, that I'm not sitting around saying "God, she's gone, how wonderful." I've been awfully tired, though. Is that tiredness a relief? A reaction? Lots has changed, certainly, in the past few weeks. It's so much easier to deal now.

May 1983

Pennie and I have lunch, and she is in rare form. "I'm in the Yellow Pages under God. Actually I'm God's secretary."

"And since he's always out, you have to handle the problems."

I ask her whether she's ever had a foster child that just didn't seem part of the family. "None do. They're not supposed to. Don't feel you've failed. Don't feel that it depends upon age. Young kids don't become part of your family any easier. Just remember that the only thing you need a mother for is to be born. Once you're born, there are other things you need—training, education. A foster parent can do those things."

I tell Pennie that Nikki said that Pennie helped her understand me better than anyone else has. Pennie told her that I'm not her mother but that I can be her friend, and why can't she let it go at that? Why can't I, I ask myself. There seems to be something in all of us that looks for family. Then we get into discussing what we want to say in our presentation.

May 1983

This tiredness does not cease. I awake with tired shoulders, neck and head, and I feel groggy for hours. I feel like I felt when I was six months pregnant with Ben.

"Is it the letting down after two years with Nikki?" I ask my therapist friends. "Is it being able to relax after being on my muscle for two years?" That's what this feels like—sinking into a calm of my own being. Getting up calm, knowing that I won't be impaled on a quill. Coming home calm, knowing that she won't be there with her phone and her stereo and her questions. I'm collapsing inward, into the quiet.

I know that I'm too aware of my external surroundings. I always have been. Sometimes I feel that I'm living life inside out. I am aware of everyone around me, including neighbors. That's waning somewhat—Nikki helped it, actually, by presenting enough need so that my awareness couldn't extend past her, through the walls of this house.

I couldn't ignore Nikki. However, I can handle her coming for an hour or two. I can give the attention for a limited period. But time doesn't stretch now, like a rubber band, the way it did when she was always here. I can deal with the demands now. They're manageable.

May 1983

Tiredness is still prevailing. Tiredness from the south. Tiredness from the north.

Nikki calls before dinner last night. "Are we eating closer to seven or seven-thirty?"

"I'm pretty much on schedule. probably a few minutes after seven, when Will gets here."

"I want to go for a bike ride. Did I tell you what happened? Schwinn wouldn't fix my bike."

"You chose not to have your bike fixed."

"No. They wouldn't fix it." The stubbornness is like a mountain face looming up in front of me.

"Whatever. They wouldn't fix, they couldn't fix, you didn't want it fixed. The point is that you didn't take care of the old bike, so you had to get a new one. Don't even bring the new one over unless you're going to put it in the basement if it rains."

"I plan to."

"Good." I slam down the receiver and then feel bad about the loss of control. I check on dinner and then sit in the nook. But I don't want to be sitting there when she tools in on this new bike, because then I can't help but see it. It is a very sore spot with me. I'm sure she went top of the line and took a chunk out of her bank account.

She gave the old bike neither daily care nor maintenance when it needed it. It sat outside in all kinds of weather because she was too lazy to put it in the basement. I don't know how many trips Will made with her to the bike shop for repairs because of carelessness or heavy hands.

At dinner Nikki chatters, and I do a pretty good job of responding. She actually washes the dishes after dinner. The next morning I notice that the wine glasses and the little china soup bowls are still there. "Look," I say to Will, "First she piled things helter-skelter in the dish drainer, and now she's ignored all those things that were waiting to be washed. I really don't know how she keeps her books, if she does keep any, but maybe she figures that she wasn't here when those particular dishes were used, so she doesn't have any reason to do them."

"If she keeps books," says Will, "that's how she'd keep them."

"Speaking of books, but not the same kind, I was reading the book by Madelaine L'Engle that Jean dropped off. There's a very interesting piece about how they took in the seven-year-old daughter of close friends. The parents had died about a year apart, and it was a number of months after the second death when they got her.

"Well, she was a hard case. She broke every rule just to test to see if there were rules, because her universe had lost its rules. The author's husband finally came up with the only punishment that worked when she began ignoring all the rules. They took the rules away. She could do whatever she wanted to. That made her so uncomfortable that she began following the rules again. Isn't that something?"

Will shakes his head. "That's why I'm not in that business."

"You prefer the cybernetic salad?" I asked, having earlier told him of Ms. L'Engle's finding that as long as the check had the "cybernetic salad," the account numbers, she could sign any name—Emily Bronte—but if it didn't, even her own name wouldn't suffice.

"Definitely," says Will.

May 1983

Nikki's setting up a problem about choir, making a mountain out of a molehill, virtually daring the director to flunk her. I am truly surprised that she's doing this, and I am angry. She's better than this. This is a shabby maneuver, a true hustle, and I don't think it's worthy of her.

But that's just one of the pictures on the wall. When I try to discuss it with her, things deteriorate into a fight. I feel so helpless to break this behavior. I lay awake last night, casting for the pattern. My sister? Probably. I would bet any money that the childhood fights that Alice and I had took this pattern. Anger and insults. And I can just see Nikki's jaw and Alice's jaw, both clenched.

Nikki has a distinct profile as she sits to my left at the table. I can tell from the profile when she's in an angry mood. When she doesn't talk back and just sticks that old lip out, I know that she knows she's wrong. She did that last night, but I didn't quit. Why can't I say "Look, we've taken a turn off the path here, and we have to get back on. Let's quit the fighting and return to sanity." Will didn't help, either. He just ambled away from the table and left us there fighting. We don't have Mara now. We've got to do this ourselves.

May 1983

Pennie calls to ask me how I thought she did in our talk last Friday. Fine, I say, and I truly think so. "Well," she says, "when I got to the part about separation, and I looked down at that word on my note card, I just couldn't handle it. I skipped that part of the talk, and I've been having trouble with it ever since."

That's something I've never had to deal with. Separation is sending a foster kid back to his own or another family and not having any further contact with that kid. Nikki's situation is uncommon in that regard. Another very common foster care problem that we haven't had is the handling of visits with the biological family. A caseworker picks up the child for a visit—maybe a few hours, maybe a day or so. The child comes back upset. How do these long-time foster parents deal with these things?

I tell Pennie that one of my friends is on a kick that she's giving too much to her family and now she's going to pay some attention to herself. That's really ludicrous when I think of the kind of giving that Pennie and others do. My friend would feel self-righteous about giving a can of succotash to a hunger center. Pennie will go out, catch a turkey, kill it, stuff it, cook it, prepare all the trimmings and will invite twenty-five people over for Thanksgiving dinner.

Pennie says that she thinks she would like working with teenagers. "If Nikki is any example, you'd be great. She says you see things better than caseworkers."

"Yeah. I'm pretty good at knowing what other people are feeling. It's as though their guts were spilled out across their foreheads. I think it's because I never had the luxury of having feelings of my own, so I was always receptive to the feelings of other people."

June 1983

Nikki called recently to say that Matt was in the hospital with severe stomach cramps or some such. I was surprised but passed it off. There are all manner of weird ailments around, including appendicitis. But Nikki called a few days later to say that Nancy had told her that Matt had a very serious heart problem.

My God, I think. He is the one who is supposed to be home free. How did this came from out of nowhere? At some point in the past, the medics must have figured that he'd escaped the problem and stopped following him. Later I run into a neighbor of the family who confirms that Matt indeed has a serious problem. "They're saying that a heart transplant is the only chance, that he doesn't have a year without one. They're talking about going to California. Most people waiting for donors are there six to eight months."

I cannot get thoughts of this family out of my head. The next time I talk to Pennie, I ask "What is it with some people that biological kids are so all-fired important? Here's a family—or at least a mom—who's wanted kids so badly that after eleven years and two degrees and bar exams in two states, had another baby instead of giving birth to a law practice. She took a one in four chance of heart disease with that baby—and lost. The little girl was born just after Nikki came to live with us. And now Matt, who was supposed to be free of heart problems. Why can't people with that strong a will for children take a foster child or adopt a child? They certainly have the will to handle problems."

"It's about ownership," says Pennie. "People have got to get rid of the idea that they can own kids. People say to me, 'How can you stand to let those foster kids go?' I tell them, 'It's going to hurt you a lot more than it does me. You'll have your kids for seventeen or eighteen years before you lose them.'" She giggles that rich giggle.

But I know that it's not that clear, either, or she wouldn't have had that trouble with the speech.

"If parents would just look at their jobs as a job. If they would stop thinking that they could own kids and make those kids whatever they want them to be, we'd all do a better job. The kid is just on loan to you."

I find myself later, thinking of ownership; the question won't leave my mind. Why are people so hell-bent on having biological children when there are so many kids out there without homes?

June 1983

Ellen made a comment yesterday that was almost identical to one that Liz had once made. "One of the things you should keep reinforcing with Nikki is that when she has children of her own, she's going to need help in dealing with them. It's not her fault, but she just doesn't have the proper background herself to enable her to parent well."

I sigh. That reminds me of Nikki's recent statement that she "beat the cat's ass" about something. My response had been, "Nikki, I certainly hope that this isn't indicative of the way you'll treat your kids."

"Oh, I didn't really beat him."

"I bet she did," said Ellen.

And I remember, too, about the cat whose jaw somehow got dislocated the weekend that Nikki was cat-sitting. She complains about her current cat. It has a bad attitude, she says.

June 1983

There are still evenings when I don't look forward to having Nikki arrive for supper. The nights when she doesn't come are almost like miniature vacations. What's been the latest "derangement," as Hercule Poirot would say? The weight. The Army, applying its charts, says that Nikki must weigh no more than one hundred and twenty-nine pounds when she enlists. I don't know what happened to the Air Force. Now it's the Army.

But here we have a girl who eats at McDonald's regularly, stuffs herself here, and, who, the other night, not only made popcorn but melted a quarter pound of margarine to pour over it. My sense of logic is assaulted by a person who eats like this in the face of a weight loss program.

Will has decided to make her a wager. "A little incentive, so to speak, in the form of a bet, to see if you can lose the weight."

"How much?"

"Twenty crossed my mind." That does indeed seem to perk up her ears. Will says that he believes that money speaks to Nikki in a way that nothing else does. He's sure that the choir brouhaha was really no more than her wish to earn a few bucks on an afternoon when an extra rehearsal was scheduled.

July 1983

Nikki and her landlady seem to be having problems. Judy raised Nikki's rent, which is a signal to me that she wants Nikki out. "She's come into my apartment," says Nikki. "She's turned off my fan. Does she have a right to do that?"

"Basically no," I tell Nikki. "She does have a right to come in for emergency measures. Otherwise she has to pick a reasonable time and notify you."

"She doesn't like my friends. She says she's scared to be in her own house with all these people around. You know my friends are okay."

Yes, basically they are. But it's probably difficult to have them in and out on a continual basis. I'll bet they are noisy. I bet they do leave the hall lights on. Welcome to the adult world, Nikki. You've got to be less abrasive. Unfortunately the sandpaper has not worn down. It will always be there. Maybe the best we can do is to get it worn down to extra-fine.

July 1983

It isn't often that I wake up early and get up, but I arise at six, do some dishes and make some tea. When I reflect on how tired I was two months ago, I can't believe I'm the same person. The last two days have been very busy work days, and there is no sign of let up. If I'd had a week like this in April or May, I might not have made it without a morning nap or something along the way.

The return of the energy seems to make it clear that its loss had to do with Nikki. Even now, when I know she's coming for dinner, I have to gear up mentally.

August 1983

Today is a nice day with Nikki, which is surprising because I came home from vacation in a depressed and strung-out mood. I probably hadn't slept well in a week, and Ben and I are still fighting the same old colds that we had three weeks ago. I am inundated with a whole lot of cases that I don't want to do, and all of them need to be done yesterday

So when she comes sailing in for supper, hair dripping wet, and mouth going, it is very nice to find that I am enjoying her. She's become an Avon Lady, she says, and I look at her book. I tell her that, as she well knows, I don't buy much in the way of make-up, but that when I'm ready to buy next, I'll buy from her. She's already picked out a number of things that she thinks Ben will like—novelty items such as pens that bend in a circle.

By the time Will comes in, she's saying that she and Vicki talked to Matt on the phone. He's right back to his usual self, saying that he's left his heart in San Francisco. "I know it's crazy," Nikki says, "but Vicki and I were wondering if you had someone else's heart inside you, you'd feel differently about people."

"That's crazy, Nikki," Will and I say almost in unison.

"I know," she says, "it's really in your head where the feelings are."

"It would make a good story," I say.

"Did I tell you that I broke up with Ralph?"

"Yes."

"Well, we didn't really break up. We were just separated."

Nikki has talked of marriage. I wish this guy would get lost. "Use Matt as a measuring stick," I say. "If a guy is like Matt, he's probably a good guy."

"There's nobody like Matt."

I'm afraid she's right. But she's got a year of school left, and maybe

Ralph will go away.

During dinner she tells us about the new place she's rented, her landlady being so immature and all. "She and her daughter will hear me on the stairs and say, 'Ding-dong, Avon calling.' How immature can someone be?"

Will and I shoot each other amused glances, but we both keep quiet. I don't even run away after dinner but stay around and talk a little bit. She does up the dishes completely voluntarily, then leaves to pick up a girl-friend because they're "going over Coventry"—the lively place of coffee-houses and boutiques.

September 1983

It's Labor Day weekend, finally, and still hot—no hint of fall. Saturday afternoon I am in the kitchen getting iced tea when I hear the front door open. "Hi," says Ben, who's playing in the living room.

"Who's that?" I ask, figuring full well who it might be. "Nikki," she answers, strolling into the kitchen

"Oh no! Why?" I ask, partly in jest but partly seriously. Will I ever be able to break myself of this pattern?

"I wanted to see if my check's come," says she, only half-way hostile.

"I told you I'd call. I wouldn't forget!" Nikki has been looking for a check from her county for a couple of weeks. It does seem to me that they've screwed up a couple of times this summer. And now that she's moved again, the cash is especially helpful. I think her own account is down to nothing.

Nikki's gotten into a house-sharing arrangement with a "business-man" who owns a house and has one other person living there.

"A 'businessman?'" I'd said to Will. "I do not like this sound of this at all." Whenever Nikki started raving about Judy, I told her that no place is perfect.

"I don't know if I like this place," says Nikki.

"What did I tell you? There's no perfect place."

"Well, the owner, Bob, boy, is he picky. Whenever I'm in the kitchen, he seems to show up. I don't think he trusts me."

"Hey, it's his house. Remember how I am about my kitchen?"

"You aren't as bad as he is. And he's changing things. Now he wants a buck a load for laundry, and I have to get my own kitchen stuff. Ralph thinks he's rude. They were playing chess, and Bob let a fart, just moved his hind end and let a fart. He didn't even say 'Excuse me.'"

"Not very classy."

"Cheryl and Steve are looking for a place. If they get enough room, I might be able to go in with them." She sees the Ms. Pacman that Ben and I have bought. "Hey, can I play?"

"Sure." I sit down with her at the nook table, and we talk as she plays. Ralph, it seems, is serious about this marrying business. He took her to look at a ring.

"You'll have to meet Ralph. You've never really met him. He can size a person up real well, like this Bob. I can't always do that."

That does sound good. But getting married at nineteen doesn't. But it ain't my business.

"I can hardly wait for school to start."

"What?" Mock horror on my part.

"Don't you remember, I was like this last year, too."

"I guess I do. We carried the old dinette table up to your room so that you could have a desk."

She stays for a couple of hours. I go upstairs to work on the word processor, occasionally coming down to check the pork chops. She's having fun with the Ms. Pacman, and we're really having a companionable time. I am truly enjoying her. As I serve dinner, she starts to leave. "If I had more, you could stay." I said. "But you'll come over for Labor Day, won't you? Will's doing a roast on the grill."

"Sure. See you then."

After dinner, Will and I watch TV as Ben plays. He's doing a great project. He's drawing a huge Christmas tree with lovely ornaments for his animals. He cuts it out and tapes it to the sunroom door. Then he decides to wrap things for presents—just toys from his shelves. But he takes pieces of paper and creates wrapping paper. The first has triangles, big and bold, huge, outlined in black like Rouault; the second has the square as a motif.

He is really blossoming. We still see some of the irritability, but basically there's a real sweetness. I praise his drawing. Is this a result of taking the lid off his pressure cooker? I've been reluctant to start his therapy again in the fall. Why not let it go until he needs it. If he needs it. I should talk to Mara.

September 1983

Lee and I talk. I give her a quick update on the move from the frying pan into the fire. "Now Nikki's talking about Steve and Cheryl and her and Ralph sharing a place. Swell, huh?"

"For sure. I'd better get up there as soon as possible." We work out an appointment time that I am to transmit to Nikki, and I will call Lee back with Nikki's new address.

Lee sounds concerned herself and a little down. "I talked to my supervisor, and she said that if Nikki moves in with Ralph, we should just stop our involvement with her and put her in charge of the money directly."

Nikki has quite a nice savings account that the agency manages for her. This is very unusual among foster children and is the result of Social Security survivor's benefits. Since the money paid out to foster parents was always less than the Social Security payment, the balance got banked.

"This may sound like a funny thing for a lawyer to say, but I'm thinking that perhaps you should look the other way for a few months. Nikki's never seemed to be in a hurry to be rid of your agency. She may actually welcome the attention. She had a good relationship with Kirsten for a lot of years. We didn't have Jane very long, but Nikki seems to respect you. I think she talks to you about things that she won't talk to me about."

"Well, up until about a month ago, we did have a pretty open relationship. But in the last month, if I ask her about Ralph, she just says that she doesn't want to talk about that and turns me off."

I sigh. "My contribution will be to meet Ralph. The last time she was here, Nikki asked if I could make pizza and Ralph could eat over.

"It was ninety degrees out at the time, and I just didn't have the energy to even think about turning on the oven. I said something like 'I'm not sure that I'm ready to meet Ralph yet.' But now I think I'd better meet him."

September 1983

I've been laughing all week about this, although it really isn't funny. Three weeks to the day after Nikki moved into the house-sharing arrangement, her landlord called. "I'd like to talk to you about your daughter."

I tense immediately and run all possible legal ramifications through my head. "She's my foster daughter."

"It's not working out with her here. I'd really like her to move as soon as possible."

"From what I've been hearing from her, she's ready to look."

"But I don't see any evidence that she is!"

As I reflect, this Bob and Carol and Ted and Alice and extra room hasn't cropped up in the last couple of discussions. Bob is being pleasant, but I get the impression that he's feeling harassed. "I'd really like to have her out by the end of the month so that I can get somebody else in. Could she come back with you until she finds a place?"

"No," I say. Kindly, gently, but firmly. In my mind's eye, I see a gallery of people rising to their feet, cheering. They hug one another. "She did it! She did it!"

"No," I say again, heady with the sound of the word. "I will not take Nikki back into my house, not even for one night. I'm a little surprised that she's driving you crazy, though. I figured that the problems I was having with her were the usual teen/mother, foster child/foster parent stuff. It's perplexing to hear that you're having problems, too."

"Those animals smell. She doesn't clean up after them. And it would help if she would take a shower once in awhile. My other tenant is complaining. You can't talk to her. I tried that. I tried to work things out, but she doesn't listen. This morning she walked right by two garbage bags. 'Why don't you take them out?' 'I'm late to school.' And she walked right out."

All of this time I am murmuring, "Yes, umhmm. Yes, I know."

Finally I say "I'll call her caseworker this morning."

"Oh, thank you. I'll give her security deposit back."

"She will need that to move," I say, figuring that I can help Nikki out on that one. "If I were you, I'd put it to her this way. Tell her that if she's out by the end of the month, you'll return her deposit right away." I figure I'll help him out, too."

When I tell Will about this conversation, I am laughing. "We had Nikki for over two years. She's got this guy on his knees in three weeks."

Then I call Lee. She's really the one that the responsibility is falling upon, so she sees less humor in the situation than I do. Lee wants to know how Nikki is doing in other areas of her life, notably Ralph.

"I got a strange mixed message when Nikki was here for dinner last night. We had a guest over, and I was bustling around, trying to serve in style, so I wasn't paying full attention." I laugh at the picture in my memory. "It was classical Nikki, though. Here I am, dishing up food, and she's poking photographs in my face. She also had the adult night class catalog, and she said she was interested in two one-night courses. One is "Planning Your Wedding!" Lee groans.

"But later, after dinner, she started talking about going on a date

Friday night with someone else. 'I thought you were planning your wedding,' I said. But she didn't give me a clear answer. She just says that Ralph says she can date other guys."

We decide that Lee will try to get in touch with Nikki later in the day. Lee is inclined to tell Nikki that if she can't make it on her own, she'll have to come back to her home county and live in a group home.

When Nikki comes in for supper, she is late, and I am rushing off to a meeting. "Did Lee reach you?" I ask in passing.

"Yes."

"Did she have any ideas?"

Silence. "Your landlord called me, and I called Lee."

"I don't know why he had to call you. I would have told you." Belligerent.

"I think he feels a little bit desperate. He says the animals smell, that you smell and that you won't listen to him."

"That room smelled when I moved in. My friends who've been there say the room smelled."

No give at all. "Let's just say that perhaps he liked the way it smelled before. He doesn't like the way it smells now. Look, I have to run. Did Lee set a date with you?"

"She's coming up Saturday morning. I told her to meet me here."

September 1983

Saturday is a glorious fall day. Nikki, Lee and I settle down to mounds of newspaper. Nikki, the inveterate listmaker has made a list of possibilities in her notebook. But first Lee talks to her a bit about approaching a landlord.

Nikki does not seem to understand that paying rent doesn't necessarily entitle one to any old behavior one chooses. Lee tells her, "A landlord may object to lots of parties. He may object to your giving keys to friends. He may object to people staying overnight. You had that problem with Judy, didn't you?"

The lip extends. Lee continues. "One thing I have to make clear. If you keep moving around and can't settle in one place for the school year, I will go to court and ask for an order that we don't have to turn your money over until you're twenty-one."

I am a little surprised at this. I'm not sure that the agency can do that, although it isn't a bad idea.

Lee goes on to say, "You need to ask a landlord questions. You need to know what behavior is acceptable. Maybe there's an old lady in the building and playing your stereo late at night will be objectionable. You need to find out now, before you move in."

While Lee and Nikki are out looking at apartments, I spend a really nice sunny Saturday morning listening to country music on the radio, watching Ben and tending the plants.

September 1983

It's been a tough week for Nikki. Bob is making life at his house miserable for her. She and Lee hunted all day Saturday without finding anything. There was one apartment that they both liked. Someone else has spoken for it, but if he doesn't put down a security deposit, Nikki will have a chance at it. But the coup de grace is that Nikki's been fired from her paper route.

My feeling is that it's a few years late in coming. She must have put on quite a show for the route man, crying and tearfully promising that she'd have the papers out by 6:30. "He said he'd try to do something for me. He said he told them I'm an orphan."

"Nikki, people have made too many allowances for you because of your background. That's why you've gotten away with a sloppy job this long. However, the fact that you're an orphan is not relevant to the fact that you don't get the papers out on time."

Lee is really bothered by the loss of the paper route. "I'm telling Nikki that she's on probation. I'm holding a slot in the group home for her, and I've found that she can finish dental assisting at a program here."

We talk a little bit about how I can help. "I won't leave Nikki high and dry on the moving, but I won't volunteer. Nikki's been talking about a woman on her paper route who gave her the cat. This woman apparently volunteered to help."

I've thought about that offer. According to Nikki, if Brenda and John had an empty third floor, they'd rent it to her. Brenda loves to drive, and Nikki can call her anytime.

"Be my guest. If it's raining, and you don't want to walk, give Brenda a call. If it's snowing, do the same. Make her put her money where her mouth is." Then I wonder if this is the way Peggy felt about me when I appeared on the scene. That I was somebody being nice and friendly to Nikki and probably assuming that everyone else is treating her badly .

September 1983

172

This morning I get a call from the landlord of the apartment that Nikki and Lee liked. His other prospective tenant backed out, so Nikki can have the place. He asks "Will there by any problems with Nikki and friends from the high school? You know, parties?"

"This is something you ought to talk with her about. Her agency worker has told her to get it very clear with landlords about what they expect. Make sure that she understands what's acceptable to you. I've been her foster mom for two years, and anything I've made a rule, she's obeyed." I don't tell him how hard it's been, but basically what I say is true.

Nikki calls later, and I tell her the good news. She seems glad, but she wants to talk about Bob. "Guess what Bob did this morning?"

"I'm not really interested in Bob."

"I was cooking French toast this morning, and I accidentally left the door from the kitchen to the living room open."

"Nikki, I don't need to hear this."

She tells me anyway. "He yelled at me about that, and then he dumped a glass of milk on my French toast."

I laugh. "Nikki, you have a knack for driving people nuts."

"He didn't have to be so rude. I told him that, and he said, 'Your mama.' I told him my mother is dead. 'Serves the bitch right,' he says."

I can't quit laughing. It must have looked like the Three Stooges.

"Compared to him, Judy is a saint." It didn't take long to elevate Judy in Nikki's hierarchy.

October 1983

Judy calls this morning in response to the letter I helped Nikki write about the return of the security deposit. My impression of her is that she's a caring person whom Nikki just pushed aside. "I felt like a warden, always going up to tell her to turn her stereo down. But I cared about her, too. She's really immature. You just can't get through to her."

Judy has plenty to say about Ralph. She thinks he's a mooch, and she thinks he's lazy. According to her, Nikki had half of the high school around most of the time. "One time I went up about the stereo, and there must have been ten kids sitting around. Nikki wasn't there. One of the kids said, 'She's over at her mom's, practicing the piano.'"

I sigh. "Nikki's been after me to have Ralph over for dinner. I've been putting it off."

"Oh, you'll like him. He won't make waves. He'll be nice and polite. But you're perceptive enough to see through it. Nikki isn't."

"Do you mean that it will be a pleasant evening?"

"Oh, yes."

"I wish that you and I had talked a long time ago."

"Me too. I wanted to talk with you. I almost tore the place apart one night looking for your number, but I couldn't find it."

I guess I didn't want to butt in after Nikki had moved. But with hindsight, it looks as though both Lee and I should have checked back with Judy.

October 1983

This has certainly been a lively week. Lee calls me one night, asking if I got an earful from Nikki about their session that day. She is quite surprised to learn that Nikki hasn't mentioned it. "She didn't tell you what her options are?"

"No."

"She has to get herself together fast. She has to be evaluated by our agency psychologist. Tonya is very concerned. She thinks Nikki is abusing alcohol and maybe drugs."

"Tonya does?"

"Yes. She says she's seen Nikki when Nikki looked terrible, washed out. She says Nikki has been spacy a few times. She says that when she saw Nikki at school today, Nikki acted inappropriately." Lee stops for a minute. "Let me ask you something. When you saw Nikki for dinner tonight, how did she look to you?"

"Fine."

"I thought so too, but Tonya thought she looked terrible when she saw her at school."

"Look, if there's a difference of perception between you and Tonya, I'd take your perception every time and twice on Sunday."

Lee seems a little more calm. "Tonya is proposing a residential treatment program for Nikki. It costs $7,000.00."

" Good God."

"I don't know what to think. She's made an absolute mess of her financial records. I've sent her close to $1,000.00 during the last two months in regular funds plus extra for moving. She can't account for more than five hundred of it. I think she may have given it to Ralph. Her checkbook is a real mess. She doesn't know what she has. Remember those papers I sent up for her to sign for Social Security? Well, we had to search for them. They were in a pile of stuff on the floor."

"That's Nikki."

"For the first time, I'm really worried about her. I'm really wondering whether she will make it. I've always figured before that she was a survivor. Now I'm worried."

"Me too. I expected some things to screw up, but I'm really surprised myself at how spectacularly she's fouled up. I worry about this Ralph, too. He seems to be a real loser. I promised Nikki that I'd meet him, and I've been putting together a pizza party. You know how excited I am about this. This coming weekend is the big date. I've asked that couple that lived downstairs at Judy's. They've been awfully nice to Nikki. And I've asked Brenda and her husband, the people that gave Nikki the cat. They've been awfully nice, too. Brenda helped Nikki move."

Lee tells me that she's almost surprised that Nikki's reaction to being moved back to her home county doesn't seem more negative.

"Do you think she's asking you to save her from this situation?"

"I don't know. I'm wondering."

"Maybe she realizes that she's in over her head. I guess you're probably asking how much time you can buy for her."

"I am."

"I'd worry about that too. I've learned so much about child development with Nikki. How do we ever give a kid back all that's been missed? For the first time, I'm beginning to understand that it might not be possible. When I can turn off the emotions of dealing with Nikki, a real person, and look at the process intellectually, it's fascinating. But dealing with it is so hard."

"You're doing a fantastic job." Lee's voice is warm.

"Bless you. There are so many times when I feel that I'm not."

We close the conversation, and I feel that both of us are facing all at once the immensity of Nikki's unpreparedness to meet the world.

October 1983

When Nikki comes in for dinner the next evening, I ask her what is going on. "What's all this about Lee taking you back to your county?"

"I found the receipt for my rent deposit," she says belligerently and sets about making a cup of tea. "Lee gave me a brochure about a drug program. I don't see what that has to do with me. I asked her what it was about, and she just said 'Read it.'"

"That's not really Lee's idea. It's Tonya's. She thinks you're abusing alcohol and maybe drugs."

"What?" Nikki is genuinely surprised and put out.

"Tonya told Lee that she's seen you when you've seemed spacy and behaved inappropriately, and it's her conclusion that you're abusing alcohol."

"Is it alcohol abuse to drink beer at a party? I never even finish a can! Drugs? I don't take pills, even. You know that!"

I do know that. I've always had to buy liquid medicines for Nikki. "Didn't Tonya ever ask you about these concerns of hers? Didn't she even talk to you about them?"

"No!" The answer is explosive. It even hits me.

"I am surprised about that. I just figured that Tonya would have discussed this with you before talking to Lee."

Will comes in at the point, and we eat dinner. I can tell that Nikki is really angry. After dinner she says "I don't trust Tonya at all. I'm not going to her as a counselor anymore. Now maybe I'm understanding why you never liked her."

"It's true that I've never liked her, but up until today that was a matter of style and training. I didn't like her approach, but I also knew that she was a new social worker. But you've got a different issue here now. This is really a question of professional ethics. I can't believe that she didn't talk with you before she talked with Lee."

"You should have seen her at the school yesterday. She tracked me down in the cafeteria and embarrassed me in front of all my friends. 'I'm your counselor. See, I'll always find you.' She hugged me and called me sweetie and dear. We moved to another table, but anyone could have heard us. Today some of my friends asked who the weird chick was."

And this is the counselor who said the Nikki's behavior at the school was inappropriate. Nikki also recounts one other incident that I hadn't known about that fits into this inappropriate category. Even though part of me is glad that Tonya is screwing up, because it validates the dislike I've always had for her, the fact is that she's hurt her client, Nikki.

"Maybe I'll go back to Mara," Nikki is saying. "She would never treat me like this. You know, Tonya never had a plan the way Mara did. She'd just let me talk about whatever I felt like at the time. Well, I'm not going back to her."

We wind down by talking about the coming pizza party.

October 1983

Nikki went for her psychological evaluation this week and stayed overnight in the agency receiving home. When she returns, she gets right into the saga. "There was a question about 'Do you feel that people are always watching you?'"

I laugh. "Bet you knew how to handle that one." I can't believe that even a paranoid would answer "Yes."

At dinner Nikki says, "Lee told me how you said that you can hardly wait to have grandchildren to get together with over the holidays."

"I what?" I am choking on my food.

"Lee said that you can hardly wait to have grandchildren."

I think that I know how that conversation actually went, but for the time being, I say, "Let's not get excited about grandchildren. I'm not looking for you to have kids until you're in your late twenties. But yes, what I told Lee was that any kid who's been here is someone that I'd expect to come back—for their wedding, with their kids, for holidays."

"Well," says Nikki, putting on an accent. "I'm going to ask Will to give me away for ze wedding."

"What do you think, Will? Are you ready to go to a wedding?"

"I can always take along my reading material." He's got the usual straight face, but a smile is lurking.

As I fold laundry later, I think that what I really wanted to say to Nikki was, "You're always part of this family. We'll always be here. You can come back at holidays, you can bring your kids." That was what I'd talked about with Lee. I'd told her of my concern that in our attempt to drive home to Nikki the fact that she has to be independent when she finishes high school, we'd lost that message. Kirsten and I had set out with a conscious plan to push Nikki toward independence. Had a side effect been to say "You leave our family when you graduate?" Leave our house, yes, but never leave our family.

Nikki comes upstairs to tell me that she has broken the plastic shade of a lamp that was in the basement. "I tripped over the cord."

When I go down later, I can't for the life of me figure how she could have tripped over the cord. It is wound around the lamp, which is on a table. Breakage. We haven't had any of that for awhile. Nikki left the mess, too. I guess I did handle that conversation badly.

October 1983

I can no longer put off the pizza dinner for Ralph. Among other things, it's no longer too warm to run the oven. I decide that I might as well make this ordeal as interesting for myself as I possibly can, so I ask

Pam and Ken. I know that Pam will keep the conversation going. And, as I told Lee, I ask Carol and Tony. They're the people who lived downstairs in Nikki's first house. I also invited Brenda and her husband. Brenda was very nice about helping Nikki move this last time. I know that Nikki won't thank her, so it might be nice to invite them to dinner.

As Judy predicted, Ralph is very polite. "Sure is a nice place you have here, ma'am." Phony. But the evening is bearable. Brenda and her husband couldn't make it, but everybody else came. Even with one couple short, we almost ran out of pizza. I'd decided to order it rather than trying to make enough for that many.

Nikki and Ralph don't hang around. There is someplace that they are going. But Carol and Tony stay and talk for awhile. Tony is doing a residency in ENT, and Carol is a dietician. She's not employed at the moment, which is why she's had time for Nikki. She thinks that Ralph is a loser, and she keeps trying to call Nikki's attention to certain things.

They're trying to rehabilitate Nikki, too. They tell of taking her with them one night for Mexican food. She ordered far more than she could eat, even though the waiter indicated that the portions were big. Then she said no thank yous when Tony paid for her meal. "I gave her a lecture," said Tony. "There were tears in her eyes when I finished."

"Good for you!" I say. Tony is a soft-spoken Texan, part Mexican. He has a gentle manner, and I can't believe that he overdid the lecture. "It's really great of you to look after her."

"She's so immature," says Carol. She's a petite woman, thirtyish, with shoulder-length hair and her own Southern accent. "She's really not old enough to be out on her own."

"I know. But after two and a half years here, something had to give. I really didn't expect her to end up with someone like Ralph, though."

"He's a hustler." Carol shakes her head.

We all wind down, the guests leave. As I clean up the kitchen, I realize that Carol's remarks have stirred my guilt. Wouldn't it have been better for Nikki to stay with us?

October 1983

Today Lee and I talk again. She doesn't have all of the results back from the psychological testing, but she's seen the pictures that Nikki drew for one part of the test. "They're scary. She drew herself as a Martian."

"She told me about that. I think she was deliberately trying to get attention. But I can see a psychologist climbing all over that—alienation, etc." I want to talk with Lee about my poor handling of Nikki's "coming back with grandchildren" remark.

"Nikki was really happy with the idea of being able to go back to your family," Lee said. "That was what she kept saying, that she'd really like to be able to go back. Then she started talking about herself. She says she has a lawyer's personality. She really sees herself in you. She described you to a T. She also wants to find a husband like Will. She thinks you have a good marriage."

"I think we do, too. You know, I can see how, on the surface, Ralph might look like Will. They're both laid back. But there are minor differences, such as Will's not having an aversion to work. We've met Ralph now, and if I hadn't heard from people who have observed him for awhile, I might have been impressed. I can see how he could fool Nikki."

We talk a bit further about whether Lee is still thinking about taking Nikki back to the home county. "I've talked to the psychologist about that. He's very hesitant about taking her away from the only family support she's got—your family."

I've been thinking about that ever since.

Thanksgiving 1983

We have a quiet, pleasant day at the farm. Will's folks are here, and my aunt and uncle come. I expected that Nikki would want to be with Ralph's family, but she asked if she could come along. We have a companionable time working on one of the many puzzles that are stashed on a shelf. She helps me with setting the table but waffles about helping my aunt and me with the dishes. "Can I help after this show I'm watching?"

"Of course, Nikki ," I say with sarcasm that I doubt she catches. Needless to say, we are through with the first round of dishes before Nikki's show is over. I tell her that she can clean up after the dessert.

Later I hear a shriek and find that Aunt Rosemary has tickled Nikki through a split in the back seam of her slacks, just below the waistband. Nikki's putting on weight. Ever the consumer, in all respects, she has now added call forwarding to her phone and gotten cable TV. The other night she forwarded her phone to the wrong number instead of the house where she was babysitting, and all of her evening's calls went to some poor old lady.

When we return, Will and his Dad drive her to her apartment. Later Mac said, "No thank you, no nothing."

"Well, there's some progress this year. She got Ben a birthday present."

November 1983

One of my Juvenile Court cases from two years has come back to court through a novel set of circumstances. I was assigned to represent Cindy when children's services was asking for temporary custody of her three children due to her physical disabilities. Unfortunately, those disabilities were severe enough so that the department did in fact get temporary custody.

However, they left the children with Cindy, and she made it for two years before she had to be hospitalized again. She called me at the time, upset that children's services was splitting up her kids. The two little ones would each be in a separate foster home, and the teen-ager, Mary, would be in an institution. Cindy had a friend that might take Mary; could I do something? Certainly, I said, but as it panned out, the friend didn't come through.

I didn't hear from Cindy again until August. The little ones had then been placed together in one foster home and that foster mom said that she'd take Mary. But the department had placed Mary in an institution, and now children's services and the institution were saying that she needed to finish the program at the institution.

The place sounded medieval. Mary had not been allowed to visit with Cindy, even though social service professionals at the hospital tried to intervene. Cindy's health had not improved, and she was now in a chronic care facility. At present Mary could only visit her mother once a month. Could I do something?

A short conversation with the children's services attorney on the case led me to the conclusion that I'd have to bring the case back into court. The inhumanity of the institution's policies was so clear that I figured we wouldn't have any trouble. Even the department attorney was empathetic. I've always enjoyed the department attorneys, although I haven't been able to say the same for all of the caseworkers.

I talked to the foster mother a number of times. She's a gem. She and her husband would like to make their life's work running a group home, but all their approaches to the system have been rebuffed. She's willing to take same really hard cases—unwed mothers with their babies. I've got one of those cases myself now at court. But children's services told her they didn't have any call for that type of home. It's in the department's interests to keep this woman licensed as a single foster home. Group homes cost more money.

In our most recent conversation, Jan, the foster mother, tells me that she has three fifteen-year-olds. Mary would be the fourth. How does she do it? I tell her that I can barely handle one teen. She says that she has a twelve-year-old that she just can't feel at peace with. "She's the kind of kid that can come in the back door from school and do six things wrong by the time she's reached her room."

"That's Nikki," I laugh. Jan is going to ask the agency to move that particular child. She feels that the girl's effect, especially the gutter language, on the younger kids in the home is bad.

"She had them playing 'pimp and hooker' the other day."

Nikki never was quite that bad, but she's come out with far more explicit sexual language than I've wanted Ben to hear.

December 1983

Mara is feeling that it's time to wrap up Ben's therapy. He still keeps his feelings in, but he's a lot more vocal than he was. He has a great teacher this year, too. I worry a bit because he doesn't seem to like school, even with a good teacher. But his teacher doesn't think that Ben has any real problem with school right now, and I am very glad to hear that.

December 1983

He did it. Judge Abernathy let Mary out of the institution. I damned near lost my faith in the system on that one. It shouldn't have taken the time and the trouble that it did. It should have moved much more quickly. But perhaps the fact that a Catholic judge let a kid out of a Catholic institution stands for something. It couldn't have been an easy decision for him to make. I got his message clearly that I shouldn't try to beat up on the people from the institution. So we had a nice little hearing that was more like a tea-party.

Then we sweated for over two weeks for a decision, and I even had to push for that. But it's over. Mary is with the foster family, and Cindy is at ease.

December 1983

Pennie and I connect by phone today. I am feeling a bit down again about my dealings with Nikki. So Pennie told me "You cared enough to let Nikki reject you, because that's what she did when she first came. But she really needed you then, more than you can possibly know. People who don't care about a kid are real casual. They don't yell at the kid. You don't yell at a kid unless you care about that kid, care what he turns out like. Don't put yourself down about what it is you didn't do for Nikki. Recognize what it is that you gave her."

Why do we take these kids, I ask? "Because you've got the guts to do what's right and what's needed. People don't understand that. Foster parents are the smallest minority in the world, and ain't nothing going to make them all right with that."

Pennie is wrestling right now with some of the reactions that she feels she's gotten since she and Vince don't have a foster kid at the moment. "You're not God anymore. How can people respect you?"

Would she ever take another kid, I ask? Yes, if she had the right physical set-up. She and Vince have started playing the lottery, and if they ever cash in, they'll buy that house with eight bedrooms and six baths. They'll hire a staff, and they'll take interns for field placement. It would be mandatory for workers in foster care to have field placements.

Vince would quit his job, and they'd become professional advocates. They'd go to those eight a.m. meetings where decisions about kids are made. "The county commissioners would begin to wonder if the sun ever sets, because they would always have shadows."

Later in the day we go down to Pam and Ken's for a tree-trimming party. One of the other guests is a woman who lives near Nikki's adoptive home and knows her. She's a warm, gray-haired mother of three. We fall into a conversation about Nikki, and, in explanation to another person who joined the conversation, I say, "Nikki is our last foster child."

Just then Ben flys by in a game with some of the other kids and adds in all happiness, "and you're talking last!" We grownups fall apart.

December 1983

I am sitting here with a cup of tea and a warm feeling, looking at a glass rectangle with "MOM" in raised letters. A picture can fit into the "O," and Nikki has given me a wallet-size senior picture cut to fit.

But I don't want to cut it, because on the back is written "To a great Mom! You'll win in the Ohio Supreme Court yet! Love, Stuffs." This is the 25% shining through, as I tried to explain to a friend who couldn't quite understand how I could take foster kids if I complained so much. I said that 75% of the time was hell, but the 25% heaven wasn't bad.

We are exchanging Christmas presents early, because Nikki's going to be with Ralph's family on Christmas. She's gotten Will a "DAD" paperweight and given Ben a little E.T. figurine. Her present is luggage, which is no surprise to her, since she'd already picked it out of the catalog. I figured that we could get three pieces: Christmas, birthday and graduation. Will's folks sent her a present, and so did Alice. Nikki seems really delighted.

Nikki won't be over again until her birthday, just after the holidays, so we plan the menu. This year she orders cheesecake instead of the fabulously rich, white-frostinged bakery birthday cakes we've all favored in the past. She asks for mint chocolate-chip to go with the cake. And Pepsi. As she leaves, I give her a big hug and a kiss, and I mean them .

January 1984

For the first time ever, Nikki is unable to finish a meal. I guess it is the combination of the cheesecake and the mint chocolate-chip, so she spends an hour on the video games before she is ready for the ice cream. If I do say so myself, the cheesecake turned out well. I don't make it often, but the recipe is fun.

As we are eating our birthday steaks, Nikki is complaining that Tonya is on her case about her schoolwork, especially world history. "How are you doing in that?" I ask.

"Horrible. I got an "F" on the last test."

"Aren't you studying?"

"Sure. I read it all before the test."

"How many times?"

"Once."

"There's no rule against reading it twice."

"Maybe."

As we talk, it seems that she's planning to take the course over in summer school if she fails, which will delay graduation. And Tonya seems to be annoying her by pushing as to exactly what she's going to do after high school.

Even though she talked about finding another counselor, she doesn't seem to have made the necessary effort to link up with one. She had me call once, about some misunderstanding, and the director of The Place said that she'd get back to me. That was weeks ago. As far as I'm concerned, Nikki doesn't have to see Tonya, but Nikki thinks Lee wants her to. No matter. I'm glad that Tonya is finally getting on Nikki's case.

Nikki isn't. "She makes me mad. I asked her if I had to have my whole life planned."

It doesn't seem that she's done much planning. She'll take some course or other at the community college and maybe get a job in a restaurant. Maybe she'll get married at the end of the summer. Bits and pieces of talk have indicated that Ralph hasn't given her the ring that he was talking about. He didn't come to her New Year's party because he had to work, and he forgot her birthday. But he's still around.

Later in the evening I find myself wondering whether this screw-up in world history is deliberate in order to put off the wedding—or to keep the Social Security money coming a few months longer.

January 1984

Ben is watching me pick up some clothes. One item is a bathrobe made of really neat material—printed with firemen, fire-engines and Dalmatians. Pam made it for her son and passed it on to Ben. Ben used to wear it outside in the sandbox because he liked it so much. "You've outgrown this! I guess we'll have to put it in the old-clothing bag."

"Let's save it. We might need it for a foster kid someday."

When I tell Will about it, I say it made me glad that Ben would still talk about another foster child. But his message is clear. The bathrobe is a boy's bathrobe, and it will only fit boys smaller than Ben.

January 1984

Nikki says that she's missed a lot of English classes—we don't get into why—but can make up the assignments by writing a composition. "What can I write about?" she asks.

"Anything. Your animals. Photography." I'm thinking that she could also write about being a foster child, something that most kids know nothing about. But I let the thought pass unsaid.

However, she pipes up with it. "I could write about all the families that I've had."

I encourage her, and we joke about a title: "The Kid with One Hundred Moms." Even Ben likes that.

Later she brings over her essays—she's written five. Three are about herself. She calls one an autobiography, and she's written it on the neat paper that Will's folks got her for Christmas, with her name in heavy black printing at the top. The second is "The Girl With Eight Families," and the third is "Out There On My Own."

She offers to let me read them. There is an idyllic quality to "Eight

Families." She'd had no trouble as a foster child because "You just become one of the family." Her placement with her grandmother hadn't worked out because they were of two different religions. Her placement at the Yanceys was going perfectly until the terrible divorce.

But I end up giving her a kiss when I read that foster families should be given credit for being willing to open their hearts and their homes. When she gets married, she'll take in foster kids and adopt as well.

January 1984

There was an intriguing message on the answering machine the other day. "Hey, Anne, I broke up with Ralph! I'll tell you about it tomorrow."

And indeed she does. It is Will's birthday, and Nikki came over for the festivities. And did she talk! It is old-style Nikki all the way. I'd been telling Ben the story of Baron Munchausen's horn, and how one day it was so cold that no notes would come out when the Baron blew the horn. Later, when his party stopped at an inn, the horn thawed out, and music was heard throughout.

If Nikki had frozen her voice on the way over here, we all would have been buried under the words that rolled out after the thaw. What I made of it is that Ralph has been a bit disappointing and that Nikki has grown less and less sure of the idea of marriage. "I don't know why I wouldn't admit that he was the wrong person. I guess I just wanted to say that I had a boyfriend."

Not that the long-range ramifications of that statement have hit her. Already she is "going with" her seventh-grade boyfriend. She saw him last summer at his sister's wedding. She called him immediately after the break-up with Ralph, and now she's going to visit him when finals are over.

Will and I have a conversation this morning about what it is that makes one person decide to break out of the background into which he was born. The vast majority never do. I recall Norman Podhoretz's beginning in *Making It*, "One of the longest journeys in the world is the journey from Brooklyn to Manhattan." Yet he chose to make that journey.

We know a man who was raised in a welfare family of sixteen or more kids. Somewhere, very early, he decided that he didn't belong in that world, so he worked his way out. He went to school, earned a couple of degrees and is very influential in his profession today.

The facet of all this that I find intriguing is that Nikki has been offered a chance to break out but hasn't taken it. Will there ever come a time when the middle-class advantages she's been exposed to will propel her forward?

Most people never have the door opened at all. Last week on a case I visited a family where a child is alleged to be abused. It was a typical welfare dwelling, not nice materially, and certainly the remaining kids in the home were fending for themselves. Mom and her boyfriend had a few noisy exchanges. The kids in that home will never have a chance. Some very few kids make their own luck and their own move. For some other very few, a door is held open, but whether a move will be made is hard to tell.

February 1984

Will picks Nikki up at the bus station Monday evening on his way home from work. For dinner we get an earful about her weekend away, and then I say I'll drive her home with her luggage. Pam and I are going to the library after that, so the three of us drive to Nikki's. She invites Pam in to look at her apartment, so we all troop in.

Our first problem is that the light in the back hallway is out. It's a real trick climbing to a third-floor apartment in the dark, but we are pretty jolly about it. That ends when Nikki opens the apartment door and finds that her lights are out, too.

While she goes to see if the people on the second floor have lights, Pam and I stand there gagging at the smell in the apartment. Part of it is the stench of the litterbox, and part seems to be coming from two huge trash bags on the kitchen floor. We can see their outlines by the moonlight that is coming in the back window.

Yes, the people on second have electricity. Nikki and I feel our way down to the basement to look at the fuse box. I've never seen that particular type of box—neither what I'd call straight fuse or straight breaker—but Nikki hauls off and gives it a whack. An additional basement light goes on.

"That's on my line! I'm not paying for that!" Nikki takes the bulb out of the socket, and we trudge back upstairs. Pam is admiring one of three chairs that Nikki had bought for $100.00. I can see Pam's mind trying new coverings on it. But the smell is so disagreeable that we make our excuses to get on to the library.

We agree that Nikki seems to be making no effort to clean up the place. I tell Pam that I can hardly believe it is the lovely apartment I saw before she moved in.

February 1984

I finally get around to my long-intended plan of calling Mrs. Evans. "I just want to touch base with you. About three weeks ago, Nikki started saying that she wasn't going to take the state boards in dental assisting this summer, and that's really worrying me."

"She told me that. I've been wanting to talk with you, too. I've had your name here on my pad. Nikki's attitude is thoroughly obnoxious. We had a sub a few weeks ago, and she was unspeakably rude to him. He left me a personal note. And when I talked to her about it, all she had to say was, 'I didn't like him.'"

Mrs. Evans goes on to say that Nikki's work has been so erratic that one day Mrs. E told her to take the next day off to think about what she was doing. "She went out on an observation, and she's telling the dentist how to run his office. 'You're a peon,' I told her. 'You do not tell anybody anything!'"

I sigh. Clearly this is Nikki at her worst. Mrs. Evans is trying to help all the students get ready for the test. First Nikki says she's not ready to take it, then she says she doesn't need any help. Her notes are at home. She can't iron her uniform because she doesn't have an iron. She has an argument for everything Mrs. Evans asks of her.

"Nikki has told me that it costs too much to take the test, but that sounds like a smoke screen to me," I say. "Has she been through that with you?"

"Yes. She told me that she lent a lot of money to somebody who wasn't going to pay it back. She was very upset."

"I was afraid of that, but she wouldn't admit it. Well, maybe the lesson was cheap at the price. She has other money she doesn't have access to yet. But we'll solve the cost thing some way. I'll call her caseworker, and I'd like to have her talk directly with you."

"That would be fine. I'd like to talk to her, too."

It's good to talk with Lee again. "Everything's okay, isn't it?"

"Afraid not," I answer. "Nikki and I have been getting along well, so I wasn't looking for trouble, but I got an earful from her dental assisting instructor today." And I relayed the conversation. "The only positive thing I can say is that Nikki's begun talking about the Air Force again. However, she's also said she plans to move to Madison this summer and go into the service in January. By that time she might have married Don."

We both sigh. Part of Lee's busyness recently has come from a job promotion, but she'll keep Nikki on her caseload for these last three months. As always, Lee is thoroughly responsive. She says she'll have a minor problem with the money in that Nikki's "everyday" account is exhausted. But she'll work something out.

"I wouldn't advertise it to Nikki, but we can always write a check and have you pay us back later."

"Great. I'm hoping to get up there to see Mrs. Evans before the end of this week."

I hang up feeling that at least the path to take the boards is now open for Nikki. We all may be pushing her down it against her will, but I don't think so. It is strange, however, that none of her future plans have involved looking for a job as a dental assistant.

February 1984

I've been thinking all of this over. What is going on with that kid? Does the anger just have to come out somewhere? That's the old anger, of course—the "Why am I a foster kid?" anger. And there's got to be some new anger at Ralph.

And it seems to be coming out at school. Will still thinks that maybe she's trying to screw up and not graduate. Maybe that's part of it. I'm just delighted that she's begun talking about the service again. I wish she didn't have to lose the weight before she can put her name on the dotted line. She went upstairs to weigh herself the other night. Not a word did she have to say about the total.

March 1984

I took a look through the TV listings last night and flew to the phone. "Pennie, can you watch PBS at eight? That show is on again, the documentary about the man in Harlem who adopted eighteen kids. Kojo Odo. Let's watch it, and I'll call you back tomorrow. I want to know what you think. I only saw the last part of it last year."

Ben, Nikki and I sit down to watch. Kojo seems so calm, warm and secure. His face is peaceful and attractive. The opening scene is a family meeting to decide whether the piece should be made. Kojo says he wants to make it because there are too many kids in foster care and in institutions, and by making the documentary, they could show that it's possible to adopt "different" kids. But he'll understand if the majority of the family is against the project.

The great bulk of the piece is on individual kids—the son with one arm, the blind son, the son with birth defects. I find myself wanting to know lots more about Kojo. Where does he work? What is his work? How has he been able to take these kids?

Are his children any different? Somehow I find myself wondering about critical mass. If a small, nuclear family took in the child with the birth defects, what would be the result? By most experiences, it would be difficult. Kojo is single. There are no parents to divide. With eighteen kids, each simply has to know that he must be self-sufficient. Is there a different dynamic in his family than in most families?

I wonder what Nikki is thinking as he says, "So many of these kids have gone from foster home to foster home. Each new move for them is like the beginning of yet another move. But when they come here, it is permanent. They're going to have to stay no matter what the struggle."

He refers very calmly and matter-of-factly to a number of struggles and battles he's had with the system. There's such peace in his manner. When I begin to talk about my battles with the system, I can feel the adrenalin rising, and I think I froth at the mouth.

Later I talk with Pennie about the program. She said they got Michael, the foster son they adopted, out of bed to watch. Pennie asked him, "Did you see where the kids were talking at the beginning about how they hated to tell people they're adopted? Did you see the one son say that he didn't like to take care of the younger kids after school, but that it was the job his father assigned to him?" Michael, eight years old, has been on a real pity party lately, says Pennie, and they figured the show let him know he's not the only kid in that boat.

Pennie liked the show, too, and also read Kojo as genuine. She thinks that maybe there is something to the idea of critical mass.

March 1984

A terrible thing has happened in a juvenile case that I was a Guardian ad Litem on last fall. Children's services got temporary custody of three children, including an infant. For once I had no problems with that, because the twenty-three year-old mom was a pothead with no discernible goal and motivation in life. She lived with her mother, who told us that even if the caseworker helped her daughter find an apartment, she'd never stay there and manage her own life.

Yesterday the attorney who'd represented the mother called me to say that she and her client had been told the baby died. Both of them wanted a full investigation, and so do I. I've made all the right calls, and children's services had already started an administrative investigation. Along with the mother, my heart keeps going out to the foster mother. I'd talked to her a couple of times, and I'd seen the baby in the grandmother's home. In my own mind, I do not doubt that foster mother's care and love for one minute. Once we talked for an hour because she was concerned about the way the baby seemed upset and restless after a day with mom at grandmother's. This seems to be just one of those tragedies. The baby had been seen at the hospital and given a prescription. Then she collapsed two nights later.

Not only does this foster mother have her own grief, but she's also , got to answer a lot of questions that no one would ask had the baby been her own child. It seems that foster parents are held to a higher standard of care than natural parents.

I remember the first summer that Nikki was here. One morning a dog on her paper route nipped her finger. There was barely a scratch, but Nikki was carrying on something fierce—mostly from indignation that the dog had the nerve to bite her.

I had her wash the finger well, and I put some antiseptic on it. Kirsten called that morning about some matter, so I told her about the incident and asked if Nikki's shots were current. Kirsten didn't think they were, so I packed her off to Ben's doctor. She said later that he looked like Wolfman Jack, a noted DJ, which is a high compliment.

I'm remembering that about two months later, a regal woman swept into my office with profuse apologies about her dog's having bitten Nikki. She'd been out of town all summer and had left a house-sitter in charge of the premises, including the dog. She insisted on giving me a ten-dollar bill for the doctor's visit. I didn't think it had cost more than seven— which I'd paid, as a lot of foster parents do, rather than wait to get children's services to pay it or to reimburse. I'd just written it off. I told her I'd give Nikki the remaining three dollars for pain and suffering.

As the lady left, she said, "Maybe now Nikki will stop riding by on her bike and shouting, 'Your dog bit me last summer!'"

March 1984

Brenda and I have lunch together. We'd been talking about doing that ever since she and her husband were unable to come to the pizza party. "You've really been great about taking Nikki places. I'm afraid I've gotten a bit hardnosed about driving. Nikki can get very demanding."

Brenda laughs. She's a warm person, with curly dark hair. "I've told

Nikki that she needs to ask me ahead of time. There've been lots of times when she's called up at the last minute, asking 'Are you busy right now?' And I always have been. But on this trip to visit Don and his sister, she asked me ten days ahead of time, and we worked things out."

"I understand you fed the cat, too, while she was gone."

Brenda frowns. "You know, I've been wondering how to talk to her about her housekeeping. That place is awful. The litterbox isn't clean, so the cat goes in the tub."

I sigh. "Unfortunately, Nikki does not pick up subtle hints. You have to come right out and tell her what's wrong. And there's a risk to that. You take the risk that she's not going to like what you have to say. It's been very hard to play the parent role with Nikki."

We talk some about her coming graduation. I tell Brenda about the big open house that we're planning, and she indicates that she'd like to help out. "I could use the help. I think Nikki wants to invite seventy-some people. That's okay, they're all legitimate names, but it's a lot of people. I just hope we have good weather!"

As we finish our tea, Brenda says, "When Nikki was looking for that third place, I felt really guilty because we have a third floor. But I just don't think I could have taken her."

I remember my early fears of Brenda wanting to "save" Nikki. "I'm not just saying this to let you off the hook, but I really feel that you'd have been putting your own children at risk if you'd taken her. Your daughter is about Ben's age, and your son is a bit younger, right?" Brenda nods. "I think Nikki can handle that fine for babysitting, but I think she would have tried to elbow your children aside if she'd seen herself as part of your family. It's great that you're doing what you're doing, being an adult friend."

We part company promising to keep in touch about the graduation day open house.

April 1984

After Ralph it's been almost like Tom, Dick and Harry. And now it's Jim. Jim is tall, good-looking, features a cowboy hat and carries a switchblade. But he has one redeeming quality. He's going into the service this month.

So now Nikki has two reasons to be interested in the service. Of course she's going to marry Jim. I always said it was the guy that showed up in April of her senior year that I'd worry about. However, if he gets

Nikki into the service, I won't let a little thing like a wedding throw me.

Nikki is really working on getting the weight off. I am truly amazed at her. "You go ahead and cook what you guys want to eat. Just get me a reduced calorie TV dinner, and I'll eat that. I can handle it."

I do believe that she'll make it this time. It appears that Jim has offered her four days in Hawaii if she gets the weight off. "That beats a twenty," I tell Will.

How long will this romance last? I watched a little exchange the other night. Jim is really fond of his cowboy hat and very careful with it. When Nikki tossed it down, he patiently corrected her. "Oh, yeah," she waved his words aside. Maybe two months.

April 1984

On precisely our third anniversary day as a family, Nikki comes in with a diamond. I don't coo over it; I am going to a meeting, Nikki is ten minutes late, Will hasn't arrived yet, and I lost the battle of getting Ben to eat dinner.

We had already decided to hold the celebration a week late anyway. That way it can double as a party for Jim before he leaves for the service. We've planned out our usual menu except that Nikki resolutely insists on a diet meal for herself. "Don't change what the rest of you have."

I'm really proud of her. The weight is starting to come off, and I hope that gives her incentive to keep going.

The celebration itself goes well. It's clear from the conversation that Jim is staying at Nikki's place. They're planning a wedding and will set the date when Jim's basic training ends. He seems like a nice guy, but I wonder how stable this relationship will be. They're into a lot of partying by their talk.

Pam comes down to join us for cake and coffee and to meet Jim. She duly admires Nikki's ring, which is a real rock. "You just glow," she tells Nikki.

Later, as Pam and I walk to the door, she says "I don't know that I would have sat at a dinner table and discussed certain sexual matters when I was engaged to Ken."

"She's always done that. I know I've complained about it, but you've never heard it before. And he's the same. But he has some manners, too. I haven't seen a young man seat all the ladies at a table for a long time."

Later I find myself wondering whether we'll be including engagement and wedding plans in our graduation day open house.

June 1984

This has been a long weekend. We're getting ready for the party next weekend. I've ordered the cake and the party trays. Nikki was with me to help choose the selection for the party trays. I think that she was impressed by the cost, because half an hour later she volunteered to come next weekend to help me clean.

Kirsten and Lee drove up this Saturday for a final meeting. They took us to lunch, and we had a great time. Lee and I had talked by phone the week before, and she had some interesting things to say. She sees Nikki's summer job as an indication that Nikki has been happy enough in our family to seek out another family.

I must say that I have some worries about this job. Nikki will be a live-in babysitter to a family with an infant, six-year-old twin girls and a nine-year-old boy. That's more than I'd want to handle! Nikki plans to stay with this family until September—or whenever Jim gets assigned to a permanent duty station. The wedding plans are completely chaotic. They may get married in Alabama in just a few weeks when Jim graduates from basic training, or maybe they'll get married in Ohio in the fall.

Mara called about the invitation to the open house. She was a bit taken aback when she heard the news of the wedding, but she also felt that Nikki is looking for her own family.

I wanted to talk with Mara about the strange thing that happened when I was reading the latest newsletter from our county's children's services department. Foster care was looking for a family for a girl who has one more year in a work-study high school program. To my absolute astonishment, I found myself wondering what she was like. I thought I'd never have the slightest interest in foster care again.

I'd told Lee about that, too, and Lee had laughed. "Now that you mention it, we have this sixteen-year-old..." And she told me of a girl who sounded a lot like Nikki. I'd told her that I just wouldn't be up to it for a few years but maybe I'd consider it then if Ben and Will were willing. Maybe a boy. A boy younger than Ben.

"But I'd need support," I told Mara, "the kind you gave us with Nikki. Foster parents have to be live-in therapists, and we need guidance about what we're doing. I don't know how people do it otherwise."

"That's the way you've chosen to foster parent. Some people don't put that kind of effort into it."

I laughed. Mara had just finished saying that at one point, when she

and her husband had a teen-age boy staying with them, ninety percent of
their conversations were about him. That's certainly how I've been about
Nikki. Maybe I should only be involved in short-term care. The drain is
so great in long-term care.

Graduation Day, June 1984

If we'd wanted a symbol to mark the end of our formal commitment
to Nikki, it would be this graduation day. Our informal commitment will
continue, of course, but Nikki's graduation does mark the end of the time
that we agreed to try to give to her.

By the time we sink into seats at the theater where the commence-
ment ceremony is held, my mind is in a complete whirl. My thoughts
remind me of the party trays we'd picked up this morning—they are a
kaleidoscope like that of the pickles, cheeses, ham, olives, corned beef and
bread.

I can't organize my thoughts at all during the ceremony. I keep trying
to spot Nikki. She's come with her home-room teacher, and she's to ride
home with us. We've invited people to the open house from four to seven,
but since it looked as though the ceremony might last longer than we'd
thought, Pam is going to be at the house to welcome the early arrivals.

Then the last graduate is cheered. As we edge out into the throng, we
catch sight of Nikki just ahead of us. But when we emerge from the front-
door funnel, she's disappeared. We stand and wait. Then I walk around
and around. Everybody pairs off like cards in one of those children's old-
maid games until virtually nobody is left.

Except us. There we stand. "This is what's symbolic." I say to Will.
"Three years and we end with a screw-up."

I am angry on the drive back to the house. I feel especially bad that
I'm not there to help Pam. I am not really surprised that Nikki is there
when we came through the back door.

"I didn't see you. We made a mistake in not picking a place to meet.
So I came with my home room teacher."

"Wasn't there another way to solve the problem? Couldn't you wait?
We did. Don't you ever do that again." I stop. There really won't be
another "again." Then I catch sight of Mara across the kitchen, and I
begin to laugh.

I go over to hug her. "Three years, and it's the same." Peggy is there,
and Vince and Pennie and everybody else who has helped me through
these years. I feel bad that I haven't had the grace not to get angry on this

last day. Do not ever tell me that human behavior is changeable. All the king's horses...

Nikki has a coterie of friends who talk on after most of the adults leave. Her sister and her sister's husband are here after all. We hadn't heard, and we were worried. In the midst of Saturday's cleaning. Nikki said. "It's sad that everybody who's coming is friends, not family." She'd seen the postcard from her grandmother, saying that she was sorry that she was unable to come.

But Nikki's sister is here. I remember Nikki's saying that her sister had seemed hurt that she couldn't come to the ceremony itself. Of Nikki's precious four tickets, two went to us, and she'd given the other two to Jim's parents. They'd called with an excuse at the last minute.

Finally Pam and I virtually push Nikki out. She is going to begin her summer job tomorrow morning, and Jim is driving her there tonight. From a message left on the answering machine, it seems that the family expected Nikki around seven. It is now about nine. "You don't want to go in too late with all your things," I say, referring to Jim's car packed with all her clothes and gifts.

All of us have final hugs on the lawn and make promises to meet at the wedding, which could be within a few weeks' time, according to Nikki, or never, according to Pam.

As I am cleaning up in the kitchen, the phone rings. It is Nikki's new employer. "Here it is ten o'clock and no Nikki. I thought she was coming around seven."

Welcome to Nikki-land. It has its own time-frames and its own rules. I wish that I could have sent Nikki to you better prepared to face the real world than she appears to be. It's not that I—and lots of other people—haven't tried; it's just that the task is so great.

Nikki's coming to help you care for your children, yet she's a child herself. I tried to tell you that when you phoned me for a reference, but I don't think that you understood. I was trying to tell you that although she'll help you with your kids, you're really gaining another child. Please take care of Nikki.

Nikki didn't marry Jim. She lost enough weight to get into the Air Force, and she spent three years at Langley Air Force Base. After leaving the Air Force, she married Randy, who has made the Air Force his career. Nikki visited us when she was pregnant with her first baby. Nikos, a Greek exchange student was with us at the time, and an instant animosity sprung up between them. We have a picture of Nikki giving Nikos the finger.

Nikki's first son was born at Langley, but she and Randy went to Germany for four years before we could meet Samuel. They were here at Christmas their first year back in the states. I loved watching Sam twirl around the day before Christmas, stopping twice to say "I'm so happy!"

They were living on Eglin Air Force Base in Florida when Thomas, the second son, arrived. We saw them at Christmas when Thomas was still a baby. I called him Pieface because he had such a round, happy face. A few years later they came back for another Christmas. That one was fun but crazy. Thomas pulled out one of the buttons from the Eames chair, which I had bought to celebrate my fiftieth birthday. Sam broke the little "shovel" that came with the fireplace set. They locked the closet in one of the bedrooms, to which there was no key, causing mild panic and creativity. We found that Sam was hitting our tabby cat Max with sticks.

During their time at Eglin, Sam was diagnosed with ADHD. I'm generally suspicious of that diagnosis, but after my own observations, I had to feel that it might be accurate. And I recalled that a few of my therapist friends had thought that Nikki had ADHD. While they were at Elmendorf Air Force Base in Alaska, Thomas was also diagnosed with ADHD.

In September of 2004 Will and I travelled to Alaska to see baby Jack at two weeks of age. I brought a baby afghan for Jack. I knitted it with bulky yarn instead of knitting worsted or the fine yarns generally used for baby blankets. The finished blanket was big enough to spread out on the floor for the baby. Nikki got out the blankets that I'd made for Sam and Thomas as well. Sam's featured alphabet blocks, and Thomas' had a heart pattern.

When I asked Sam what he'd like for Christmas, to my amazement he said that he'd like a blanket like Jack's. Jack's was white, and Sam decided on navy blue for his color. So I knitted a larger version in navy yarn and got it to Sam by Christmas. Then Thomas said that he'd like a blanket too, and he wanted his to be fire-engine red. It took some looking to come up with that exact shade of red, but eventually Thomas got his blanket too. Red, white and blue. Perfect for a military family.

At first I was surprised that the older boys also wanted blankets. But then I thought about what blankets mean to us. We can pull them around us and relax. They'll keep us warm and safe. A blanket could be a metaphor for a family. Nikki has a family now, and we have a son-in-law and grandchildren. I'm very proud of what Nikki has been able to do.